# family favourites

Published in 2007 by Murdoch Books Pty Limited.
www.murdochbooks.com.au

Murdoch Books Australia
Pier 8/9, 23 Hickson Road
Millers Point NSW 2000
Phone: + 61 (0) 2 8220 2000
Fax: + 61 (0) 2 8220 2558

Murdoch Books UK Limited
Erico House, 6th Floor
93–99 Upper Richmond Road
Putney, London SW15 2TG
Phone: + 44 (0) 20 8785 5995
Fax: + 44 (0) 20 8785 5985

Chief Executive: Juliet Rogers
Publishing Director: Kay Scarlett

Design Manager: Vivien Valk
Design: Heather Menzies
Project Manager: Colette Vella
Editor: Gordana Trifunovic
Production: Maiya Levitch
Introduction text: Leanne Kitchen
Recipes developed by the Murdoch Books Test Kitchen

ISBN 978 1 921259 75 3

A CIP catalogue record for this book is available from the British Library

Printed by i-Book Printing Ltd. in 2007. PRINTED IN CHINA.

IMPORTANT: Those who might be at risk from the effects of salmonella poisoning (the elderly, pregnant women, young children and those suffering from immune deficiency diseases) should consult their doctor with any concerns about eating raw eggs.

CONVERSION GUIDE: You may find cooking times vary depending on the oven you are using. For fan-forced ovens, as a general rule, set the oven temperature to 20°C (35°F) lower than indicated in the recipe. We have used 20 ml (4 teaspoon) tablespoon measures. If you are using a 15 ml (3 teaspoon) tablespoon, for most recipes the difference will not be noticeable. However, for recipes using baking powder, gelatine, bicarbonate of soda (baking soda), small amounts of flour, add an extra teaspoon for each tablespoon specified.

# family favourites

## A test kitchen cookbook

MURDOCH BOOKS

# contents

Anyone who cooks for their family will tell you it's a non-stop whirl. Every night, there's that predicted chorus of 'what's for dinner?' to deal with and satisfy. In the mornings, lunches get packed for the work or school day ahead while on other occasions, there are snacks, impromptu meals, sweet treats, barbecue foods or perhaps even a special dinner party to produce. For all those who regularly cook, it can be a challenge to keep the fare interesting and varied. Sometimes, we simply crave dishes that are familiar, straightforward and comforting, such as those our grandmothers might have made. At other times though, it can be fun to experiment and challenge taste buds by producing something a little less expected. Luckily, the gastronomic world is shrinking and, with wider ranges of ingredients and fresh produce now easily procurable, we have unprecedented choices about what we will cook and eat.

As the contents of this fantastically useful book will attest, our cooking can take us anywhere we please. For those times when nothing but the homey simplicity of a turkey pot roast, a sausage sandwich or some crunchy potato wedges will do, there's a recipe at hand here. For those other days when we want to stretch beyond the limits of our geography or our family traditions, we can turn our meal times into a fascinating journey by incorporating the foods and flavours of other lands; there are plenty of ideas and recipes here. Some of these dishes that have exotic origins (risotto, curries, kebabs, guacamole or tacos, for example) have become mainstream. Others remain more exotic but no less doable—teriyaki from Japan, for instance, linguine pesto from regional Italy, or the Indonesian rice classic called Nasi Goreng—and all without the aid of any supermarket short-cuts, either. And when the challenges of home cooking stretch beyond the everyday and a special tea-time cake or a swish, multi-course dinner for guests is needed, there's endless inspiration to be found between these covers. With so many diverse options, influences and ingredients at the modern-day cook's disposal, nourishing family and friends has never been such an adventure.

# family favourites

Meat and three veg meals (of which roast meat and gravy, casseroles, and sausages with mash are prime examples) may be the Anglo-saxon bedrock of family dining but these days, immigrant contributions such a stir-fries, curries, pilafs and pasta dishes are, thankfully, equally as mainstream.

# pumpkin soup

serves 4

## ingredients

500 ml (17 fl oz/2 cups) vegetable stock
750 g (1 lb 10 oz) butternut pumpkin (squash),
  cut into 1.5 cm ($^5/_8$ in) cubes
2 onions, chopped
2 garlic cloves, halved
$^1/_4$ teaspoon ground nutmeg
3 tablespoons pouring (whipping) cream

## method

Put the stock and 500 ml (17 fl oz/2 cups) water in a large heavy-based saucepan and bring to the boil. Add the pumpkin, onion and garlic and return to the boil. Reduce the heat and cook for 15 minutes, or until the pumpkin is soft.

Drain the vegetables through a colander, reserving the liquid. Purée the pumpkin mixture in a blender until smooth (you may need to add some of the reserved liquid). Return the pumpkin purée to the pan and stir in enough of the reserved liquid to reach the desired consistency. Add the nutmeg and season to taste.

Ladle the soup into four bowls and pour some cream into each bowl to create a swirl pattern on the top. Serve with warm crusty bread.

# pea and ham soup

serves 6–8

## ingredients

500 g (1 lb 2 oz/2$^1$/$_4$ cups) yellow or
    green split peas
1$^1$/$_2$ tablespoons olive oil
2 onions, chopped
1 carrot, diced
3 celery stalks, finely chopped
1 kg (2 lb 4 oz) ham bones or a smoked ham hock,
    chopped
1 bay leaf
2 thyme sprigs
lemon juice, to taste (optional)

## method

Put the split peas in a large bowl, cover with cold water and soak for 6 hours. Drain well.

Heat the oil in a large saucepan, add the onion, carrot and celery and cook over low heat for 6–7 minutes, or until the vegetables are soft.

Add the peas, ham bones, bay leaf, thyme and 2.5 litres (85 fl oz/10 cups) cold water and bring to the boil. Reduce the heat and simmer, stirring occasionally, for 2 hours, or until the peas are tender, removing any scum that rises to the surface. Remove the bay leaf and thyme and discard.

Remove the ham bones from the soup, cool slightly, then remove the meat from the bones and discard the bones.

Return the ham to the soup and reheat. Season to taste and add lemon juice, if desired.

# vegetable soup

serves 6

## ingredients

105 g (3$^1$/$_2$ oz/$^1$/$_2$ cup) dried red kidney beans or
 borlotti beans
1 tablespoon olive oil
1 leek, halved lengthways and chopped
1 small onion, diced
2 carrots, chopped
2 celery stalks, chopped
1 large zucchini (courgette), chopped
1 tablespoon tomato paste (concentrated purée)
1 litre (35 fl oz/4 cups) vegetable stock
400 g (14 oz) butternut pumpkin (squash),
 cut into 2 cm ($^3$/$_4$ in) cubes
2 potatoes, cut into 2 cm ($^3$/$_4$ in) cubes
3 tablespoons chopped flat-leaf (Italian) parsley

## method

Put the beans in a large bowl, cover with cold water and soak overnight. Rinse, then transfer to a saucepan. Cover with cold water and cook for 45 minutes, or until just tender. Drain well.

Heat the olive oil in a saucepan. Add the leek and onion and cook over medium heat for 2–3 minutes without browning. Add the carrot, celery and zucchini and cook for 3–4 minutes. Add the tomato paste and stir for 1 minute. Pour in the vegetable stock and 1.25 litres (44 fl oz/5 cups) water and bring to the boil. Reduce the heat to low and simmer for 20 minutes.

Add the pumpkin, potato, parsley and beans and simmer for a further 20 minutes, or until the vegetables are tender and the beans are cooked. Season well. Serve with crusty bread.

# minestrone

serves 4

## ingredients

80 g (2³/₄ oz/¹/₂ cup) macaroni
1 tablespoon olive oil
1 leek, sliced
2 garlic cloves, crushed
1 carrot, sliced
1 boiling (waxy) potato, chopped
1 zucchini (courgette), sliced
2 celery stalks, sliced
100 g (3¹/₂ oz) green beans, cut into short lengths
425 g (15 oz) tinned chopped tomatoes
2 litres (70 fl oz/8 cups) vegetable or beef stock
2 tablespoons tomato paste (concentrated purée)
425 g (15 oz) tinned cannellini beans, rinsed
    and drained
2 tablespoons chopped flat-leaf (Italian) parsley
shaved parmesan cheese, to serve

## method

Bring a saucepan of water to the boil, add the macaroni and cook for 10–12 minutes, or until *al dente*. Drain.

Meanwhile, heat the oil in a large heavy-based saucepan. Add the leek and garlic and cook over medium heat for 3–4 minutes.

Add the carrot, potato, zucchini, celery, green beans, tomato, stock and tomato paste. Bring to the boil, then reduce the heat. Simmer for 10 minutes, or until the vegetables are tender.

Stir in the cooked pasta and the cannellini beans. Spoon into bowls and garnish with the parsley and parmesan cheese.

# lentil and silverbeet soup

serves 6

## ingredients

### chicken stock

1 kg (2 lb 4 oz) chicken trimmings (necks, ribs, wings), fat removed
1 small onion, roughly chopped
1 bay leaf
3–4 flat-leaf (Italian) parsley sprigs
1–2 oregano or thyme sprigs

280 g (10 oz/1$^1$/$_2$ cups) brown lentils, washed
850 g (1 lb 14 oz) silverbeet (Swiss chard)
3 tablespoons olive oil
1 large onion, finely chopped
4 garlic cloves, crushed
25 g (1 oz/$^1$/$_2$ cup) finely chopped coriander (cilantro) leaves
4 tablespoons lemon juice
lemon wedges, to serve

## method

To make the stock, place all the ingredients in a large saucepan. Add 3 litres (102 fl oz/12 cups) water and bring to the boil. Skim any scum from the surface. Reduce the heat and simmer for 2 hours. Strain the stock, and discard the trimmings, onion and herbs. Chill overnight.

Skim any fat from the stock. Place the lentils in a large saucepan, add the stock and 1 litre (35 fl oz/4 cups) water. Bring to the boil, then reduce the heat and simmer, covered, for 1 hour.

Meanwhile, remove the stems from the silverbeet and shred the leaves. Heat the oil in a saucepan over medium heat and cook the onion for 3 minutes, or until transparent. Add the garlic and cook for 1 minute. Add the silverbeet and toss for 2–3 minutes. Stir mixture into the lentils. Add the coriander and lemon juice, season, and simmer, covered, for 15–20 minutes. Serve with the lemon wedges.

# creamy chicken and corn soup

serves 4–6

## ingredients

20 g ($^3/_4$ oz) butter
1 tablespoon olive oil
500 g (1 lb 2 oz) boneless, skinless chicken
   thighs, trimmed and thinly sliced
2 garlic cloves, chopped
1 leek, chopped
1 large celery stalk, chopped
1 bay leaf
$^1/_2$ teaspoon thyme
1 litre (35 fl oz/4 cups) chicken stock
3 tablespoons sherry
550 g (1 lb 4 oz) corn kernels (fresh, canned
   or frozen)
1 large roasting (floury) potato, cut into 1 cm
   ($^1/_2$ in) cubes
185 ml (6 fl oz/$^3/_4$ cup) pouring (whipping) cream,
   plus extra, to drizzle
snipped chives, to garnish

## method

Melt the butter and oil in a large saucepan over high heat. Cook the chicken in batches for 3 minutes, or until lightly golden and just cooked through. Place in a bowl, cover and refrigerate until needed.

Reduce the heat to medium and stir in the garlic, leek, celery, bay leaf and thyme. Cook for 2 minutes, or until the leek softens—do not allow the garlic to burn. Add the stock, sherry and 500 ml (17 fl oz/2 cups) water and stir, scraping up any sediment stuck to the bottom of the pan. Add the corn and potato and bring to the boil. Reduce the heat and simmer for 1 hour, skimming any scum off the surface. Cool slightly.

Remove the bay leaf and purée the soup. Return to the cleaned pan, add the cream and chicken and stir over medium–low heat for 2–3 minutes, or until heated through—do not boil. Season. Drizzle with extra cream and garnish with chives. Serve with crusty bread.

# Vietnamese beef soup

serves 4

## ingredients

400 g (14 oz) rump steak, trimmed
$^1/_2$ onion
$1^1/_2$ tablespoons fish sauce
1 star anise
1 cinnamon stick
pinch of ground white pepper
1.5 litres (52 fl oz/6 cups) beef stock
300 g (10$^1/_2$ oz) fresh thin rice noodles
3 spring onions (scallions), thinly sliced
15 g ($^1/_2$ oz) Vietnamese mint leaves
90 g (3$^1/_4$ oz/1 cup) bean sprouts, trimmed
1 small white onion, cut in half and thinly sliced
1 small red chilli, thinly sliced on the diagonal
lemon wedges, to serve

## method

Wrap the rump steak in plastic wrap and freeze for 40 minutes.

Meanwhile, put the onion, fish sauce, star anise, cinnamon stick, pepper, stock and 500 ml (17 fl oz/2 cups) water in a large saucepan. Bring to the boil, then reduce the heat, cover and simmer for 20 minutes. Discard the onion, star anise and cinnamon stick.

Cover the noodles with boiling water and gently separate the strands. Drain and refresh under cold water.

Remove the meat from the freezer and thinly slice across the grain.

Divide the noodles and spring onion among four deep bowls. Top with the beef, mint, bean sprouts, onion and chilli. Ladle the hot broth over the top and serve with the lemon wedges.

# asparagus risotto

serves 4

## ingredients

1 kg (2 lb 4 oz) asparagus spears
1 litre (35 fl oz/4 cups) chicken stock
4 tablespoons olive oil
1 onion, finely chopped
360 g (12$^3$/$_4$ oz/1$^2$/$_3$ cups) risotto rice
85 g (3 oz) parmesan cheese, grated
3 tablespoons thick (double/heavy) cream

## method

Wash the asparagus and remove the woody ends. Separate the tender tips from the stems.

Cook the asparagus stems in boiling water for about 8 minutes, or until very tender. Drain and put in a blender with the chicken stock. Blend for 1 minute, then put in a saucepan, bring to the boil and maintain at a low simmer.

Cook the asparagus tips in boiling water for 1 minute. Drain and refresh in iced water.

Heat the olive oil in a wide, heavy-based saucepan. Add the onion and cook until softened but not browned. Add the rice and reduce the heat to low. Season and stir briefly to thoroughly coat the rice. Stir in a ladleful of the simmering stock and cook over medium heat, stirring continuously. When the stock has been absorbed, stir in another ladleful. Continue this process for about 20 minutes, until all the stock has been added and the rice is *al dente*.

Add the parmesan cheese and cream, and gently stir in the asparagus tips. Season and serve hot.

# quiche lorraine

serves 8

## ingredients

### tart pastry
220 g (7³/₄ oz) plain (all-purpose) flour
150 g (5¹/₂ oz) unsalted butter, chilled and diced
1 egg yolk

25 g (1 oz) butter
300 g (10¹/₂ oz) bacon slices, diced
250 ml (9 fl oz/1 cup) double (thick/heavy) cream
3 eggs
freshly grated nutmeg

## method

To make the tart pastry, sift the flour and a pinch of salt into a bowl, add the butter and rub in until the mixture resembles breadcrumbs. Add the egg yolk and a little cold water and mix with a palette knife until the dough starts to come together. Bring the dough together with your hands and shape into a ball. Wrap in plastic wrap and put in the fridge for at least 30 minutes.

Roll out the pastry into a circle on a lightly floured surface. Preheat the oven to 200°C (400°F/Gas 6). Line a 25 cm (10 in) fluted loose-based tart tin with the pastry. Line the pastry shell with a crumpled piece of greaseproof paper and baking beads (use dried beans or rice if you don't have beads). Blind bake the pastry for 10 minutes, remove the paper and beads and bake for a further 3–5 minutes, or until the pastry is just cooked but still very pale. Reduce the oven to 180°C (350°F/Gas 4).

Melt the butter in a small frying pan and cook the bacon until golden. Drain on paper towels.

Mix together the cream and eggs, add the nutmeg and season. Scatter the bacon into the pastry shell and then pour in the egg mixture. Bake for 30 minutes, or until the filling is set. Leave in the tin for 5 minutes before serving.

# Mediterranean burgers

serves 4

## ingredients

1 large red capsicum (pepper)
500 g (1 lb 2 oz) minced (ground) lamb
1 egg, lightly beaten
1 small onion, grated
3 garlic cloves, crushed
2 tablespoons pine nuts, chopped
1 tablespoon finely chopped mint
1 tablespoon finely chopped flat-leaf (Italian)
    parsley
1 teaspoon ground cumin
2 teaspoons chilli sauce
1 tablespoon olive oil
4 pide (Turkish/flat bread) rolls
220 g ($7^3/_4$ oz/1 cup) hummus
100 g ($3^1/_2$ oz) baby rocket (arugula)
1 small Lebanese (short) cucumber, cut into
    ribbons
chilli sauce, to serve (optional)

## method

Cut the capsicum into large pieces, removing the seeds and membrane. Place, skin-side-up, under a hot grill (broiler) until the skin blackens and blisters. Cool in a plastic bag, then peel and cut into thick strips.

Combine the lamb, egg, onion, garlic, pine nuts, fresh herbs, cumin and chilli sauce in a large bowl. Mix with your hands and roll into four even-sized balls. Press the balls into large patties about 9 cm ($3^1/_2$ in) in diameter.

Heat the oil in a large frying pan and cook the patties over medium heat for 6 minutes each side, or until well browned and cooked through, then drain on paper towels.

Halve the rolls and toast both sides. Spread the cut sides of the rolls with hummus, then lay rocket leaves, roasted capsicum and cucumber ribbons over the base. Place a patty on the salad and top with the other half of the roll. Serve with chilli sauce.

# macaroni cheese

serves 4

## ingredients

390 g (13$^3$/$_4$ oz/2$^1$/$_2$ cups) macaroni
75 g (2$^3$/$_4$ oz) pancetta, diced
500 ml (17 fl oz/2 cups) pouring (whipping) cream
125 g (4$^1$/$_2$ oz/1 cup) grated cheddar cheese
260 g (9$^1$/$_4$ oz/2 cups) grated gruyère cheese
100 g (3$^1$/$_2$ oz/1 cup) grated parmesan cheese
1 garlic clove, crushed
2 teaspoons dijon mustard
$^1$/$_2$ teaspoon paprika
2 tablespoons snipped chives, plus extra,
   to garnish

## method

Bring a large saucepan of lightly salted water to the boil. Add the macaroni and cook until *al dente*. Drain. Cover and keep warm.

Meanwhile, put the pancetta in a large saucepan and cook over high heat, stirring, for 4 minutes, or until well browned and slightly crisp. Drain on paper towels. Reduce the heat to medium, stir in the cream and simmer. Add the cheeses, garlic, mustard and paprika, and stir for 5 minutes, or until the cheeses have melted and the sauce has thickened. Season.

Add the macaroni and pancetta and stir for 1 minute, or until heated through. Stir in the chives. Garnish with the extra chives to serve.

# fettucine carbonara

serves 4–6

## ingredients

8 bacon slices
500 g (1 lb 2 oz) fettucine
4 eggs
50 g ($1^3/_4$ oz/$^1/_2$ cup) freshly grated parmesan
  cheese
315 ml (10 fl oz/$1^1/_4$ cups) pouring (whipping)
  cream

## method

Cut the bacon into thin strips. Cook in a heavy-based frying pan over medium heat until crisp. Drain on paper towels.

Add the pasta to a large saucepan of rapidly boiling salted water and cook until *al dente*. Drain and return to the pan.

While the pasta is cooking, beat the eggs, parmesan and cream in a bowl until well combined. Stir the bacon through the mixture. Pour the sauce over the hot pasta and toss gently until the sauce coats the pasta.

Return the pan to very low heat and cook for $^1/_2$–1 minute, or until the sauce has slightly thickened.

# fried rice

serves 4

## ingredients

350 g (12 oz/1$^3$/$_4$ cups) long-grain rice
1 tablespoon vegetable or peanut oil
2 eggs, beaten
3 Chinese sausages (lap cheong), thinly sliced
    on the diagonal
100 g (3$^1$/$_2$ oz) snake (yard-long) beans, cut into
    2 cm ($^3$/$_4$ in) lengths
6 spring onions (scallions), finely chopped
2 garlic cloves, crushed
2 teaspoons grated fresh ginger
160 g (5$^1$/$_2$ oz) small raw prawns (shrimp), peeled
    and deveined
100 g (3$^1$/$_2$ oz/$^2$/$_3$ cup) frozen peas, thawed
2 tablespoons soy sauce
2 spring onions (scallions), extra, thinly sliced
    on the diagonal

## method

Wash the rice under cold running water until the water runs clear. Bring a large saucepan of water to the boil, add the rice and cook for 10–12 minutes, or until tender. Drain and rinse under cold water to remove any excess starch. Spread out on a flat tray and refrigerate for 2 hours, or preferably overnight.

Heat a wok over high heat, add half the oil and swirl to coat. Add the egg, swirling to coat the side of the wok. When the egg is almost set, roll it up in the wok, turn off the heat, then remove. Roughly chop and set aside.

Reheat the wok over high heat, add the remaining oil and swirl to coat. Add the Chinese sausage and snake beans and stir-fry for 2–3 minutes. Add the spring onion, garlic and ginger and stir-fry for 1 minute. Add the prawns and stir-fry for 1–2 minutes, or until cooked. Stir in the rice and peas and toss until well combined and heated through. Stir in the soy sauce and serve garnished with the chopped egg and extra spring onion.

# butter chicken

serves 4–6

## ingredients

2 tablespoons peanut oil

1 kg (2 lb 4 oz) boneless, skinless chicken thighs,
   quartered

60 g (2$^1$/$_4$ oz) butter or ghee

2 teaspoons garam masala

2 teaspoons sweet paprika

2 teaspoons ground coriander

1 tablespoon finely chopped fresh ginger

$^1$/$_4$ teaspoon chilli powder

1 cinnamon stick

6 cardamom pods, bruised

350 g (12 oz) tomato passata (puréed tomatoes)

1 tablespoon sugar

60 g (2$^1$/$_4$ oz/$^1$/$_4$ cup) plain yoghurt

125 ml (4 fl oz/$^1$/$_2$ cup) pouring (whipping) cream

1 tablespoon lemon juice

rice and pappadums, to serve

## method

Heat a wok until very hot, add 1 tablespoon oil and swirl to coat. Stir-fry the chicken thigh in two batches for 4 minutes each, or until browned. Remove from the pan and set aside.

Reduce the heat, add the butter to the wok and melt. Add the garam masala, sweet paprika, coriander, ginger, chilli powder, cinnamon stick and cardamom pods, and stir-fry for 1 minute, or until fragrant. Return the chicken to the wok and mix to coat in the spices.

Add the tomato and sugar, and simmer, stirring, for 15 minutes, or until the chicken is tender and the sauce has thickened.

Add the yoghurt, cream and juice and simmer for 5 minutes, or until the sauce has thickened slightly. Serve with rice and pappadums.

# potato gnocchi with tomato and basil sauce

serves 4–6

## ingredients

**tomato sauce**
1 tablespoon oil
1 onion, chopped
1 celery stalk, chopped
2 carrots, chopped
850 g (1 lb 14 oz) tinned crushed tomatoes
1 teaspoon sugar
30 g (1 oz) basil, chopped

**potato gnocchi**
1 kg (2 lb 4 oz) all-purpose potatoes
30 g (1 oz) butter
250 g (9 oz/2 cups) plain (all-purpose) flour
2 eggs, beaten

freshly grated parmesan cheese, to serve

## method

To make the tomato sauce, heat the oil in a large frying pan, add the onion, celery and carrot and cook for 5 minutes, stirring regularly. Add the tomato and sugar and season to taste. Bring to the boil, reduce the heat to very low and simmer for 20 minutes. Cool slightly and process, in batches, in a food processor until smooth. Add the basil and set aside.

To make the potato gnocchi, peel the potatoes, chop roughly and boil until very tender. Drain thoroughly and mash until smooth. Using a wooden spoon, stir in the butter and flour, then beat in the eggs. Allow to cool.

Turn onto a floured surface and divide into two. Roll each into a long sausage shape. Cut into short pieces and press each piece with the back of a fork.

Cook the gnocchi, in batches, in a large saucepan of boiling salted water for about 2 minutes, or until the gnocchi rise to the surface. Using a slotted spoon, drain the gnocchi, and transfer to serving bowls. Serve with the tomato sauce and freshly grated parmesan.

# beer-battered fish with crunchy chips

serves 4

## ingredients

**batter**

155 g (5$^1$/$_2$ oz/1$^1$/$_4$ cups) plain (all-purpose) flour
375 ml (13 fl oz/1$^1$/$_2$ cups) beer

4 roasting (floury) potatoes, cut into 1 cm
   ($^1$/$_2$ in) wide chips (fries)
oil, for deep-frying
4 skinless firm white fish fillets, such as cod or
   haddock
cornflour (cornstarch), for coating
lemon wedges, to serve

## method

Sift the flour into a large bowl and make a well in the centre. Gradually pour in the beer, whisking to make a smooth batter. Cover and set aside.

Soak the potatoes in cold water for 10 minutes. Drain and pat dry. Fill a deep-fat fryer or large saucepan one-third full of oil and heat to 160°C (315°F), or until a small cube of white bread browns in 30 seconds. Cook batches of chips for 4–5 minutes, or until lightly golden. Remove with a slotted spoon and drain on crumpled paper towels.

Dust the fish with cornflour, dip into the batter and shake off any excess. Deep-fry in batches for 5–7 minutes, or until golden and the fish is cooked through. Turn with tongs if necessary. You can check that the fish is cooked by cutting into the centre of one of the pieces—the flesh should be moist and opaque. Drain on crumpled paper towels. Keep warm in a low oven while you cook the chips again. Reheat the oil to 180°C (350°F), or until a cube of bread browns in 15 seconds. Cook the chips for 1–2 minutes, in batches, until crisp and golden. Drain on crumpled paper towels. Serve the fish with lemon wedges and the chips.

# curried lamb chops

serves 4

## ingredients

8 lamb chops
2 tablespoons oil
2 onions, sliced
2 garlic cloves, crushed
1 tablespoon curry powder
1 tablespoon plain (all-purpose) flour
425 g (15 oz) tinned tomatoes
70 g ($2^1/_2$ oz/$^1/_4$ cup) fruit chutney
2 large carrots, cut into 1 cm ($^1/_2$ in) slices
2 tablespoons chopped flat-leaf (Italian) parsley,
   to serve

## method

Trim the meat of excess fat and sinew. Heat the oil in a heavy-based frying pan and add the lamb. Cook over medium-high heat for 2 minutes each side, or until well browned. Drain on paper towels.

Add the onion and garlic to the pan and stir for 2 minutes, or until soft. Add the curry powder and flour and stir for 1 minute.

Return the chops to the pan with undrained crushed tomatoes, 375 ml (13 fl oz/$1^1/_2$ cups) of water, chutney and carrots and bring to the boil.

Reduce the heat. Simmer, covered, for 40 minutes or until the chops are tender, stirring occasionally. Sprinkle with the parsley.

# rissoles with gravy

serves 4

## ingredients

500 g (1 lb 2 oz) minced (ground) beef
1 onion, finely chopped
1 garlic clove, crushed
2 tablespoons tomato sauce (ketchup)
1 teaspoon dried mixed herbs
1 egg, lightly beaten
80 g (2$^3$/$_4$ oz/1 cup) fresh breadcrumbs
2 tablespoons oil

### gravy

2 tablespoons plain (all-purpose) flour
500 ml (17 fl oz/2 cups) chicken stock
1 tablespoon tomato paste (concentrated purée)
2 tablespoons chopped flat-leaf (Italian) parsley

## method

Put the beef, onion, garlic, tomato sauce, herbs, egg and breadcrumbs in a bowl. Mix using your hands until combined.

Divide the mixture into 8 portions and shape into patties.

Heat the oil in a large heavy-based frying pan. Add the rissoles 4 at a time. Cook over high heat for 1 minute each side, turning once. Reduce the heat to medium, cook for 2 minutes each side or until cooked through. Remove the rissoles from the pan, drain on paper towels, and keep warm.

To make the gravy, blend the flour with chicken stock and tomato paste until the mixture is smooth. Add to the pan juices. Stir over medium heat for 3 minutes, or until the gravy boils and thickens. Strain, stir in the chopped parsley and serve with the rissoles.

# tandoori chicken with cardamom rice

serves 4

## ingredients

250 ml (9 fl oz/1 cup) plain yoghurt, plus extra
   to serve
60 g (2$^1$/$_4$ oz/$^1$/$_4$ cup) ready-made tandoori paste
2 tablespoons lemon juice
1 kg (2 lb 4 oz) boneless, skinless chicken breast,
   cut into 4 cm (1$^1$/$_2$ in) cubes
1 tablespoon oil
1 onion, finely diced
300 g (10$^1$/$_2$ oz/1$^1$/$_2$ cups) long-grain rice
2 cardamom pods, bruised
750 ml (26 fl oz/3 cups) hot chicken stock
400 g (14 oz) English spinach leaves

## method

Soak eight wooden skewers in water for 30 minutes to prevent burning during cooking. Combine the yoghurt, tandoori paste and lemon juice in a non-metallic dish. Add the chicken and coat well, then cover and marinate for at least 10 minutes.

Meanwhile, heat the oil in a saucepan. Add the onion and cook for 3 minutes, then add the rice and cardamom pods. Cook, stirring often, for 3–5 minutes, or until the rice is slightly opaque. Add the hot chicken stock and bring to the boil. Reduce the heat to low, cover, and cook the rice for 15 minutes.

Heat a barbecue plate or oven grill (broiler) to very hot. Thread the chicken cubes onto the skewers, leaving the bottom quarter of the skewers empty. Cook on each side for 5 minutes, or until cooked through.

Wash the spinach and put in a large saucepan with just the water clinging to the leaves. Cook, covered, over medium heat for 1–2 minutes, or until the spinach has wilted. Uncover the rice, fluff up with a fork and serve with the spinach, chicken and extra yoghurt.

# chicken and winter vegetable pie

serves 6

## ingredients

1 kg (2 lb 4 oz) boneless, skinless chicken thighs,
     cut into 2 cm ($^3/_4$ in) cubes
1 tablespoon plain (all-purpose) flour
4 tablespoons olive oil
1 large leek, finely sliced
2 celery stalks, chopped
2 garlic cloves, crushed
2 carrots, chopped
200 g (7 oz) pumpkin (winter squash), chopped
2 dried mace blades
500 ml (17 fl oz/2 cups) chicken stock
3 tablespoons pouring (whipping) cream
3 tablespoons chopped flat-leaf (Italian) parsley
2 sheets frozen puff pastry, thawed
1 egg, lightly beaten

## method

Put the chicken and flour in a large plastic bag and shake until the chicken is coated in flour.

Heat half the oil in a large saucepan and cook the chicken over medium heat, in batches, for 5 minutes, or until browned.

Heat the remaining oil in the same pan and cook the leek, celery and garlic for 4 minutes, or until the leek is tender. Return the chicken to the pan with the carrots, pumpkin, mace and stock. Bring to the boil. Reduce the heat and simmer, uncovered, for 30 minutes. Stir in the cream and parsley.

Preheat the oven to 180°C (350°F/Gas 4). Cut strips of pastry from one sheet, wide enough to fit the rim of a 23 cm (9 in) pie dish. Press into place, joining where necessary. Cut two pieces from the remaining pastry and join onto the whole sheet, so it is large enough to cover the pie dish.

Spoon the chicken mixture into the pie dish and top with puff pastry, pressing into the pastry rim. Trim the edges and press around the edge of the pastry to seal. Using a knife, cut two steam vents in the top of the pie. Brush the pie with egg. Bake in the oven for 30 minutes, or until the pastry is golden brown.

# lasagne

serves 6

## ingredients

### meat sauce
1 tablespoon olive oil
750 g (1 lb 10 oz) minced (ground) beef
1 onion, finely chopped
2 celery stalks, finely chopped
400 g (14 oz) tinned chopped tomatoes
2 tablespoons tomato paste (concentrated purée)
1 teaspoon dried mixed herbs
1–2 teaspoons sugar

### béchamel sauce
60 g ($2^1/_4$ oz) butter
3 tablespoons plain (all-purpose) flour
750 ml (26 fl oz/3 cups) milk

375 g (13 oz) fresh lasagne sheets
125 g ($4^1/_2$ oz/1 cup) grated cheddar cheese

## method

Preheat the oven to 180°C (350°F/Gas 4). Heat half the oil in a large frying pan and brown the meat in batches. Remove from the pan. Add the remaining oil and cook the onion and celery until soft. Return the meat to the pan and add all other ingredients. Bring to the boil, then reduce the heat and simmer, covered, for 20 minutes.

Melt the butter in a saucepan over low heat. Stir in the flour and cook for 1 minute. Remove from the heat and gradually stir in the milk. Return to the heat and stir constantly until the sauce boils and thickens. Reduce the heat and simmer for 2 minutes.

Lightly brush a 2.5 litre (85 fl oz/10 cup) ovenproof dish with oil. Spoon one-third of the meat sauce into the dish. Top with a single layer of the lasagne sheets, then spoon on one-third of the béchamel sauce. Repeat layering twice more, and top with cheddar cheese.

Bake in the oven for 25 minutes, or until golden and heated through.

# spaghetti bolognese

serves 4–6

## ingredients

2 tablespoons olive oil
2 garlic cloves, crushed
1 large onion, chopped
1 carrot, finely chopped
1 celery stalk, finely chopped
500 g (1 lb 2 oz) lean minced (ground) beef
500 ml (17 fl oz/2 cups) beef stock
375 ml (13 fl oz/1$^1$/$_2$ cups) red wine
850 g (1 lb 14 oz) tinned chopped tomatoes
1 teaspoon sugar
3 tablespoons finely chopped flat-leaf (Italian)
   parsley
500 g (1 lb 2 oz) spaghetti
grated parmesan cheese, to serve

## method

Heat the olive oil in a large, deep frying pan. Add the garlic, onion, carrot and celery and stir over low heat for 5 minutes, or until the vegetables are tender.

Increase the heat, then add the beef. Stir with a wooden spoon to break up any lumps. Add the stock, wine, tomatoes, sugar and parsley. Bring to the boil, then reduce the heat and simmer for 1$^1$/$_2$ hours, stirring occasionally. Season.

Just before serving, cook the spaghetti in a large saucepan of boiling, salted water until *al dente*. Drain and serve with the meat sauce and the parmesan cheese.

# cannelloni

serves 4

## ingredients

### meat sauce

3 tablespoons olive oil
1 onion, finely chopped
2 garlic cloves, crushed
120 g ($4^1/_4$ oz) bacon, finely chopped
60 g ($2^1/_4$ oz) button mushrooms, finely chopped
$^1/_4$ teaspoon dried basil
220 g ($7^3/_4$ oz) minced (ground) pork
220 g ($7^3/_4$ oz) minced (ground) veal
1 tablespoon chopped flat-leaf (Italian) parsley
200 g (7 oz) tinned chopped tomatoes
250 ml (9 fl oz/1 cup) beef stock
3 tablespoons dried breadcrumbs
1 egg

### tomato sauce

2 tablespoons olive oil
1 small onion, finely chopped
2 garlic cloves, crushed
800 g (1 lb 12 oz) tinned chopped tomatoes
1 teaspoon chopped basil

10 sheets fresh lasagne, about 17 x 12 cm
   ($6^1/_2$ x $4^1/_2$ in)
4 large slices prosciutto, cut in half
60 g ($2^1/_4$ oz) fontina cheese, grated
200 ml (7 fl oz) thick (double/heavy) cream
60 g ($2^1/_4$ oz) parmesan cheese, grated

## method

To make the meat sauce, heat the oil in a frying pan and cook the onion, garlic and bacon over medium heat for 6 minutes. Stir in the mushrooms and basil, cook for 2–3 minutes, then add the pork and veal. Cook, stirring often, until the meat has changed colour. Season, add the parsley, tomatoes and stock, cover and simmer for 1 hour. Remove the lid and simmer for a further 30 minutes. Cool, then stir in the breadcrumbs and egg.

To make the sauce, heat the oil in a frying pan and cook the onion and garlic for 6 minutes, or until softened. Stir in the tomatoes and basil. Add 250 ml (9 fl oz/1 cup) water and season. Simmer for 30 minutes, or until thick.

Cook the lasagne in a large saucepan of boiling salted water until *al dente*. Preheat the oven to 190°C (375°F/Gas 5). Grease a shallow 30 x 18 cm (12 x 7 in) ovenproof dish and spoon the sauce over the base. Place a half slice of prosciutto over each pasta sheet. Top with fontina. Spoon an eighth of the meat filling across one end of the pasta sheet. Starting from this end, roll the pasta up tightly to enclose the filling. Place the filled rolls, seam side down, in a row in the dish.

Beat together the cream and parmesan and season. Spoon over the cannelloni. Bake for 20 minutes, or until browned.

# chicken cacciatora

serves 4

## ingredients

3 tablespoons olive oil
1 large onion, finely chopped
3 garlic cloves, crushed
1 celery stalk, finely chopped
150 g (5$^1$/$_2$ oz) pancetta, finely chopped
125 g (4$^1$/$_2$ oz) button mushrooms, thickly sliced
4 chicken drumsticks
4 boneless, skinless chicken thighs
90 ml (3 fl oz) dry vermouth or dry white wine
800 g (1 lb 12 oz) tinned chopped tomatoes
$^1$/$_4$ teaspoon brown sugar
1 oregano sprig, plus 4–5 sprigs, to garnish
1 rosemary sprig
1 bay leaf

## method

Heat half the oil in a large casserole dish. Add the onion, garlic and celery and cook, stirring occasionally, over low heat for 6–8 minutes, or until the onion is golden.

Add the pancetta and mushrooms, increase the heat and cook, stirring occasionally, for 4–5 minutes. Spoon out onto a plate and set aside.

Add the remaining olive oil to the dish and lightly brown the chicken pieces, a few at a time. Season. Spoon off any excess fat and return all the pieces to the dish. Add the vermouth, increase the heat and cook until the liquid has almost evaporated.

Add the tomatoes, sugar, oregano, rosemary, bay leaf and 75 ml (2$^1$/$_4$ fl oz) cold water. Bring to the boil, then stir in the reserved pancetta mixture. Cover and leave to simmer for 20 minutes, or until the chicken is tender.

If the liquid is too thin, remove the chicken from the dish increase the heat and boil until thickened. Discard the herb sprigs and season. Add the extra oregano sprigs and serve.

# steak and kidney pie

serves 6

## ingredients

60 g (2¼ oz/½ cup) plain (all-purpose) flour,
  seasoned
1.5 kg (3 lb 5 oz) chuck steak, cut into 2 cm
  (¾ in) cubes
500 g (1 lb 2 oz) kidney, cut into 2 cm
  (¾ in) cubes
2 tablespoons olive oil
2 onions, chopped
125 g (4½ oz) button mushrooms, quartered
40 g (1½ oz) butter
250 ml (9 fl oz/1 cup) beef or veal stock
185 ml (6 fl oz/¾ cup) stout
2 tablespoons worcestershire sauce
1 tablespoon anchovy essence
1 tablespoon chopped flat-leaf (Italian) parsley
600 g (1 lb 5 oz) frozen puff pastry, thawed
1 egg, lightly beaten

## method

Place the flour in a bowl. Toss the steak and kidney pieces through the flour and shake off any excess. Heat the oil in a large saucepan over medium heat. Add the onion and cook for 5 minutes. Add the mushrooms and cook for 5 minutes. Remove from the pan.

Melt a third of the butter in the saucepan, add a third of the beef and kidney and cook over medium heat, turning occasionally, for 5 minutes, or until brown. Remove and repeat twice with the remaining butter, beef and kidney. Return all the meat to the saucepan, add the stock and stout, stir and bring slowly to boil. Reduce the heat and simmer for 2 hours. Remove from the heat, leave to cool, then add the onion and mushrooms, worcestershire sauce, anchovy essence and parsley.

Preheat the oven to 180°C (350°F/Gas 4). Place the filling into a 20 cm (8 in) ceramic pie dish. Roll out the pastry between two sheets of baking paper to fit the top of the pie dish. Moisten the rim of the dish with milk and place the pastry over the filling. Press firmly into place and brush with egg. Decorate with pastry scraps, brush with egg and bake for 40–45 minutes, or until golden.

# lamb cutlets with onion marmalade

serves 4

## ingredients

40 g ($1^1/_2$ oz) butter
4 tablespoons olive oil
4 onions, finely sliced
2 teaspoons brown sugar
2 teaspoons thyme leaves
2 tablespoons flat-leaf (Italian) parsley, finely
    chopped
12 French-trimmed lamb cutlets
2 tablespoons lemon juice

## method

Heat the butter and half the olive oil together in a saucepan.
Add the onion, sugar and thyme and stir well. Turn the heat
to low, cover the saucepan and cook the onion, stirring it
occasionally for 30–35 minutes, or until it is very soft and
golden. Season well, stir the parsley through and keep warm
over low heat.

Heat the remaining oil in a frying pan and, when hot, add the
cutlets in a single layer. Fry for 2 minutes on each side, or until
the lamb is browned. Add the lemon juice and season well.

Put a small pile of the onion and herb marmalade on each plate
and place the cutlets around it.

# chicken and pork paella

serves 6

## ingredients

3 tablespoons olive oil
1 large red capsicum (pepper), seeded and cut
   into 5 mm ($^1/_4$ in) strips
600 g (1 lb 5 oz) boneless, skinless chicken
   thighs, cut into 3 cm ($1^1/_4$ in) cubes
200 g (7 oz) chorizo sausage, cut into 2 cm
   ($^3/_4$ in) slices
200 g (7 oz) mushrooms, thinly sliced
3 garlic cloves, crushed
1 tablespoon lemon zest
700 g (1 lb 9 oz) tomatoes, roughly chopped
200 g (7 oz) green beans, cut into 3 cm ($1^1/_4$ in)
   lengths
1 tablespoon chopped rosemary
2 tablespoons chopped flat-leaf (Italian) parsley
$^1/_4$ teaspoon saffron threads dissolved in
   3 tablespoons hot water
440 g ($15^1/_2$ oz/2 cups) short-grain rice
750 ml (26 fl oz/3 cups) hot chicken stock
6 lemon wedges

## method

Heat the oil in a large deep frying pan or paella pan over medium heat. Add the capsicum and cook for 6 minutes, or until soft. Remove from the pan.

Add the chicken to the pan and cook for 10 minutes, or until brown on all sides. Remove. Add the sausage to the pan and cook for 5 minutes, or until golden on all sides. Remove.

Add the mushrooms, garlic and lemon zest and cook over medium heat for 5 minutes. Stir in the tomato and capsicum and cook for a further 5 minutes, or until the tomato is soft.

Add the beans, rosemary, parsley, saffron mixture, rice, chicken and sausage. Stir briefly and then add the stock.

Reduce the heat and simmer for 30 minutes. Remove the pan from the heat, cover and leave to stand for 10 minutes. Serve with lemon wedges.

# green chicken curry

serves 4

## ingredients

250 ml (9 fl oz/1 cup) coconut cream
4 tablespoons green curry paste
8 boneless, skinless chicken thighs or 4 chicken
    breasts, cut into pieces
250 ml (9 fl oz/1 cup) coconut milk
4 Thai eggplants (aubergines) or ½ purple
    eggplant, cut into chunks
2 tablespoons shaved palm sugar (jaggery) or
    brown sugar
2 tablespoons fish sauce
4 makrut (kaffir) lime leaves, torn
1 handful Thai basil leaves
1–2 large red chillies, sliced
coconut milk or cream, for drizzling

## method

Heat a wok over a low heat, add the coconut cream and bring to the boil. Stir until the oil separates out.

Add the green curry paste, stir for 1 minute, then add the chicken. Cook the chicken until it turns opaque, then add the coconut milk and eggplant. Cook for 1–2 minutes, or until the eggplant is tender. Add the sugar, fish sauce, lime leaves and half of the basil, then mix together.

Garnish with the rest of the basil, the chilli and a drizzle of coconut milk or cream. Serve with rice.

# pork chops pizzaiola

serves 4

## ingredients

4 pork chops
4 tablespoons olive oil
600 g (1 lb 5 oz) ripe tomatoes
3 garlic cloves, crushed
3 basil leaves, torn into pieces
1 teaspoon finely chopped flat-leaf (Italian)
    parsley, to serve

## method

Using scissors or a knife, cut the pork fat at 5 mm ($^1/_4$ in) intervals around the rind. Brush the chops with 1 tablespoon of the olive oil and season well.

Remove the stems from the tomatoes and score a cross in the bottom of each one. Blanch in boiling water for 30 seconds. Transfer to cold water, peel the skin away from the cross and chop the tomatoes.

Heat 2 tablespoons of the oil in a saucepan over low heat and add the garlic. Soften for 1–2 minutes, then add the tomato and season. Increase the heat, bring to the boil and cook for 5 minutes or until thick. Stir in the basil.

Heat the remaining oil in a large frying pan with a tight-fitting lid. Brown the chops in batches over medium-high heat for 2 minutes on each side. Place in a slightly overlapping row down the centre of the pan and spoon the sauce over the top, covering the chops completely.

Cover the pan and cook over low heat for about 5 minutes. Sprinkle with parsley to serve.

# lamb pilaff

serves 4

## ingredients

1 large eggplant (aubergine), cut into 1 cm
   ($^1/_2$ in) cubes
125 ml ($4^1/_2$ oz/$^1/_2$ cup) olive oil
1 large onion, finely chopped
1 teaspoon ground cinnamon
2 teaspoons ground cumin
1 teaspoon ground coriander
300 g ($10^1/_2$ oz/$1^1/_2$ cups) long-grain rice
500 ml (17 fl oz/2 cups) chicken or vegetable
   stock
500 g (1 lb 2 oz) minced (ground) lamb
$^1/_2$ teaspoon allspice
2 tablespoons olive oil, extra
2 tomatoes, cut into wedges
3 tablespoons toasted pistachio nuts
2 tablespoons currants
2 tablespoons chopped coriander (cilantro)
   leaves, to garnish

## method

Put the eggplant in a colander, sprinkle with salt and leave for
1 hour. Rinse and squeeze dry. Heat 2 tablespoons of the oil in
a large, deep frying pan with a lid, add the eggplant and cook
over medium heat for 8–10 minutes. Drain on paper towels.

Heat the remaining oil, add the onion and cook for about
4–5 minutes, or until soft. Stir in half each of the cinnamon,
cumin and ground coriander. Add the rice and stir to coat,
then add the stock, season and bring to the boil. Reduce the
heat and simmer, covered, for 15 minutes.

Put the lamb in a bowl with the allspice and remaining cumin,
cinnamon and ground coriander. Season and mix. Roll into
balls the size of macadamia nuts. Heat the extra oil in the
frying pan and cook the meatballs in batches over medium
heat for 5 minutes each batch. Drain on paper towels.

Add the tomato to the pan and cook, for 3–5 minutes, or until
golden. Remove from the pan. Stir the eggplant, pistachios,
currants and meatballs through the rice. Serve the pilaff with
the tomato and coriander.

# sausages cooked with lentils

serves 4

## ingredients

3 tablespoons olive oil
8 Italian sausages
1 onion, chopped
3 garlic cloves, thinly sliced
2 tablespoons finely chopped rosemary
800 g (1 lb 12 oz) tinned tomatoes
16 juniper berries, lightly crushed
1 teaspoon freshly grated nutmeg
1 bay leaf
1 dried chilli
200 ml (7 fl oz) red wine
100 g ($3^1/_2$ oz) green lentils
extra rosemary, to garnish

## method

Heat the olive oil in a large saucepan and cook the sausages for 5–10 minutes, browning well all over. Remove the sausages and set aside.

Reduce the heat to low, add the onion and garlic to the pan and cook until the onion is soft and translucent, but not browned. Stir in the rosemary, then add the tomatoes and cook gently until the sauce has thickened.

Add the juniper berries, nutmeg, bay leaf, chilli, red wine and 400 ml (14 fl oz) water. Bring to the boil, then add the lentils and the cooked sausages. Stir well, cover the saucepan and simmer gently for about 40 minutes, or until the lentils are soft. Remove the bay leaf and chilli before serving. Garnish with the extra rosemary.

# mexican chicken bake

serves 4

## ingredients

165 g (5$^3$/$_4$ oz/$^3$/$_4$ cup) short-grain rice
300 g (10$^1$/$_2$ oz) tinned red kidney beans, drained
   and thoroughly rinsed
3$^1$/$_2$ tablespoons chopped coriander (cilantro)
   leaves
1 tablespoon oil
600 g (1 lb 5 oz) boneless, skinless chicken
   thighs, unrolled
400 g (14 oz) ready-made spicy taco sauce
250 g (9 oz/2 cups) grated cheddar cheese
125 g (4$^1$/$_2$ oz/$^1$/$_2$ cup) sour cream

## method

Preheat the oven to 180°C (350°F/Gas 4). Lightly grease a 7 x
21 cm (2$^3$/$_4$ x 8$^1$/$_4$ in) deep round ceramic casserole dish. Bring
a large saucepan of water to the boil, add the rice and cook for
10–12 minutes, stirring occasionally. Drain.

In the prepared dish, combine the beans and 1$^1$/$_2$ tablespoons
of the coriander, then add the rice and mix together. Lightly
press the mixture so the beans are mixed into the rice and the
mixture is flat.

Heat the oil in a large frying pan over medium–high heat. Sauté
the chicken thighs for 3 minutes each side. Add the spicy taco
sauce, and cook for a further 3 minutes.

To assemble, spread half the cheese over the rice. Arrange
the thighs and sauce on top in a star shape, sprinkle with
1$^1$/$_2$ tablespoons coriander, then sprinkle with cheese. Cover
with foil.

Bake for 35–40 minutes, or until the mixture is bubbling and
the cheese is melted and slightly browned—remove the foil for
the last 5 minutes. Cut into four servings and scoop out
carefully, keeping the layers intact. Serve sprinkled with the
remaining coriander and a dollop of sour cream.

# meat loaf

serves 6

## ingredients

125 g (4$^1$/$_2$ oz) bacon slices, trimmed and chopped
500 g (1 lb 2 oz) minced (ground) beef
500 g (1 lb 2 oz) minced (ground) pork
1 onion, coarsely grated
2 garlic cloves, crushed
160 g (5$^3$/$_4$ oz/2 cups) fresh breadcrumbs
2 teaspoons thyme leaves
1 egg, lightly beaten
1 tablespoon red wine vinegar
2 teaspoons soft brown sugar

## method

Preheat the oven to 180°C (350°F/Gas 4). Lightly grease a loaf tin then line with a single sheet of baking paper, leaving the paper to overhang on the long sides of the tin.

Heat a non-stick frying pan over medium heat. Add the bacon, and cook, stirring, until crispy. Drain on paper towels.

Place the meat, onion, garlic, breadcrumbs, thyme, egg, vinegar, sugar and bacon in a large bowl. Season and mix together using your hands. Don't overmix or the meat loaf will become too dense when it is cooked.

Spoon the mixture into the tin and press down gently. Smooth the top and bake for 1 hour 10 minutes, or until browned and cooked through. Test if it is cooked by pushing a metal skewer or sharp knife into the centre, leaving it for 3 seconds, and then pulling it out and holding it against your wrist. If it is really hot, it is cooked through, if not, cook a little longer. Leave for 5 minutes and pour the cooking juices into a bowl. Lift out the meat loaf using the overhanging baking paper. Cut into slices with a serrated knife and drizzle with the cooking juices.

# beef in black bean sauce

serves 4

## ingredients

4 tablespoons tinned salted black beans in
    soy sauce
750 g (1 lb 10 oz) rump steak
1 tablespoon peanut oil
1 tablespoon sesame oil
1 large onion, thinly sliced
1 garlic clove, finely chopped
4 cm x 1 cm (1$^1$/$_2$ in x $^1$/$_2$ in) piece of fresh ginger,
    peeled and finely chopped
1 small fresh red chilli, finely chopped
2 teaspoons cornflour (cornstarch)
2 tablespoons dark soy sauce
1 teaspoon sugar
3 tablespoons beef stock
1 spring onion (scallion), thinly sliced on the
    diagonal, to garnish

## method

Rinse and then soak the black beans in cold water for 5 minutes. Drain and roughly mash the beans with a fork.

Trim the steak of all fat and sinew, then cut the meat in thin slices across the grain.

Heat a saucepan over medium heat and add half each of the peanut and sesame oils. Add the beef in two batches, and stir each for 2 minutes, or until well browned. Transfer the beef and any liquid to a bowl. Heat the remaining oils, add the onion and stir for 2 minutes. Add the garlic, ginger and chilli, and stir for 1 minute.

Mix the cornflour with 1 teaspoon water, then return the beef and any cooking liquid to the pan with the black beans, soy sauce, sugar, stock and cornflour paste. Stir for 1–2 minutes, or until the sauce boils and thickens. Garnish with the spring onions and serve with steamed rice.

# honey chicken

serves 4

## ingredients

500 g (1 lb 2 oz) boneless, skinless chicken
    thighs, cut into cubes
1 egg white, lightly beaten
40 g ($1^1/_2$ oz/$^1/_3$ cup) cornflour (cornstarch)
3 tablespoons vegetable oil
2 onions, thinly sliced
1 green capsicum (pepper), cubed
2 carrots, cut into batons
100 g ($3^1/_2$ oz) snow peas (mangetout), sliced
90 g ($3^1/_4$ oz/$^1/_4$ cup) honey
2 tablespoons toasted almonds

## method

Dip the chicken cubes into the egg white, then lightly dust with the cornflour, shaking off any excess.

Heat a wok over high heat, add $1^1/_2$ tablespoons of the oil and swirl to coat the side of the wok. Add the chicken in two batches and stir-fry each batch for 4–5 minutes, or until the chicken is golden brown and just cooked. Remove the chicken from the wok and drain on crumpled paper towels.

Reheat the wok over high heat, add 1 tablespoon of the oil and stir-fry the sliced onion for 3–4 minutes, or until slightly softened. Add the green capsicum and carrot, and cook, tossing constantly, for 3–4 minutes, or until tender. Stir in the sliced snow peas and cook for 2 minutes.

Ensure that the wok is still very hot, then pour in the honey and toss with the vegetables until well coated. Return the chicken to the wok and toss thoroughly until heated through and well coated in the honey. Remove the wok from the heat and season well. Serve immediately, sprinkled with the toasted almonds. Serve with steamed white rice.

# linguine pesto

serves 4–6

## ingredients

100 g (3$^1$/$_2$ oz/2 cups) basil leaves
2 garlic cloves, crushed
40 g (1$^1$/$_2$ oz/$^1$/$_4$ cup) pine nuts, toasted
185 ml (6 fl oz/$^3$/$_4$ cup) olive oil
50 g (1$^3$/$_4$ oz/$^1$/$_2$ cup) grated parmesan cheese
500 g (1 lb 2 oz) linguine
shaved or grated parmesan cheese, extra,
    to serve

## method

Finely chop the basil, garlic and pine nuts together in a food processor. With the motor running, add the oil in a steady stream until mixed to a smooth paste. Transfer to a bowl, stir in the parmesan and season to taste.

Cook the pasta in a large saucepan of rapidly boiling salted water until *al dente*. Drain and return to the pan. Toss enough of the pesto through the pasta to coat well. Serve sprinkled with parmesan.

# spaghetti marinara

serves 4

## ingredients

**tomato sauce**
2 tablespoons olive oil
1 onion, finely chopped
1 carrot, finely chopped
2 garlic cloves, crushed
400 g (14 oz) tinned chopped tomatoes
125 ml ($4^1/_2$ fl oz/$^1/_2$ cup) white wine
1 teaspoon sugar

3 tablespoons white wine
3 tablespoons fish stock
1 garlic clove, crushed
12 black mussels, cleaned
375 g (13 oz) spaghetti
30 g (1 oz) butter
125 g ($4^1/_2$ oz) squid, cleaned and cut into rings
125 g ($4^1/_2$ oz) skinless cod fillet, cut into
   bite-sized pieces
200 g (7 oz) prawns (shrimp), peeled and deveined
1 handful flat-leaf (Italian) parsley, chopped
200 g (7 oz) tinned clams, drained

## method

To make the tomato sauce, heat the oil in a saucepan, then cook the onion and carrot over medium heat for 10 minutes, or until lightly browned. Add the garlic, tomato, wine and sugar. Bring to the boil, then reduce the heat and gently simmer for 30 minutes, stirring occasionally.

Heat the wine, stock and garlic in a large saucepan. Add the mussels. Cover and shake the pan over high heat for 5 minutes. After 3 minutes, start removing any opened mussels and set them aside. After 5 minutes, discard any unopened mussels and reserve the cooking liquid.

Cook the spaghetti in a large saucepan of boiling salted water until *al dente*. Drain and keep warm.

Meanwhile, melt the butter in a frying pan and stir-fry the squid, cod and prawns in batches for 2 minutes, or until just cooked. Remove from the heat and add to the tomato sauce along with the reserved cooking liquid, mussels, parsley and clams. Gently heat through, then toss the sauce with the pasta and serve.

# sweet and sour pork

serves 4

## ingredients

600 g (1 lb 5 oz) pork loin, cubed
2 eggs
120 g (4$^1$/$_4$ oz) cornflour (cornstarch)
1 tablespoon oil
1 onion, cubed
1 red capsicum (pepper), cubed
2 spring onions (scallions), cut into lengths
250 ml (9 fl oz/1 cup) clear rice vinegar or
   white vinegar
4 tablespoons tomato sauce (ketchup)
220 g (7$^3$/$_4$ oz/1 cup) sugar
2 tablespoons oil, extra

## method

Put the pork cubes and egg in a bowl with 4 tablespoons of the cornflour. Stir to coat the pork well, then tip into a sieve and shake off any excess cornflour.

Heat a wok over a high heat, add 1 tablespoon of oil and heat until it just starts to smoke. Add the onion and cook for 1 minute. Add the red capsicum and spring onion and cook for a further 1 minute. Add the rice vinegar, tomato ketchup and sugar, reduce the heat and stir until the sugar has dissolved. Bring to the boil and simmer for about 3 minutes.

Mix 2 tablespoons of cornflour with 2 tablespoons of water. Add to the sweet and sour mixture, then simmer for 1 minute, or until the sauce thickens slightly. Pour the sauce into a bowl.

Heat half the remaining oil in a non-stick frying pan over medium heat. Once the oil is hot, slide in half the pork cubes into the pan and cook until they are browned and crisp. Remove from the pan. Repeat with the remaining oil and pork. Return the pork to the pan and add the sauce. Heat until the sauce is bubbling.

# lemon chicken

serves 6

## ingredients

500 g (1 lb 2 oz) boneless, skinless chicken breast
1 tablespoon light soy sauce
1 tablespoon shaoxing rice wine
1 spring onion (scallion), finely chopped
1 tablespoon finely chopped ginger
1 garlic clove, finely chopped
1 egg, lightly beaten
100 g ($3^1/_2$ oz) cornflour (cornstarch)
oil, for deep-frying

### lemon sauce

2 tablespoons lemon juice
2 teaspoons sugar
$^1/_2$ teaspoon salt
$^1/_2$ teaspoon roasted sesame oil
3 tablespoons chicken stock or water
$^1/_2$ teaspoon cornflour (cornstarch)

## method

Cut the chicken into slices. Place in a bowl, add the soy sauce, rice wine, spring onion, ginger and garlic, and toss lightly. Marinate in the fridge for at least 1 hour, or overnight.

Add the egg to the chicken mixture and toss lightly to coat. Drain any excess egg and coat the chicken pieces with the cornflour.

Fill a wok one-quarter full of oil. Heat the oil to 190°C (375°F), or until a small cube of white bread browns in 10 seconds. Add half the chicken, a piece at a time, and fry, stirring constantly, for $3^1/_2$–4 minutes, or until golden brown. Remove with a wire sieve or slotted spoon and drain. Repeat with the remaining chicken. Reheat the oil and return all the chicken to the wok. Cook until crisp and golden brown. Drain the chicken. Pour off the oil and wipe out the wok.

To make the lemon sauce, combine the lemon juice, sugar, salt, sesame oil, stock and cornflour.

Reheat the wok over medium heat until hot, add the lemon sauce and stir constantly until thickened. Add the chicken and toss lightly in the sauce.

# madras beef curry

serves 6

## ingredients

1 tablespoon vegetable oil
2 onions, finely chopped
3 garlic cloves, finely chopped
1 tablespoon grated ginger
4 tablespoons madras curry paste
1 kg (2 lb 4 oz) chuck steak, trimmed and cut into
   3 cm (1$^1/_4$ in) cubes
60 g (2$^1/_4$ oz/$^1/_4$ cup) tomato paste (concentrated
   purée)
250 ml (9 fl oz/1 cup) beef stock
6 all-purpose potatoes, halved
155 g (5$^1/_2$ oz/1 cup) frozen peas

## method

Preheat the oven to 180°C (350°F/Gas 4). Heat the oil in a large heavy-based 3 litre (102 fl oz/12 cup) flameproof casserole dish. Cook the onion over medium heat for 4–5 minutes. Add the garlic and ginger and cook, stirring, for 5 minutes or until the onion is lightly golden, taking care not to burn it.

Add the curry paste and cook, stirring, for 2 minutes or until fragrant. Increase the heat to high. Add the meat and stir constantly for 2–3 minutes, or until the meat is well coated. Add the tomato paste and stock and stir well.

Bake, covered, for 50 minutes, stirring 2–3 times during cooking. Add a little water if necessary. Reduce the oven to 160°C (315°F/Gas 2–3). Add the potato and cook for 30 minutes, then add the peas. Cook for a further 10 minutes, or until the potato is tender. Serve hot with steamed jasmine rice.

# chicken and leek cobbler

serves 4–6

## ingredients

50 g (1³/₄ oz) butter
1 kg (2 lb 4 oz) boneless, skinless chicken breast,
    cut into thick strips
1 large leek, trimmed and finely sliced
1 celery stalk, finely sliced
1 tablespoon plain (all-purpose) flour
250 ml (9 fl oz/1 cup) chicken stock
250 ml (9 fl oz/1 cup) pouring (whipping) cream
3 teaspoons dijon mustard
3 teaspoons drained and rinsed green peppercorns

### topping

400 g (14 oz) all-purpose potatoes, quartered
165 g (5¹/₂ oz/1¹/₃ cups) self-raising flour
¹/₂ teaspoon salt
30 g (1 oz/¹/₄ cup) grated mature cheddar
100 g (3¹/₂ oz) cold butter, chopped
1 egg yolk, lightly beaten, to glaze

## method

Melt half the butter in a frying pan. Add the chicken and cook until golden. Remove from the pan. Add the remaining butter and cook the leek and celery until soft. Return the chicken to the pan. Sprinkle the flour over the chicken and stir for 1 minute. Remove from the heat and stir in the stock and cream. Mix. Return to the heat. Bring to the boil, then simmer for 20 minutes. Add the mustard and peppercorns and season. Transfer the mixture to a 1.25–1.5 litre (44–52 fl oz/5–6 cup) capacity casserole dish. Preheat the oven to 200°C (400°F/Gas 6).

To make the topping, cook the potatoes in a saucepan of boiling water until tender. Drain and mash. Place the flour and salt in a food processor and add the cheese and butter. Process in short bursts until the mixture forms crumbs. Add to the mashed potato and bring together to form a dough.

Roll out the dough on a floured surface, until it is 1 cm (¹/₂ in) thick. Cut into circles with a 6 cm (2¹/₂ in) diameter pastry cutter. Keep re-rolling the pastry scraps until all the dough is used. Lift the circles up with your fingers, and arrange them so that they overlap on top of the cooled chicken and leek filling.

Brush the dough circles with the egg yolk and add a little milk. Bake for 30 minutes, or until the pastry is golden.

# cottage pie

serves 4

## ingredients

30 g (1 oz) butter
1 kg (2 lb 4 oz) finely chopped lean beef or lean
    minced (ground) beef
1 large onion, chopped
1 large carrot, diced
140 g ($4^2/_3$ oz/$^1/_2$ cup) tomato sauce
425 g (15 oz) tinned chopped tomatoes
3 tablespoons beef or vegetable stock
115 g (4 oz/$^3/_4$ cup) peas
3 large all-purpose potatoes, chopped
30 g (1 oz) butter
1–2 tablespoons milk

## method

Heat a little oil and half the butter in a frying pan. Add the meat, in batches, and stir constantly until browned, breaking up any lumps with a wooden spoon. Transfer to a bowl and set aside.

Add the remaining butter and a little extra oil to the pan. Stir in the onion and carrot and cook over medium heat for 3–4 minutes, or until lightly browned. Return the meat to the pan. Stir in the tomato sauce, tomatoes and stock and mix well. Reduce the heat and simmer for 10–15 minutes, or until the liquid has reduced and mixture thickened. Stir in the peas and cook for 2 minutes. Remove from the heat.

Add the potatoes to a large saucepan of water. Bring to the boil, then reduce the heat and cook for 5–10 minutes or until soft. Drain, add the butter and milk and season. Mash until smooth and creamy.

Preheat the oven to 180°C (350°F/Gas 4). Spoon the beef and vegetable mixture into an ovenproof dish and spread the mashed potato over the top. Place the dish on top of a baking tray and bake for 20 minutes, or until the potato topping is golden brown.

# minced pork with spicy cellophane noodles

serves 4

## ingredients

200 g (7 oz) minced (ground) pork
1 teaspoon cornflour (cornstarch)
1$^1/_2$ tablespoons light soy sauce
2 tablespoons Chinese rice wine
1 teaspoon sesame oil
150 g (5$^1/_2$ oz) cellophane noodles (mung bean
    vermicelli)
2 tablespoons oil
4 spring onions (scallions), finely chopped
1 garlic clove, crushed
1 tablespoon finely chopped ginger
2 teaspoons chilli bean sauce
185 ml (6 fl oz/$^3/_4$ cup) chicken stock
1/2 teaspoon sugar
2 spring onions (scallions), green part only, extra,
    thinly sliced on the diagonal

## method

Combine the pork, cornflour, 1 tablespoon of the soy sauce,
1 tablespoon of the rice wine and $^1/_2$ teaspoon of the sesame
oil in a bowl, using a fork or your fingers. Cover with plastic
wrap and marinate for 10–15 minutes.

Meanwhile, place the noodles in a heatproof bowl, cover with
boiling water and soak for 3–4 minutes, or until softened.
Drain well.

Heat a wok over high heat, add the oil and swirl to coat.
Cook the spring onion, garlic, ginger and chilli bean sauce
for 10 seconds, then add the mince mixture and cook for
2 minutes, stirring to break up any lumps. Stir in the stock,
sugar, $^1/_2$ teaspoon salt, and the remaining soy sauce, rice
wine and sesame oil.

Add the noodles to the wok and toss to combine. Bring to
the boil, then reduce the heat to low and simmer, stirring
occasionally, for 7–8 minutes, or until the liquid is almost
completely absorbed. Garnish with the extra spring onion
and serve.

# beef cooked in guinness with celeriac purée

serves 4

## ingredients

2 tablespoons oil
1 kg (2 lb 4 oz) chuck steak, cubed
2 onions, chopped
1 garlic clove, crushed
2 teaspoons brown sugar
2 teaspoons plain (all-purpose) flour
125 ml (4 fl oz/$^1\!/_2$ cup) Guinness
375 ml (13 fl oz/1$^1\!/_2$ cups) beef stock
1 bay leaf
2 thyme sprigs
1 celeriac
1 all-purpose potato, cubed
250 ml (9 fl oz/1 cup) milk
20 g ($^3\!/_4$ oz) butter
4 slices baguette, toasted
1 teaspoon dijon mustard

## method

Preheat the oven to 180°C (350°F/Gas 4). Heat half of the oil in a frying pan over a high heat and fry the meat in batches until it is browned all over. Add more oil as you need it. Put the meat in a casserole dish.

Add the onion to the frying pan and fry it gently over a low heat. When the onion starts to brown, add the garlic and brown sugar and cook until the onion is brown. Stir in the flour, then transfer to the casserole dish.

Put the Guinness and stock in the frying pan and bring it to the boil, then pour into the casserole dish. Add the bay leaf and thyme to the casserole dish and season well. Bring to the boil, cover with a lid and put the casserole in the oven for 2 hours.

Peel and chop the celeriac. Put the pieces into a bowl of water. Put the potato and celeriac in a saucepan with the milk and bring to the boil. Cover and cook for 15 minutes, then mash everything together with the milk. Season and add the butter.

Spread the bread with the mustard and serve with the beef ladled over and the celeriac purée on the side.

# curried sausages

serves 6

## ingredients

9 thick beef or pork sausages
1 tablespoon vegetable oil
20 g ($^3/_4$ oz) butter
2 teaspoons grated ginger
3 garlic cloves, crushed
2 large onions, sliced
3 teaspoons curry powder
1 teaspoon garam masala
2 teaspoons tomato paste (concentrated purée)
1 tablespoon plain (all-purpose) flour
625 ml ($21^1/_2$ fl oz/$2^1/_2$ cups) hot chicken stock
2 bay leaves

## method

Place the sausages in a saucepan, cover with cold water and bring to the boil. Lower the heat and simmer for 3 minutes. Remove from the heat and allow the sausages to cool in the water. Drain, pat dry, and cut into 2 cm ($^3/_4$ in) pieces.

Heat the oil in a large frying pan over high heat and cook the sausages for 2–3 minutes, or until golden all over. Drain on paper towels.

Using the same pan, melt the butter, then add the ginger, garlic and onion. Cook over medium heat for about 5 minutes, or until the onion is soft and golden. Add the curry powder and garam masala and cook for 1 minute, or until fragrant. Stir in the tomato paste and cook for 1 minute, then add the flour. Stir to combine, then gradually pour in the stock, taking care that no lumps form. Bring to a simmer, add the bay leaves and the sausages and cook over low heat for 15 minutes, or until thickened. Season and serve with mashed potato.

# chilli con carne

serves 4

## ingredients

2 teaspoons ground cumin
$^1/_2$ teaspoon ground allspice
1–2 teaspoons chilli powder
1 teaspoon paprika
1 tablespoon vegetable oil
1 large onion, finely chopped
2 garlic cloves, crushed
2 small red chillies, seeded and finely chopped
500 g (1 lb 2 oz) minced (ground) beef
400 g (14 oz) tinned whole tomatoes
2 tablespoons tomato paste (concentrated purée)
425 g (15 oz) tinned red kidney beans, drained
    and rinsed
250 ml (9 fl oz/1 cup) beef stock
1 tablespoon chopped oregano
1 teaspoon sugar
tortilla and guacamole, to serve

## method

Heat a small frying pan over medium heat and dry-fry the cumin, allspice, chilli and paprika for 1 minute, or until fragrant. Remove from the pan.

Heat the oil in a large saucepan over medium heat and cook the onion for 2–3 minutes, or until soft. Add the garlic and chilli and cook for 1 minute. Add the beef and cook over high heat for 4–5 minutes, or until the meat is browned, breaking up any lumps with a fork.

Add the tomatoes, tomato paste, kidney beans, stock, oregano, sugar and spices. Reduce the heat and simmer, stirring occasionally and gently breaking up the tomatoes, for 1 hour, or until reduced and thickened. Season and serve with tortillas and guacamole.

# Irish stew

serves 4

## ingredients

20 g ($^3/_4$ oz) butter
1 tablespoon vegetable oil
8 lamb neck chops, trimmed
4 bacon slices, cut into strips
1 teaspoon plain (all-purpose) flour
600 g (1 lb 5 oz) potatoes, peeled and cut into
thick slices
3 carrots, cut into thick slices
1 onion, cut into 16 wedges
1 small leek, cut into thick slices
150 g ($5^1/_2$ oz) savoy cabbage, thinly sliced
500 ml (17 fl oz/2 cups) beef stock
2 tablespoons finely chopped flat-leaf (Italian)
parsley

## method

Heat the butter and oil in a flameproof casserole dish or a large heavy-based saucepan over high heat. Add the chops and cook for 1–2 minutes on each side, or until browned, then remove from the dish. Add the bacon and cook for 2–3 minutes, or until crisp. Remove with a slotted spoon, leaving the drippings in the dish.

Sprinkle the flour into the dish and stir to combine. Remove from the heat and layer half the potato, carrot, onion, leek, cabbage and bacon in the base of the dish. Arrange the chops in a single layer over the bacon and cover with layers of the remaining vegetables and bacon.

Pour in enough of the stock to cover, then bring to the boil over high heat. Reduce the heat, cover, and simmer for $1^1/_2$ hours, or until the meat is very tender and the sauce is slightly reduced. Season well and serve sprinkled with the parsley.

# lamb shanks with chickpeas

serves 4

## ingredients

1 tablespoon oil
4 large or 8 small lamb shanks
2 onions, finely chopped
2 garlic cloves, crushed
1 tablespoon harissa
1 cinnamon stick
800 g (1 lb 12 oz) tinned chopped tomatoes
600 g (1 lb 5 oz) tinned chickpeas, drained
90 g (3$^1/_4$ oz) green olives
$^1/_2$ tablespoon preserved lemon or lemon zest,
    finely chopped
2 tablespoons mint, chopped

## method

Heat the oil in a large casserole dish over medium heat and fry the lamb shanks until browned. Add the onion and garlic and fry for 2–3 minutes, or until the onion starts to soften.

Add the harissa and cinnamon to the casserole and season. Stir together, then add the chopped tomato and bring to the boil. Add more water if necessary. Cover with a lid and reduce the heat until the liquid is simmering. Cook for 50 minutes.

Add the chickpeas, olives and lemon to the pan. Season to taste and continue cooking, uncovered, for a further 20–30 minutes. By this time, the lamb should be very tender and almost falling off the bone. If it isn't, just keep cooking, checking every 5 minutes until it is. Using a large spoon, scoop any orange-coloured oil off the top, then stir in the mint. Serve with extra harissa, if desired.

# tuna mornay

serves 4

## ingredients

60 g (2¼ oz) butter
2 tablespoons plain (all-purpose) flour
500 ml (17 fl oz/2 cups) milk
½ teaspoon dry mustard
90 g (3¼ oz/¾ cup) grated cheddar cheese
600 g (1 lb 5 oz) tinned tuna in brine, drained
2 tablespoons finely chopped flat-leaf (Italian)
    parsley
2 eggs, hard-boiled and chopped
4 tablespoons fresh breadcrumbs
ground paprika, for dusting

## method

Preheat the oven to 180°C (350°F/Gas 4). Melt the butter in a small saucepan, add the flour and stir over low heat for 1 minute. Remove from the heat and slowly pour in the milk, stirring until you have a smooth sauce. Return the pan to the heat and stir constantly until the sauce boils and thickens. Reduce the heat and simmer for another 2 minutes. Remove the pan from the heat, whisk in the mustard and two-thirds of the cheese. Whisk until you have a smooth, rich cheesy sauce.

Roughly flake the tuna with a fork, then tip it into the cheesy sauce, along with the parsley and egg. Season, then spoon the mixture into four 250 ml (9 fl oz/1 cup) ovenproof ramekins.

Mix together the breadcrumbs and the rest of the cheese, then sprinkle it over the mornay. Add a hint of colour by dusting the top very lightly with paprika. Place in the oven for 20 minutes, or until the topping is golden brown.

# veal schnitzel with dill potato salad

serves 4

## ingredients

750 g (1 lb 10 oz) all-purpose potatoes, unpeeled
500 g (1 lb 2 oz) veal leg steaks
60 g (2$^1$/$_4$ oz/$^1$/$_2$ cup) seasoned plain (all-purpose)
  flour
2 eggs, lightly beaten
100 g (3$^1$/$_2$ oz/1 cup) dry breadcrumbs
125 ml (4 fl oz/$^1$/$_2$ cup) virgin olive oil
2 tablespoons lemon juice
1$^1$/$_2$ tablespoons finely chopped dill
200 g (7 oz) mixed salad leaves

## method

Cook the potatoes in a large saucepan of boiling water for 15–20 minutes, or until tender. Drain, then cut into quarters lengthways and cover to keep warm.

Meanwhile, beat the veal between two sheets of plastic wrap to 5 mm ($^1$/$_4$ in) thickness. Coat the veal in the flour and shake off the excess. Dip the veal in the egg, then coat in breadcrumbs. Place the schnitzel on a flat tray, cover and freeze for 5 minutes.

Heat 3 tablespoons of the oil in a large frying pan. Cook the veal in two batches over medium–high heat for 2–3 minutes on each side, or until golden and cooked through. Drain on crumpled paper towels and keep warm.

Whisk the lemon juice, dill and remaining oil together in a bowl and pour over the potatoes. Season and toss gently. Serve the schnitzel with the potatoes and a mixed salad.

# spinach and ricotta ravioli

serves 4

## ingredients

1 tablespoon olive oil
1 red onion, finely chopped
1 garlic clove, crushed
200 g (7 oz) baby English spinach leaves, coarsely
　chopped
250 g (9 oz/1 cup) ricotta cheese
2 egg yolks, beaten
2 tablespoons grated parmesan cheese
freshly grated nutmeg
48 won ton wrappers
40 g (1$^1$/$_2$ oz) butter
2 tablespoons sage leaves

## method

Heat the oil in a frying pan over low heat and add the onion and garlic. Fry for 2–3 minutes, or until the onion is soft and translucent. Add the spinach and stir until wilted.

Stir the spinach mixture into the ricotta, along with the egg yolk, parmesan and some nutmeg and season.

Brush a little water around the edge of a won ton wrapper and put a teaspoon of filling in the centre. Fold the wrapper over to make a half moon shape and press the edges firmly together. Put the ravioli on a tea towel (dish towel) laid out on a work surface and repeat with the remaining wrappers.

Bring a large saucepan of water to the boil and cook the ravioli for 2–3 minutes. They will float to the surface when they are ready. Scoop out carefully with a slotted spoon and drain in a colander. Melt the butter in a small saucepan, add the sage and sizzle for a few minutes until the butter browns slightly. Put the ravioli in bowls and pour the butter and sage over.

# teriyaki chicken

serves 4

## ingredients

4 small boneless chicken breasts, skin on (about
    170 g/6 oz each)
3 tablespoons soy sauce
2 tablespoons sake
1$^1$/$_2$ tablespoons mirin
1$^1$/$_2$ tablespoons soft brown sugar
3 teaspoons finely grated fresh ginger
300 g (10$^1$/$_2$ oz/1$^1$/$_2$ cups) long-grain rice
2 tablespoons finely chopped chives
2 tablespoons oil

## method

Pound each chicken breast between sheets of plastic wrap with a mallet until 1 cm ($^1$/$_2$ in) thick. Put the soy sauce, sake, mirin, sugar and 1 teaspoon ginger in a flat non-metallic dish and stir until the sugar has dissolved. Add the chicken and turn to coat. Cover and refrigerate for 1 hour, turning once halfway through.

Bring a large saucepan of water to the boil. Add the rice and cook for 12 minutes, stirring occasionally. Drain. Stir in the chives and remaining ginger, then cover until ready to serve.

Drain the chicken, reserving the marinade. Heat the oil in a deep frying pan and cook the chicken, skin side down, over medium heat for 5 minutes, until the skin is crisp. Turn and cook for 4 minutes.

Add the marinade and 3 tablespoons water to the pan and scrape up any sediment. Bring to the boil over high heat, then add the chicken and juices. Cook for 5–6 minutes, until cooked through, turning once.

Serve the chicken whole or sliced, drizzled with the sauce.

# beef pot roast

serves 6

## ingredients

300 g (10$^1$/$_2$ oz) pickling onions
2 carrots
3 parsnips, peeled
40 g (1$^1$/$_2$ oz) butter
1.5 kg (3 lb 5 oz) piece of silverside,
    trimmed of fat
3 tablespoons dry red wine
1 large tomato, finely chopped
250 ml (9 oz/1 cup) beef stock

## method

Put the onions in a heatproof bowl and cover with boiling water. Leave for 1 minute, then drain well. Allow to cool then peel off the skins.

Cut the carrots and parsnips in half lengthways then into even-sized pieces. Heat half the butter in a large saucepan that will tightly fit the meat, add the onions, carrot and parsnip and cook, stirring, over high heat until browned. Remove from the pan. Add the remaining butter to the pan and add the meat, browning well all over. Increase the heat to high and pour in the wine. Bring to the boil, then add the tomato and stock. Return to the boil, then reduce the heat to low, cover and simmer for 2 hours, turning once. Add the vegetables and simmer, covered, for 1 hour.

Remove the meat from the pan and put it on a board ready for carving. Cover with foil and leave it to stand.

Increase the heat to high and boil the pan juices with the vegetables for 10 minutes to reduce and thicken slightly. Skim off any excess fat, and season to taste. Slice the meat and arrange on a serving platter with the vegetables. Drizzle with the pan juices. Serve with mustard on the side.

# goulash

serves 6

## ingredients

100 g (3$^1$/$_2$ oz) bacon slices, julienned
1 onion, chopped
2 tomatoes, peeled and chopped
1 garlic clove, chopped
$^1$/$_2$ teaspoon caraway seeds, lightly crushed
1$^1$/$_2$ tablespoons sweet paprika
1 kg (2 lb 4 oz) lamb fillet, trimmed and cut into
    2 cm ($^3$/$_4$ in) pieces
1 bay leaf
250 ml (9 fl oz/1 cup) vegetable stock
450 g (1 lb) chat potatoes, cut into 2 cm ($^3$/$_4$ in)
    pieces
100 g (3$^1$/$_2$ oz) fresh or frozen peas
3 tablespoons sour cream
sweet paprika, extra, to garnish

## method

Place the bacon in a 4 litre (135 fl oz/16 cup) casserole dish and cook over medium heat for 4–5 minutes. Add the onion and cook for 2 minutes, then add the tomato and cook for 1 minute.

Stir in the garlic, caraway seeds, paprika, lamb, bay leaf and stock. Bring to the boil, then reduce the heat to low, and simmer, covered, for 40 minutes.

Add the potato and cook, uncovered, for 15 minutes, or until tender. Add the peas and cook for 5 minutes, or until tender. Stir in the sour cream and gently heat, without boiling. Garnish with paprika and serve with rye bread.

# lamb koftas in spicy tomato sauce

serves 4

## ingredients

3 tablespoons vegetable oil
2 large onions, finely chopped
3 garlic cloves, finely chopped
1$\frac{1}{2}$ tablespoons garam masala
$\frac{1}{2}$ teaspoon chilli powder
400 g (14 oz) tinned chopped tomatoes
1 tablespoon tomato paste (concentrated purée)
500 ml (17 fl oz/2 cups) beef stock
270 ml (9$\frac{1}{2}$ fl oz) tinned coconut milk
500 g (1 lb 2 oz) minced (ground) lamb
1 large handful mint, finely chopped, plus extra, to garnish
1 large handful coriander (cilantro) leaves, finely chopped, plus extra, to garnish
1 egg, lightly beaten
juice of 1 lime
steamed basmati rice, to serve

## method

Heat the oil in a large heavy-based frying pan. Cook the onion for 5 minutes, or until lightly brown. Add the garlic, garam masala and chilli powder. Cook, stirring for 2–3 minutes, or until aromatic. Remove half of the onion mixture to a large bowl and set aside to cool.

Add the chopped tomatoes and tomato paste to the remaining onion in the frying pan, stirring. Simmer for 5 minutes, then add the stock and coconut milk. Bring to the boil, then remove from the heat, cover and set aside.

Add the lamb, herbs and beaten egg to the cooled onion mixture. With wet hands, roll the meat into 28 walnut-sized balls. Cover and refrigerate for 30 minutes.

Heat the sauce to simmering point. Add the kofta balls and cook over low heat for 1 hour, or until cooked through and the sauce has reduced and thickened. Gently stir the kofta balls occasionally. Stir in the lime juice. Garnish with the extra herbs and serve with basmati rice.

# chicken casserole with mustard and tarragon

serves 4–6

## ingredients

3 tablespoons olive oil
1 kg (2 lb 4 oz) boneless, skinless chicken thighs,
    halved, then quartered
1 onion, finely chopped
1 leek, sliced
1 garlic clove, finely chopped
350 g (12 oz) button mushrooms, sliced
$1/2$ teaspoon dried tarragon
375 ml (13 fl oz/$1^1/2$ cups) chicken stock
185 ml (6 fl oz/$^3/4$ cup) pouring (whipping) cream
2 teaspoons lemon juice
2 teaspoons dijon mustard

## method

Preheat the oven to 180°C (350°F/Gas 4). Heat 1 tablespoon of the oil in a flameproof casserole dish over medium heat, and cook the chicken in two batches for 6–7 minutes each, or until golden. Remove from the dish.

Add the remaining oil to the casserole dish and cook the onion, leek and garlic over medium heat for 5 minutes, or until soft. Add the mushrooms and cook for 5–7 minutes, or until they are soft and browned and most of the liquid has evaporated. Add the tarragon, chicken stock, cream, lemon juice and mustard, bring to the boil and cook for 2 minutes. Return the chicken pieces to the dish and season well. Cover.

Place the casserole in the oven and cook for 1 hour, or until the sauce has reduced and thickened. Season and serve with potatoes and a green salad.

# pork chops with apples and cider

serves 4

## ingredients

1 tablespoon oil
2 onions, sliced
2 golden delicious apples, cored and cut
    into wedges
2 teaspoons caster (superfine) sugar
10 g ($^1/_4$ oz) butter
4 thick pork chops, snipped around the edges
4 tablespoons cider
4 tablespoons pouring (whipping) cream

## method

Heat the oil in a large non-stick frying pan, add the onion and fry for about 5 minutes, or until soft and just beginning to brown. Remove from the pan.

Add the apple wedges to the pan and fry for 1–2 minutes — they should not break up, but should start to soften and brown. Add the sugar and butter and shake around in the pan until the apples start to caramelize. Transfer the apples to the plate with the onion.

Put the pork chops in the frying pan, add a bit of seasoning and fry for 4 minutes on each side, or until they are cooked through. Put the onion and apple back in the pan and heat, then add the cider and bring to a simmer. Once the liquid is bubbling, add the cream and shake the pan. Let it bubble for 1 minute, then season well and serve with potatoes and a green salad.

# pasta with pork and fennel sausages

serves 4

## ingredients

6 Italian pork and fennel sausages (about 550 g/
    1 lb 4 oz)
1 tablespoon olive oil
1 small red onion, finely chopped
2–3 garlic cloves, crushed
$1/2$ teaspoon chilli flakes
300 g ($10^1/2$ oz) field or button mushrooms,
    thinly sliced
800 g (1 lb 12 oz) tinned diced tomatoes
1 tablespoon finely chopped thyme
500 g (1 lb 2 oz) penne rigate
grated parmesan cheese, to serve

## method

Split the sausages open, remove and crumble the filling and discard the skins.

Heat the oil in a large saucepan over medium–high heat and cook the onion for 3–4 minutes, or until fragrant and transparent. Add the garlic, chilli flakes, mushrooms and crumbled sausage meat. Cook over high heat, stirring gently to mash the sausage meat, for 4–5 minutes, or until the meat is evenly browned. If necessary, use a tablespoon to remove any excess fat from the pan, leaving about a tablespoon of oil. Continue to cook, stirring once or twice, for 10 minutes.

Stir in the tomato and thyme, then bring the sauce to the boil. Cover and cook over medium–low heat for 20 minutes, stirring occasionally.

Meanwhile, cook the penne rigate in a large saucepan of rapidly boiling salted water until *al dente*. Drain well, then add to the sauce, stirring to combine. Serve with parmesan.

# Thai noodle salad

serves 4

## ingredients

250 g (9 oz) dried instant egg noodles
500 g (1 lb 2 oz) cooked large prawns (shrimp),
    peeled and deveined, tails intact
5 spring onions (scallions), sliced
2 tablespoons chopped coriander (cilantro)
1 red capsicum (pepper), diced
100 g (3½ oz) snowpeas (mangetout), julienned
4 lime wedges

### dressing

2 tablespoons grated fresh ginger
2 tablespoons soy sauce
2 tablespoons sesame oil
4 tablespoons red wine vinegar
1 tablespoon sweet chilli sauce
2 garlic cloves, crushed
4 tablespoons kecap manis

## method

Cook the egg noodles in a saucepan of boiling water for
2 minutes, or until tender. Drain thoroughly, then leave to
cool in a large serving bowl.

Whisk all the dressing ingredients together in a bowl and
gently mix through the cooled noodles. Add the prawns, spring
onion, coriander, capsicum and snowpeas. Toss gently and
serve with lime wedges.

# satay chicken stir-fry

serves 4

## ingredients

300 g (10$^1/_2$ oz/1$^1/_2$ cups) jasmine rice

1$^1/_2$ tablespoons peanut oil

6 spring onions (scallions), cut into 3 cm (1$^1/_4$ in) lengths

800 g (1 lb 12 oz) boneless, skinless chicken breast, thinly sliced on the diagonal

1–1$^1/_2$ tablespoons Thai red curry paste

90 g (3$^1/_4$ oz/$^1/_3$ cup) crunchy peanut butter

270 ml (9$^1/_2$ fl oz) coconut milk

2 teaspoons soft brown sugar

1$^1/_2$ tablespoons lime juice

## method

Bring a large saucepan of water to the boil. Add the rice and cook for 12 minutes, stirring occasionally. Drain well.

Meanwhile, heat a wok until very hot, add 1 teaspoon of the peanut oil and swirl to coat. When hot, add the spring onion and stir-fry for 30 seconds, or until softened slightly. Remove from the wok. Add a little extra peanut oil to the wok as needed and stir-fry the chicken in three batches for about 1 minute per batch, or until the meat just changes colour. Remove from the wok.

Add a little more oil to the wok, add the curry paste and stir-fry for 1 minute, or until fragrant. Add the peanut butter, coconut milk, sugar and 250 ml (9 fl oz/1 cup) water and stir well. Bring to the boil and boil for 3–4 minutes, or until thickened and the oil starts to separate—reduce the heat slightly if the sauce spits at you. Return the chicken and the spring onion to the wok, stir well and cook for 2 minutes, or until heated through. Stir in the lime juice and season. Serve with the rice and a green salad.

# roast lamb

serves 4

## ingredients

2 rosemary sprigs
3 garlic cloves
75 g (2$^1$/$_2$ oz) pancetta
2 kg (4 lb 8 oz) leg of lamb, shank bone cut off
   just above the joint, trimmed of excess fat
   and tied
1 large onion
125 ml (4 fl oz/$^1$/$_2$ cup) olive oil
375 ml (13 fl oz/1$^1$/$_2$ cups) dry white wine

## method

Preheat the oven to 230°C (450°F/Gas 8). Strip the leaves off the rosemary sprigs and chop with the garlic and pancetta until paste-like. Season.

With the point of a sharp knife, make incisions about 1 cm ($^1$/$_2$ in) deep all over the lamb. Rub the rosemary filling over the surface of the lamb, pushing it into the incisions.

Cut the onion into four thick slices and put them in the centre of a roasting tin. Place the lamb on top and gently pour the olive oil over it. Roast for 15 minutes. Reduce the temperature to 180°C (350°F/Gas 4) and pour in 250 ml (9 fl oz/1 cup) of the wine. Roast for 1$^1$/$_2$ hours for medium–rare, or longer if you prefer. Baste a couple of times and add a little water if the juices start to burn in the tin. Transfer the lamb to a carving platter and leave to rest for 10 minutes.

Remove the onion and spoon off the excess fat from the tin. Place over high heat on the stovetop, pour in the remaining wine and cook for 3–4 minutes, or until the sauce reduces and thickens. Season. Slice the lamb and serve with the sauce spooned over the top.

# shepherd's pie

serves 4

## ingredients

1 tablespoon oil
1 onion, finely chopped
1 carrot, finely chopped
1 kg (2 lb 4 oz) minced (ground) lamb,
    raw or cooked
plain (all-purpose) flour, for thickening
2 tablespoons tomato sauce (ketchup)
2 beef stock cubes
worcestershire sauce
6 all-purpose potatoes, cut into chunks
4 tablespoons milk
20 g (³/₄ oz) butter

## method

Preheat the oven to 200°C (400°F/Gas 6). Heat the oil in a frying pan, add the onion and carrot and fry until starting to brown. Add the meat and cook, turning, mashing out any large lumps with the back of a fork.

When the meat is browned all over, add a little flour and stir. Add the ketchup and sprinkle on the stock cube. Add about 500 ml (17 fl oz/2 cups) of water and mix to combine. Bring the mixture to the boil, then reduce the heat and simmer gently for 30 minutes, or until thick. Season and add the worcestershire sauce.

Meanwhile, cook the potato chunks in simmering water for 12 minutes, or until they are tender. When they are soft, drain and mash them with the milk and plenty of seasoning. Pour the meat into a large ovenproof dish or four individual dishes and dollop the potato on top. Dot some butter over the potato and bake for about 20 minutes, by which time the top of the potato should be lightly browned. Serve with peas.

# moussaka

serves 4–6

## ingredients

2 large eggplants (aubergines), about 800 g
   (1 lb 12 oz), sliced lengthways into 1.5 cm
   (⁵/₈ in) thick pieces
1 tablespoon olive oil
1 large onion, chopped
1 garlic clove, crushed
500 g (1 lb 2 oz) minced (ground) beef
125 ml (4 fl oz/¹/₂ cup) red wine
125 g (4¹/₂ oz/¹/₂ cup) tomato paste (concentrated
   purée)
pinch of ground cinnamon
2 teaspoons chopped oregano
3 tablespoons chopped flat-leaf (Italian) parsley
2 tablespoons grated parmesan cheese
2 tablespoons dry breadcrumbs

### Sauce

20 g (³/₄ oz) butter
40 g (1¹/₂ oz/¹/₃ cup) plain (all-purpose) flour
500 ml (17 fl oz/2 cups) milk
pinch of ground nutmeg
1 tablespoon grated parmesan cheese

## method

Preheat the oven to 200°C (400°F/Gas 6). Spread the eggplant slices on two foil-lined baking sheets and brush both sides using a little of the oil. Bake for 10 minutes, turn the slices and bake for a further 10 minutes. Allow to cool.

Heat the remaining oil in a large saucepan. Add the onion and garlic and cook for 4–5 minutes. Increase the heat to high and brown the beef for 5 minutes. Stir in the wine, tomato paste, cinnamon, oregano and a quarter of the parsley. Season. Reduce to a simmer, stirring occasionally, for 15–20 minutes. Remove from the heat.

To make the sauce, melt the butter in a saucepan. Stir in the flour and cook over low heat for 2–3 minutes. Slowly whisk in the milk, cooking for 6–8 minutes until thickened. Remove from the heat and add the nutmeg, parmesan and ¹/₂ teaspoon salt.

Grease an 18 x 28 cm (7 x 11 in) rectangular casserole dish. Line the base with a layer of eggplant, then top with the beef. Cover with the remaining eggplant, then pour over the sauce. Mix together the parmesan, breadcrumbs and remaining parsley, season, then sprinkle over the top. Bake for 30 minutes, or until golden.

# spaghetti with meatballs

serves 4

## ingredients

### meatballs

500 g (1 lb 2 oz) minced (ground) beef
40 g (1¹/₂ oz/¹/₂ cup) fresh breadcrumbs
1 onion, finely chopped
2 garlic cloves, crushed
2 teaspoons worcestershire sauce
1 teaspoon dried oregano
30 g (1 oz/¹/₄ cup) plain (all-purpose) flour
2 tablespoons olive oil

### sauce

800 g (1 lb 12 oz) tinned chopped tomatoes
1 tablespoon olive oil
1 onion, finely chopped
2 garlic cloves, crushed
2 tablespoons tomato paste (concentrated purée)
125 ml (4 fl oz/¹/₂ cup) beef stock
2 teaspoons sugar

500 g (1 lb 2 oz) spaghetti
grated parmesan cheese, to serve (optional)

## method

Combine the beef, breadcrumbs, onion, garlic, worcestershire sauce and oregano in a bowl and season. Use your hands to mix the ingredients together well. Roll level tablespoons of the mixture into balls, dust lightly with the flour and shake off the excess. Heat the oil in a deep frying pan and cook the meatballs in batches, turning frequently, until browned all over. Drain well.

To make the sauce, purée the tomatoes in a food processor or blender. Heat the oil in a frying pan. Add the onion and cook over medium heat for a few minutes until soft and just lightly golden. Add the garlic and cook for a further 1 minute. Add the puréed tomatoes, tomato paste, stock and sugar to the pan and stir to combine. Bring the mixture to the boil, and add the meatballs. Reduce the heat and simmer for 15 minutes, turning the meatballs once. Season.

Meanwhile, cook the spaghetti in a large saucepan of boiling water until just tender. Drain, divide among serving plates and top with the meatballs and sauce. Serve with grated parmesan, if desired.

# silverside with parsley sauce

serves 6

## ingredients

1.5 kg (3 lb 5 oz) corned silverside
1 teaspoon black peppercorns
5 cloves
2 bay leaves, torn
2 tablespoons soft brown sugar

### parsley sauce

50 g ($1^3/_4$ oz) butter
$1^1/_2$ tablespoons plain (all-purpose) flour
400 ml (14 fl oz) milk
125 ml (4 fl oz/$^1/_2$ cup) beef stock
2 tablespoons chopped flat-leaf (Italian) parsley

## method

Soak the corned beef in cold water for 45 minutes, changing the water 3–4 times.

Lift the beef out of the water and put in a large heavy-based saucepan with the peppercorns, cloves, bay leaves, brown sugar and enough cold water to just cover it. Bring to the boil, then reduce the heat to low and simmer for $1^1/_2$–$1^3/_4$ hours. Turn the meat over every half hour and keep an eye on the water level—you'll probably need to add some more. Remove the meat from the pan and let it rest for 15 minutes.

To make the parsley sauce, melt the butter in a saucepan over medium heat and then stir in the flour and continue stirring for 1 minute. Remove from the heat and pour in the milk and stock, whisking until smooth. Return the pan to the heat and cook, whisking constantly, until the sauce boils and thickens. Reduce the heat and simmer for a further 2 minutes before stirring in the parsley. Season. Serve over slices of silverside with steamed vegetables.

# zucchini pasta bake

serves 4

## ingredients

200 g (7 oz) risoni
40 g (1¹/₂ oz) butter
4 spring onions (scallions), thinly sliced
400 g (14 oz) zucchini (courgettes), grated
4 eggs
125 ml (4 fl oz/¹/₂ cup) pouring (whipping) cream
100 g (3¹/₂ oz) ricotta cheese
100 g (3¹/₂ oz/²/₃ cup) grated mozzarella cheese
75 g (2¹/₂ oz/³/₄ cup) grated parmesan cheese

## method

Preheat the oven to 180°C (350°F/ Gas 4). Cook the pasta in a large saucepan of rapidly boiling water until *al dente*. Drain well.

Meanwhile, heat the butter in a frying pan, add the spring onion and cook for 1 minute, then add the zucchini and cook for a further 4 minutes, or until soft. Cool slightly.

Combine the eggs, cream, ricotta, mozzarella, risoni and half of the parmesan, then stir in the zucchini mixture. Season well. Spoon into four 500 ml (17 fl oz/2 cup) greased ovenproof dishes. Sprinkle with the remaining parmesan and cook for 25–30 minutes, or until firm and golden.

# sausage and bean hotpot with roasted orange sweet potato

serves 4

## ingredients

1 kg (2 lb 4 oz) spicy Italian-style sausages

2 garlic cloves, roughly chopped

800 g (1 lb 12 oz) tinned cannellini beans

850 g (1 lb 14 oz) tinned crushed tomatoes

2 teaspoons dijon mustard

750 g (1 lb 10 oz) orange sweet potato, cut into 3 cm (1¼ in) cubes

2 tablespoons olive oil

2 tablespoons coarsely chopped flat-leaf (Italian) parsley

## method

Preheat the oven to 200°C (400°F/Gas 6). Cook the sausages in a large frying pan over medium heat for 5–7 minutes, or until golden. Cut into 5 cm (2 in) pieces and place in a 4 litre (135 fl oz/16 cup) casserole dish. Add the garlic, beans, tomato, mustard and 2 tablespoons water to the dish and season. Stir well and cover with a lid. Place in the oven.

Meanwhile, toss the sweet potato with the oil and place in a baking dish. Sprinkle with salt. Place in the oven with the casserole dish and bake for 25 minutes. Uncover the casserole dish and bake for a further 10–15 minutes, or until the hotpot is golden and bubbling and the sweet potato is soft and lightly golden brown. Serve the hotpot garnished with the parsley and the sweet potato on the side.

# fish pie

serves 4

## ingredients

800 g (1 lb 12 oz) skinless ling fillets, cut into
    large chunks
375 ml (13 fl oz/1$^{1}/_{2}$ cups) milk
30 g (1 oz) butter
1 onion, finely chopped
1 garlic clove, crushed
2 tablespoons plain (all-purpose) flour
2 tablespoons lemon juice
2 teaspoons lemon zest
1 tablespoon chopped dill

### potato topping
500 g (1 lb 2 oz) roasting (floury) potatoes, diced
3 tablespoons milk or pouring (whipping) cream
1 egg, lightly beaten
30 g (1 oz) butter
60 g (2$^{1}/_{4}$ oz) cheddar cheese, finely grated

## method

Preheat the oven to 180°C (350°F/Gas 4). To make the potato topping, steam the potatoes until tender. Mash, then push to one side of the pan, add the milk and heat gently. Beat the milk into the potato until it is fluffy, then season and stir in the egg and butter. Mix in half the cheddar, then set aside and keep warm.

Put the fish in a frying pan and cover with the milk. Bring to the boil, then reduce the heat and simmer for 2 minutes, or until the fish is opaque and flaky. Drain, reserving the milk, and put the fish in a 1.5 litre (52 fl oz/6 cup) ovenproof dish.

Melt the butter in a saucepan and cook the onion and garlic for 2 minutes. Stir in the flour and cook for 1 minute, or until pale and foaming. Remove from the heat and gradually stir in the reserved milk. Return to the heat and stir constantly until it boils and thickens. Reduce the heat and simmer for 2 minutes. Add the lemon juice, zest and dill, and season. Mix with the fish. Spoon the topping over the fish and top with the remaining cheddar. Bake for 35 minutes, or until golden.

# beef pie

serves 6

## ingredients

90 g (3 oz/$^3$/$_4$ cup) plain (all-purpose) flour
40 g (1$^1$/$_2$ oz/$^1$/$_3$ cup) self-raising flour
90 g (3$^1$/$_4$ oz) butter, chopped
2 bacon slices, chopped
1 small onion, finely chopped
750 g (1 lb 10 oz) lean minced (ground) beef
2 tablespoons plain (all-purpose) flour, extra
375 ml (12 fl oz/1$^1$/$_2$ cups) beef stock
125 g (4$^1$/$_2$ oz/$^1$/$_2$ cup) tomato paste (concentrated
    purée)
2 tablespoons worcestershire sauce
2 teaspoons dried mixed herbs
1 tablespoon dry mustard
375 g (12 oz) frozen puff pastry
1 egg, lightly beaten

## method

Mix the flours and butter in a food processor until fine and crumbly. Add 1 tablespoon of water and process until the mixture comes together, adding more water if necessary. Turn out onto a floured surface and gather it into a ball. Cover with plastic wrap and refrigerate for 30 minutes. Roll the pastry on a sheet of baking paper until large enough to cover the base and sides of a greased 23 cm (9 in) round pie dish and refrigerate.

Heat some oil in a frying pan and cook the bacon and onion for 5 minutes. Add the beef and cook for 4 minutes, or until browned. Stir in the flour for 1 minute.

Add the stock, paste, sauce, herbs and mustard and bring to the boil. Reduce the heat and simmer, stirring occasionally, for 8 minutes, or until most of the liquid has evaporated. Cool, then place in the pastry shell. Preheat the oven to 210°C (415°F/Gas 6–7).

On a floured surface, roll out the puff pastry until it is large enough to cover the pie. Brush the edge of the pie shell with egg, place the pastry on top and trim the edges. Make cuts around the edge, cutting right through the pastry, and 4 cuts in the top. Brush with egg. Bake for 15 minutes. Reduce the heat to 180°C (350°F/Gas 4) and bake for 25 minutes, or until golden.

# rice noodles with beef, black beans and capsicums

serves 4

## ingredients

300 g (10$^1$/$_2$ oz) rump steak
1 garlic clove, crushed
3 tablespoons oyster sauce
2 teaspoons sugar
2 tablespoons soy sauce
100 ml (3$^1$/$_2$ fl oz) black bean sauce
2 teaspoons cornflour (cornstarch)
$^3$/$_4$ teaspoon sesame oil
1.2 kg (2 lb 11 oz) fresh or 600 g (1 lb 5 oz) dried
    flat rice noodles
1$^1$/$_2$ tablespoons oil
2 red capsicums (peppers), sliced
1 green capsicum (pepper), sliced
1 handful coriander (cilantro) leaves

## method

Cut the steak across the grain into thin slices and put it in a bowl with the garlic, oyster sauce, sugar, soy sauce, black bean sauce, cornflour and sesame oil. Mix to combine, making sure the slices are all well coated.

If you are using dried rice noodles, soak in boiling water for 10 minutes, or until opaque and soft. If the noodles are particularly dry, they may need a little longer. Drain well.

Heat the oil in a wok or frying pan and, when hot, add the capsicums. Stir-fry the capsicums for 1–2 minutes, or until starting to soften, then add the meat mixture and cook for 1 minute. Add the noodles and toss together well. Continue cooking until the meat is cooked through. Toss in the coriander leaves and stir, then remove from the heat.

# lamb's fry and bacon

serves 4

## ingredients

500 g (1 lb 2 oz) lamb's fry
plain (all-purpose) flour, for coating
30 g ( 1 oz) butter
1 tablespoon oil
2 onions, sliced
4 bacon slices
375 ml (13 fl oz/1$^1$/$_2$ cups) chicken stock
1 teaspoon worcestershire sauce
2 tablespoons chopped flat-leaf (Italian) parsley,
    to serve

## method

Peel off the outer membrane of lamb's fry with your fingers and discard. Cut the lamb's fry into 1 cm ($^1$/$_2$ in) slices. Dust with seasoned flour. Shake off the excess flour and reserve 2 tablespoons.

Heat the butter and oil in a frying pan. Add the onion. Stir over medium heat for 2 minutes, or until soft. Remove the onion from the pan and set aside.

Add the bacon to the pan, stir over medium heat for 2 minutes or until crisp. Remove from the pan and set aside.

Add the lamb's fry to the pan and cook over medium–high heat for 1 minute on each side, or until lightly browned, turning once. Return the onion to the pan.

Blend the chicken stock, worcestershire sauce and reserved flour. Pour into the pan and bring to the boil. Reduce the heat to low, simmer for 3 minutes or until the lab's fry is tender and the sauce has thickened. Stir in the cooked bacon and heat through. Serve immediately with the parsley.

# surf 'n' turf

serves 4

## ingredients

**lemon mustard sauce**
30 (1 oz) butter
1 spring onion (scallion), finely chopped
1 garlic clove, crushed
1 tablespoon plain (all-purpose) flour
250 ml (9 fl oz/1 cup) milk
2 tablespoons pouring (whipping) cream
1 tablespoon lemon juice
2 teaspoons dijon mustard

2 tablespoons oil
1 large green lobster tail, shelled
4 beef scotch fillets
170 g (6 oz) tinned crab, drained

## method

To make the lemon mustard sauce, heat the butter in a saucepan and add the onion and garlic. Stir over medium heat for 1 minute, or until the onion is soft.

Add the milk gradually to the saucepan, stirring until the mixture is smooth. Stir constantly over medium heat until the mixture boils and thickens. Simmer for 1 minute. Remove from the heat, stir in the cream, lemon juice and mustard. Keep warm.

Heat the oil in a frying pan. Add the lobster tail. Cook over medium heat for 3 minutes on each side, or until just cooked through. Remove from the pan and keep warm.

Add the steaks to the pan, cook over high heat for 2 minutes on each side to seal, turning once. Cook each side for a further 1 minute, or until done to your liking. Drain on paper towels.

To serve, place the steaks on plates, top with crab then sliced lobster. Pour lemon mustard sauce over and garnish with spring onion.

# Vietnamese chicken salad

serves 4

## ingredients

2 boneless, skinless chicken breasts or 4 chicken
   thighs, cooked
2 tablespoons lime juice
$1^{1}/_{2}$ tablespoons fish sauce
$^{1}/_{4}$ teaspoon sugar
1–2 bird's eye chillies, finely chopped
1 garlic clove, crushed
2 French shallots, finely sliced
2 handfuls bean sprouts, trimmed
1 large handful shredded Chinese cabbage (wong
   bok)
4 tablespoons Vietnamese mint or mint leaves,
   finely chopped

## method

Shred the cooked chicken.

Mix together the lime juice, fish sauce, sugar, chilli, garlic
and shallot.

Bring a saucepan of water to the boil and throw in the bean
sprouts. After 10 seconds, drain them and rinse under cold
water to stop them cooking any longer.

Mix the bean sprouts with the Chinese cabbage, Vietnamese
mint and chicken. Pour the dressing over the salad and toss
everything together well.

# rigatoni with chorizo and tomato

serves 4

## ingredients

2 tablespoons olive oil
1 onion, sliced
250 g (9 oz) chorizo sausage, sliced
425 g (15 oz) tinned crushed tomatoes
125 ml (4 fl oz/$^1/_2$ cup) dry white wine
$^1/_2$–1 teaspoon chopped chilli, optional
375 g (13 oz) rigatoni
2 tablespoons chopped flat-leaf (Italian) parsley
2 tablespoons freshly grated parmesan cheese

## method

Heat the oil in a frying pan. Add the onion and stir over low heat until tender.

Add the sausage to the pan and cook, turning, for 2–3 minutes. Add the tomato, wine, chilli and season. Stir well. Bring to the boil, reduce the heat and simmer for 15–20 minutes.

While the sauce is cooking, cook the rigatoni in a large saucepan of rapidly boiling salted water until *al dente*. Drain and return to the pan. Add the sauce to the hot pasta. Toss well to combine. Serve sprinkled with the combined parsley and grated parmesan.

# souvlake

serves 4

## ingredients

1 kg (2 lb 4 oz) boned leg lamb, trimmed, cut into
    2 cm (³/₄ in) cubes
3 tablespoons olive oil
2 teaspoons finely grated lemon zest
4 tablespoons lemon juice
125 ml (4 fl oz/¹/₂ cup) dry white wine
2 teaspoons dried oregano
2 large garlic cloves, finely chopped
2 bay leaves
250 g (9 oz/1 cup) Greek-style natural yoghurt
2 garlic cloves, crushed, extra

## method

Place the lamb in a non-metallic bowl with 2 tablespoons oil, the lemon zest and juice, wine, oregano, garlic, bay leaves and some black pepper. Toss, then cover and refrigerate overnight.

Place the yoghurt and extra garlic in a bowl, mix well and leave for 30 minutes.

Drain the lamb and thread onto 8 skewers. Cook on a barbecue or chargrill plate, brushing with the remaining oil, for about 7–8 minutes. Serve with the yoghurt.

# sausages and mash with gravy

serves 4

## ingredients

4 tablespoons olive oil
200 g (7 oz) French shallots, thinly sliced
1 tablespoon plain (all-purpose) flour
125 ml (4 fl oz/$^1/_2$ cup) red wine
375 ml (13 fl oz/1$^1/_2$ cups) beef stock
1 tablespoon dijon mustard
1.5 kg (3 lb 5 oz) potatoes, chopped
150 g (5$^1/_2$ oz) butter
8 thick pork sausages (about 100 g/3$^1/_2$ oz each)
450 g (1 lb) green beans, topped and tailed

## method

Heat 2 tablespoons of the oil in a large frying pan over medium heat. Add the shallots and cook for 5 minutes, stirring often until soft. Add the flour and cook for 30 seconds. Increase the heat, pour in the wine and stock and bring to the boil. Reduce the heat and simmer for 10 minutes, or until the gravy thickens. Stir in the mustard, then reduce the heat to medium–low and simmer gently until the sausages and mash are ready.

Cook the potatoes in boiling water until tender. Drain, return to the pan and add 1 tablespoon olive oil and 120 g (4$^1/_4$ oz) of the butter. Mash until smooth, then season.

While the potatoes are cooking, prick the sausages with a fork. Heat a large frying pan over medium–high heat, add the remaining oil and the sausages. Cook for 10 minutes, or until cooked through, turning often.

Bring a saucepan of lightly salted water to the boil, add the beans and cook for 4 minutes, or until just tender. Whisk the remaining butter into the gravy and season. Place a mound of mash on each plate, top with the sausages and gravy, and serve with the beans on the side.

# stir-fried chicken with ginger and cashews

serves 4

## ingredients

1$^1$/$_2$ tablespoons oil
8 spring onions (scallions), cut into pieces
3 garlic cloves, crushed
8 cm (3 in) piece ginger, finely shredded
2 boneless, skinless chicken breasts, cut into
   strips
2 red capsicums (peppers), cut into strips
150 g (5$^1$/$_2$ oz) snow peas (mangetout)
100 g (3$^1$/$_2$ oz) cashew nuts
2 tablespoons soy sauce
1$^1$/$_2$ teaspoons sesame oil

## method

Heat the oil in a wok until it is smoking. Add the spring onion, garlic and ginger and stir for a few seconds. Add the chicken and stir until it has turned white. Add the red capsicum and continue stirring, then add the snow peas and cashews and stir-fry for a further 1–2 minutes.

Add the soy sauce and sesame oil and toss together. Serve with rice or noodles and more soy sauce, if desired.

# nasi goreng

serves 4

## ingredients

2 eggs
4 tablespoons oil
3 garlic cloves, finely chopped
1 onion, finely chopped
2 red chillies, seeded and very finely chopped
1 teaspoon shrimp paste
1 teaspoon coriander seeds
$1/2$ teaspoon sugar
400 g (14 oz) raw prawns (shrimp), peeled
    and deveined
200 g (7 oz) rump steak, finely sliced
200 g (7 oz/1 cup) long-grain rice, cooked and
    cooled
2 teaspoons kecap manis
1 tablespoon soy sauce
4 spring onions (scallions), finely chopped
$1/2$ lettuce, finely shredded
1 Lebanese (short) cucumber, thinly sliced
3 tablespoons crisp fried onions

## method

Beat the eggs and $1/4$ teaspoon of salt until foamy. Heat a frying pan and brush with a little oil. Pour about one-quarter of the mixture into the pan and cook for 1–2 minutes over medium heat, or until the omelette sets. Turn the omelette over and cook the other side for about 30 seconds. Remove the omelette from the pan and repeat with the remaining mixture. When the omelettes are cold, roll them up, cut into fine strips and set aside.

Combine the garlic, onion, chilli, shrimp paste, coriander and sugar in a food processor, and process until a paste is formed.

Heat 1–2 tablespoons of the oil in a wok. Add the paste and cook over high heat for 1 minute. Add the prawns and steak, and stir-fry for 2–3 minutes.

Add the remaining oil and the cold rice to the wok. Stir-fry until the rice is heated through. Add the kecap manis, soy sauce and spring onion, and stir-fry for a further 1 minute.

Arrange the lettuce around the outside of a large platter. Put the rice in the centre, and garnish with the omelette, cucumber slices and crisp fried onion. Serve immediately.

# pasta with beef ragù

## ingredients

100 g (3½ oz) streaky bacon or pancetta (not trimmed), finely chopped
1 onion, finely chopped
3 garlic cloves, crushed
1 bay leaf
800 g (1 lb 12 oz) lean minced (ground) beef
500 ml (17 fl oz/2 cups) red wine
90 g (3¼ oz/⅓ cup) tomato paste (concentrated purée)
400 g (14 oz) tagliatelle
freshly grated parmesan cheese, to serve

## method

Heat a large deep frying pan, add the bacon or pancetta and cook over medium–high heat for 2 minutes, or until soft and just starting to brown. Add the onion, garlic and bay leaf and cook for 2 minutes, or until the onion is soft and just starting to brown.

Add the beef and stir for about 4 minutes, or until the beef browns, breaking up any lumps with the back of a wooden spoon. Add the wine, tomato paste and 250 ml (9 fl oz/1 cup) water and stir well. Bring to the boil, then reduce the heat and simmer, covered, for 40 minutes. Remove the lid and cook for another 40 minutes, or until reduced to a thick, glossy sauce.

Bring a large saucepan of salted water to the boil and cook the pasta until *al dente*. Drain. Serve the sauce over the pasta with the grated parmesan.

# pastitsio

serves 6–8

## ingredients

2 tablespoons oil
4 garlic cloves, crushed
2 onions, chopped
1 kg (2 lb 4 oz) minced (ground) beef
1 kg (2 lb 4 oz) tinned peeled tomatoes, chopped
250 ml (9 fl oz/1 cup) dry red wine
250 ml (9 fl oz/1 cup) beef stock
1 bay leaf
1 teaspoon dried mixed herbs
350 g (12 oz) ziti pasta
3 eggs, lightly beaten
500 g (1 lb 2 oz) Greek-style yoghurt
200 g (7 oz) kefalotyri cheese, grated
$^1/_2$ teaspoon ground nutmeg
60 g ($2^1/_4$ oz/$^1/_2$ cup) grated cheddar cheese

## method

Heat the oil in a large heavy-based pan, and cook the garlic and onion over medium heat for 5 minutes, or until the onion is soft. Add the beef and cook over high heat until browned, then drain off any excess fat. Add the tomato, wine, stock, bay leaf and herbs and bring to the boil. Reduce the heat and simmer for 40 minutes. Season well.

Preheat the oven to 180°C (350°F/Gas 4). Meanwhile, cook the pasta in a large pan of rapidly boiling water until *al dente*. Drain well and spread in the base of a large ovenproof dish. Pour in half the egg and top with the sauce.

Combine the yoghurt, remaining egg, kefalotyri and nutmeg and pour over the top. Sprinkle with the cheddar and bake for 40 minutes, or until golden brown. Leave to stand for 10 minutes before serving.

# lemon and thyme roasted chicken with zucchini

serves 4

## ingredients

1 x 1.8 kg (4 lb) chicken
12 garlic cloves, unpeeled
10 lemon thyme sprigs
1 lemon, halved
1 tablespoon olive oil
8 small zucchini (courgettes), halved lengthways
2 tablespoons chopped flat-leaf (Italian) parsley
1 tablespoon plain (all-purpose) flour
250 ml (9 fl oz/1 cup) chicken stock

## method

Remove the giblets and any large fat deposits from inside the chicken, then pat it dry inside and out with paper towels. Season the cavity and stuff with the garlic cloves and thyme. Rub the skin with the cut lemon, then brush with 2 teaspoons of the oil and season.

Preheat a kettle or covered barbecue to medium indirect heat. Position the chicken on the barbecue, close the hood and roast the chicken for 1 hour, or until the juices run clear when pierced with a skewer between the thigh and the body.

Toss the zucchini with the remaining olive oil and season. Arrange the zucchini on the grill around the chicken, cover the kettle and cook the chicken and the zucchini for 20 minutes, or until the zucchini is tender. Put the zucchini in a serving dish and sprinkle with the parsley. When the chicken is ready, remove from the barbecue, cover loosely with foil and leave to rest for 10 minutes. Remove the garlic from the chicken cavity.

# on the barbecue

Thanks to **mild, sunny, outdoorsy weather** and some wonderful meats and fish, **barbecuing** has become a **culinary obsession**. Food never tastes better than when it is cooked outside. The **delicious aroma of food sizzling** on a barbecue and flame-grilled flavour is hard to resist! It's also the perfect excuse to **gather friends and family around.**

# corn with chilli lime butter

serves 6

## ingredients

6 corn cobs, husks and silks removed
75 g (2½ oz) butter, at room temperature
1 tablespoon finely chopped coriander (cilantro)
    leaves
1 small red chilli, finely chopped
2 teaspoons lime juice
6 lime wedges

## method

Preheat a barbecue grill plate or chargrill pan to hot. Lightly brush the hotplate with oil and grill the cobs for about 15 minutes, turning often, until tender and flecked with brown.

Meanwhile, put the butter in a small bowl and mash with a fork. Add the coriander, chilli and lime juice and mix together until well combined.

When the cobs are cooked, secure corn holders in each end and spread each cob with some chilli lime butter. Season with salt and serve each cob with a wedge of lime for squeezing over the top.

# gourmet sausage sandwiches

makes 12

## ingredients

### yoghurt and coriander dressing
3 tablespoons Greek-style yoghurt
2 tablespoons finely chopped coriander (cilantro)
2 teaspoons lemon juice

### mustard mayonnaise
3 tablespoons whole-egg mayonnaise
2 tablespoons dijon mustard

### wholegrain tomato sauce
3 tablespoons tomato sauce
2 tablespoons wholegrain mustard

4 pork sausages
4 chicken sausages
4 beef sausages
1 tablespoon olive oil
2 red onions, sliced
2 red apples, cored and thinly sliced
150 g (5$^1$/$_2$ oz) mixed lettuce leaves
12 pocket pitta breads, split at the top

## method

To make the dressings, combine the ingredients for the yogurt and coriander dressing, mustard mayonnaise and wholegrain tomato sauce in separate small bowls. Cover and refrigerate until needed.

Preheat a barbecue grill plate or flat plate to medium. Fry the sausages for about 10 minutes, or until cooked through, turning during cooking. Keep warm.

Heat the oil on the barbecue flat plate. Cook the onion on one area of the hotplate and the apples on another for 5 minutes, or until they begin to soften and turn golden. Remove from the heat and set aside.

Put some lettuce leaves in each pitta bread pocket. Slice the pork sausages in half lengthways and divide among 4 pitta pockets. Add some barbecued onion and all the apple and drizzle with mustard mayonnaise. Slice the chicken sausages in half and divide among 4 pitta pockets. Add some barbecued onion and drizzle with the yoghurt and coriander dressing. Slice the beef sausages and divide among the remaining pitta pockets. Add the remaining onion and drizzle with the wholegrain tomato sauce. Wrap in napkins and serve.

# greek salad

serves 4

## ingredients

4 tomatoes, cut into wedges
1 telegraph (long) cucumber, peeled, halved, seeded and diced into small cubes
2 green capsicums (peppers), cut into strips
1 red onion, finely sliced
16 kalamata olives
250 g (9 oz) firm feta cheese, cut into cubes
3 tablespoons flat-leaf (Italian) parsley
12 mint leaves
125 ml (4 fl oz/$^1/_2$ cup) olive oil
2 tablespoons lemon juice
1 garlic clove, crushed

## method

Put the tomato, cucumber, capsicum, onion, olives, feta and half the parsley and mint leaves in a large bowl. Toss together.

Combine the oil, lemon juice and garlic in a small screw-top jar, season well and shake until thoroughly combined. Pour the dressing over the salad, toss well and serve scattered with the remaining parsley and mint.

# beef satay

serves 4

## ingredients

650 g (1 lb 7 oz) rump steak, finely sliced
lime wedges, to serve
2 tablespoons chopped coriander (cilantro)
    leaves, to serve

### satay sauce

2 teaspoons peanut oil
1 small onion, finely chopped
2 tablespoons chopped lemon grass,
    white part only
2 tablespoons finely grated fresh galangal
1 red bird's eye chilli, finely chopped
140 g (5 oz) crunchy peanut butter
250 ml (9 fl oz/1 cup) coconut milk

## method

Soak 12 bamboo skewers in cold water for 20 minutes. Thread the beef evenly onto the skewers.

To make the satay sauce, heat the oil in a small saucepan over medium heat and cook the onion, stirring, for 3 minutes, or until soft. Add the lemon grass, galangal and chilli and cook, stirring, for 1 minute, or until fragrant. Stir in the peanut butter and coconut milk and cook over low heat until well combined and heated through.

Heat an oiled barbecue grill plate or chargrill pan over high heat. Lightly brush the beef with oil. Cook the skewers for about 3 minutes on each side, or until browned and cooked as desired.

Serve the beef with the satay sauce and lime wedges and sprinkle with the coriander.

# chilli lamb cutlets

serves 4

## ingredients

4 garlic cloves, crushed
1 tablespoon grated ginger
1 teaspoon oil
1 teaspoon sambal oelek
2 teaspoons ground coriander
2 teaspoons ground cumin
2 tablespoons soy sauce
2 teaspoons sesame oil
2 tablespoons sweet chilli sauce
2 tablespoons lemon juice
12 lamb cutlets
steamed rice, to serve

## method

Combine the garlic, ginger, oil, sambal oelek, coriander, cumin, soy sauce, sesame oil, sweet chilli sauce and lemon juice in a bowl. Season.

Place the cutlets in a non-metallic dish and pour on the marinade, coating all sides. Leave to marinate for 20 minutes.

Cook the cutlets on a very hot chargrill pan or barbecue chargrill plate for 3 minutes each side, or until cooked to your liking. Serve with steamed rice.

# fresh beetroot and goat's cheese salad

serves 2

### ingredients

2 beetroot bulbs, with leaves
100 g (3$^1$/$_2$ oz) green beans, trimmed
50 g (1$^3$/$_4$ oz) goat's cheese

### caper dressing
2 teaspoons red wine vinegar
1 tablespoon extra virgin olive oil
1 garlic clove, crushed
2 teaspoons capers, rinsed, drained and
    coarsely chopped

### method

Trim the leaves from the beetroot. Scrub the bulbs and wash the leaves well. Bring a large saucepan of water to the boil, add the beetroot, then reduce the heat and simmer, covered, for about 30 minutes, or until tender. Drain and allow to cool. Wearing gloves to protect your hands from staining, peel the skins off the beetroot and cut the bulbs into wedges.

Meanwhile, bring a saucepan of lightly salted water to the boil, add the beans and blanch until bright green and just tender, about 2–3 minutes. Remove with tongs and plunge into a bowl of cold water. Drain well.

Add the beetroot leaves to the saucepan of boiling water and cook for about 3–5 minutes, or until the leaves and stems are tender. Drain, plunge into a bowl of cold water, then drain well again.

To make the caper dressing, put the vinegar, oil, garlic and capers in a small screw-top jar with $^1$/$_4$ teaspoon each of salt and cracked black pepper. Shake vigorously until well combined.

Divide the beans, beetroot and beetroot leaves between two plates. Crumble the goat's cheese over the top and drizzle with the dressing.

# jumbo spicy lamb burgers

serves 4

## ingredients

2 red capsicums (peppers)
1 eggplant (aubergine), cut into 8 thick slices
3 tablespoons olive oil
3 teaspoons ground cumin
2 teaspoons ground coriander
1 teaspoon ground cardamom
$1/2$ teaspoon ground cinnamon
3 tablespoons chopped coriander (cilantro)
    stems and leaves
750 g (1 lb 10 oz) minced (ground) lamb
1 small red onion, diced
oil, for brushing
8 thick slices sourdough bread
200 g (7 oz) ready-made baba ghanoush
60 g ($2^1/4$ oz) baby rocket (arugula) leaves
125 g ($4^1/2$ oz/$1/2$ cup) whole-egg mayonnaise
3 garlic cloves, crushed

## method

Heat the grill (broiler) to high. Cut the capsicums into quarters, discarding the seeds and membrane. Arrange skin side up on the grill tray and grill until the skin blackens and blisters. Leave to cool in a plastic bag, then peel away the skin.

Meanwhile, preheat a barbecue flat plate, grill plate or chargrill pan to high. Toss the eggplant in the oil to coat and cook for 2–3 minutes on each side, or until golden and softened. Remove from the heat. Reduce the heat to medium.

Dry-fry the ground cumin, coriander, cardamom and cinnamon in a frying pan over medium heat for 1 minute, or until fragrant. Put the fried spices in a bowl with the chopped coriander, lamb and onion and season with salt and pepper. Mix until well combined, then form into four burgers about 1 cm ($1/2$ in) thick.

Brush the hotplate with oil and cook the lamb burgers for 4–5 minutes on each side, or until cooked through.

Meanwhile, grill the bread until toasted on both sides. Spread the baba ghanoush over 4 of the slices and top with the rocket, eggplant, capsicum and lamb burgers. Mix the mayonnaise and garlic together and dollop over the burgers. Top with the remaining bread halves and serve immediately.

# marinated baby octopus salad

serves 4

## ingredients

750 g (1 lb 10 oz) baby octopus
4 tablespoons olive oil
2 garlic cloves, crushed
1 red capsicum (pepper), thinly sliced
1 tablespoon sweet chilli sauce
2 tablespoons chopped coriander (cilantro)
2 tablespoons lime juice

## method

Using a small knife, carefully cut between the head and tentacles of the octopus, just below the eyes. Grasp the body of the octopus and push the beak out and up through the centre of the tentacles with your finger. Cut the eyes form the head of the octopus by slicing a small disc off with a sharp knife. Discard the eye section. To clean the octopus head, carefully slit through one side, avoiding the ink sac and scrape out any gut from inside. Rinse under running water to remove any remaining grit. Put in a mixing bowl. Add the oil and garlic, mix, then cover and marinate in the refrigerator for 1–2 hours.

Heat a barbecue grill or chargrill pan to very hot. Cook the baby octopus for about 3–5 minutes, in batches, or until just tender. Drain well on crumpled paper towels.

Put the capsicum, sweet chilli sauce, coriander and lime juice in a serving bowl. Add the octopus and mix together. Serve warm or cold.

# seared tuna and white bean salad

serves 4

## ingredients

400 g (14 oz) tuna steaks
1 small red onion, thinly sliced
1 tomato, seeded and chopped
1 small red capsicum (pepper), thinly sliced
800 g (1 lb 12 oz) tinned cannellini beans, rinsed
    and drained
2 garlic cloves, crushed
1 teaspoon chopped thyme
4 tablespoons finely chopped flat-leaf (Italian)
    parsley
oil, for brushing
100 g (3$^1/_2$ oz) baby salad leaves or baby rocket
    (arugula) leaves
1 teaspoon lemon zest strips

### warm vinaigrette
1$^1/_2$ tablespoons lemon juice
4 tablespoons extra virgin olive oil
1 teaspoon honey

## method

Put the tuna steaks on a plate, sprinkle both sides with plenty of cracked black pepper, cover with plastic wrap and refrigerate until needed.

Toss the onion, tomato and capsicum in a large mixing bowl with the beans, garlic, thyme and parsley.

To make the warm vinaigrette, put the lemon juice, oil and honey in a small saucepan. Bring to the boil, then simmer, stirring, for 1 minute, or until the honey has dissolved. Remove from the heat but keep warm.

Brush a barbecue hotplate or chargrill pan with a little oil and heat until very hot. Cook the tuna steaks for 1–2 minutes on each side, depending on their thickness—they should still be pink in the middle. Slice into large cubes and add to the beans. Pour the warm dressing over the top and toss well.

Divide the beans and tuna between four serving plates. Top with the salad leaves, scatter with the lemon zest and serve.

# spice-rubbed pork kebabs with garlic sauce

serves 4

## ingredients

800 g (1 lb 12 oz) pork neck fillet, trimmed
2 teaspoons fennel seeds
2 teaspoons coriander seeds
1 tablespoon olive oil

**garlic sauce**
4 garlic cloves, coarsely chopped
1 thick slice of white bread, crusts removed
3 tablespoons olive oil
$1^1/_2$ tablespoons lemon juice

lemon wedges and pitta bread, to serve

## method

Soak eight wooden skewers in cold water for 1 hour. Cut the pork into 2 cm ($^3/_4$ in) cubes. Dry-fry the fennel and coriander seeds for about 30 seconds, or until they are fragrant, then grind them in a spice grinder or mortar and pestle. Mix the ground spices with the olive oil and toss the pork in it until the meat is well coated. Cover and refrigerate for 2 hours.

To make the garlic sauce, crush the garlic cloves in a mortar and pestle with $^1/_2$ teaspoon salt until you have a smooth paste. Tear the bread into pieces and leave in a bowl with enough warm water to cover. Soak for 5 minutes then squeeze out the bread and add to the garlic, a little at a time, pounding until you have a smooth paste. Add the olive oil, 1 tablespoon at a time, then add 3 tablespoons of boiling water, one tablespoon at a time, and stir in the lemon juice.

Thread the pork onto the soaked skewers and season the kebabs well. Preheat the barbecue chargrill plate to medium–high direct heat and grill the kebabs for 10 minutes, or until they are cooked through, turning them halfway through the cooking time. Drizzle the kebabs with a little garlic sauce and put the rest of the sauce in a small bowl to serve at the table. Serve with the lemon wedges and warm pitta bread.

# honeyed prawn and scallop skewers

makes 8

## ingredients

500 g (1 lb 2 oz) raw medium prawns (shrimp)
250 g (9 oz) scallops

### marinade
3 tablespoons honey
2 tablespoons soy sauce
3 tablespoons barbecue sauce
2 tablespoons sweet sherry

## method

Soak 8 wooden skewers in water for 30 minutes.

Peel the prawns, leaving the tails intact. Gently pull out the dark vein from each prawn back, starting at the head end.

Slice or pull off any vein, membrane or hard white muscle from the scallops, leaving any roe attached.

Thread the prawns and scallops alternately onto the skewers (about 2 prawns and 3 scallops per skewer). Place in a shallow non-metallic dish. Combine the honey, soy sauce, barbecue sauce and sherry in a jug and pour over the skewers. Cover and marinate in the refrigerator for 3 hours, or overnight.

Preheat the barbecue. Cook the skewers on a lightly greased barbecue flatplate, turning several times, for 5 minutes, or until cooked through. Brush frequently with marinade while cooking.

# watercress salad

serves 4

## ingredients

500 g (1 lb 2 oz) watercress, washed
1 Lebanese (short) cucumber, peeled, halved,
    seeded and thinly sliced
3 celery stalks, cut into thin batons
1 red onion, thinly sliced and separated into rings
30 g (1 oz) chives, snipped
3 oranges
60 g ($2^1/_4$ oz/$^1/_2$ cup) chopped pecan nuts
    or walnuts

### mustard citrus dressing

3 tablespoons olive oil
3 tablespoons lemon juice
2 teaspoons grated orange zest
1 teaspoon seeded mustard
1 tablespoon honey

## method

Pick the watercress into small sprigs, discarding the coarser stems. Toss in a large bowl with the cucumber, celery, onion and chives.

Peel the oranges, removing all the bitter white pith, and cut the flesh into segments between the membrane. Add the segments to the salad.

Put all the mustard citrus dressing ingredients in a small screw-top jar, season with black pepper and shake vigorously. Pour over the salad, toss, sprinkle with the nuts and serve.

# barbecued squid with salsa verde

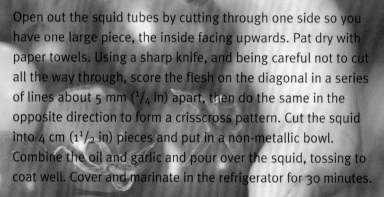

serves 4

## ingredients

4 squid tubes, cleaned
3 tablespoons olive oil
3 garlic cloves, crushed
150 g (5$\frac{1}{2}$ oz) mixed lettuce leaves
250 g (9 oz) cherry tomatoes, halved

### salsa verde

2 large handfuls flat-leaf (Italian) parsley
2 tablespoons chopped dill
2 tablespoons extra virgin olive oil
2 tablespoons olive oil
1 tablespoon dijon mustard
2 garlic cloves, crushed
1 tablespoon red wine vinegar
1 tablespoon baby capers, rinsed and drained
4 anchovy fillets, drained

## method

Open out the squid tubes by cutting through one side so you have one large piece, the inside facing upwards. Pat dry with paper towels. Using a sharp knife, and being careful not to cut all the way through, score the flesh on the diagonal in a series of lines about 5 mm ($\frac{1}{4}$ in) apart, then do the same in the opposite direction to form a crisscross pattern. Cut the squid into 4 cm (1$\frac{1}{2}$ in) pieces and put in a non-metallic bowl. Combine the oil and garlic and pour over the squid, tossing to coat well. Cover and marinate in the refrigerator for 30 minutes.

Put all the salsa verde ingredients in a food processor and blend until just combined. Set aside until ready to use.

Preheat a barbecue flat plate to high. Drain the squid and cook for 1–2 minutes, or until curled up and just cooked through. Put the squid in a bowl with the salsa verde and toss until well coated. Arrange the lettuce and tomatoes on four serving plates, top with the squid, then season and serve.

# barbecued steaks filled with bocconcini and semi-dried tomatoes

serves 6

## ingredients

6 New York-style (boneless sirloin) steaks
200 g (7 oz) semi-dried (sun-blushed) tomatoes, chopped
200 g (7 oz) bocconcini (fresh baby mozzarella cheese), chopped
2 garlic cloves, crushed
2 tablespoons finely chopped flat-leaf (Italian) parsley
oil, for brushing

## method

Cut a slit along the side of each steak to form a pocket. Combine the tomato, bocconcini, garlic and parsley in a small bowl and season. Fill each steak with the mixture and secure with toothpicks to hold the filling in.

Preheat a barbecue grill plate or chargrill pan to medium. Just before cooking, brush the steaks lightly with oil and season. Grill the steaks for 3–4 minutes on each side for medium–rare, or until cooked to your liking, turning only once. Remove the toothpicks and serve with vegetables or a salad.

# caramelized onion and potato salad

serves 2

## ingredients

1 tablespoon olive oil
3 red onions, thinly sliced
500 g (1 lb 2 oz) kipfler or new potatoes, unpeeled
2 bacon slices
15 g ($^1/_2$ oz) chives, snipped

**lemon mayonnaise**
125 g ($4^1/_2$ oz/ $^1/_2$ cup) ready-made whole-egg
    mayonnaise
2 teaspoon dijon mustard
$^1/_2$ lemon, juiced
1 tablespoon sour cream

## method

Heat the oil in a large heavy-based frying pan. Add the onion and cook, stirring, over low heat for 40 minutes, or until soft and caramelized.

Cut any large potatoes into large chunks (leave the small ones whole). Cook in boiling water for 10 minutes, or until just tender, then drain. Place in a large bowl with the onion and most of the chives and mix well.

Meanwhile, grill (broil) the bacon slices until crisp. Drain on paper towels. Allow to cool slightly, then chop coarsely.

Whisk together the lemon mayonnaise ingredients, pour over the salad and toss to coat. Divide between two plates and sprinkle with the bacon and reserved chives.

# veal stacks with mozzarella

serves 4

## ingredients

1 small eggplant (aubergine)
125 g (4$^{1}/_{2}$ oz/$^{1}/_{2}$ cup) tomato passata (puréed tomatoes)
1 garlic clove, crushed
$^{1}/_{4}$ teaspoon sugar
oil, for brushing
4 x 150 g (5$^{1}/_{2}$ oz) butterflied veal loin steaks
50 g (1$^{3}/_{4}$ oz) baby rocket (arugula) leaves
75 g (2$^{1}/_{2}$ oz/$^{1}/_{2}$ cup) coarsely grated mozzarella cheese

## method

Slice the eggplant into 5 mm ($^{1}/_{4}$ in) thick rounds. Put in a colander and sprinkle generously with salt to draw out the juice. Leave for 20 minutes, then rinse well under cold running water and pat dry with paper towels.

Put the passata, garlic and sugar in a small bowl. Season to taste and set aside.

Preheat a barbecue grill plate, flat plate or chargrill pan to high. Brush both sides of each eggplant slice with a little oil and cook for about 15 minutes, turning once, or until lightly browned on both sides. Remove from the heat.

Heat the grill (broiler) to high. Brush the veal steaks with a little oil, season, then grill on the hotplate for about 3–5 minutes on each side, or until nicely browned and cooked to your liking. Remove from the heat.

Arrange the rocket, eggplant slices, passata mixture and mozzarella on top of each steak. Put the steaks on the grill plate under the hot grill and cook for 1 minute, or until the cheese is golden. Serve hot.

# king prawns with dill mayonnaise

serves 4

## ingredients

### marinade
125 ml (4 fl oz/$^1$/$_2$ cup) olive oil
4 tablespoons lemon juice
2 tablespoons wholegrain mustard
2 tablespoons honey
2 tablespoons chopped dill

16–20 raw king prawns (shrimp)

### dill mayonnaise
185 g (6$^1$/$_2$ oz/$^3$/$_4$ cup) mayonnaise
2 tablespoons chopped dill
1$^1$/$_2$ tablespoons lemon juice
1 gherkin, finely chopped
1 teaspoon chopped capers
1 garlic clove, crushed

## method

To make the marinade, combine the olive oil, lemon juice, mustard, honey and dill, pour over the unpeeled prawns and coat well. Cover and refrigerate for at least 2 hours, turning occasionally.

To make the mayonnaise, whisk together the mayonnaise, dill, lemon juice, gherkin, capers and garlic. Cover and refrigerate.

Cook the drained prawns on a hot, lightly oiled barbecue grill or flat plate in batches for 4 minutes, turning frequently until pink and cooked through. Serve with the dill mayonnaise.

# coleslaw

serves 8–10

## ingredients

$^1/_2$ green cabbage
$^1/_4$ red cabbage
3 carrots, coarsely grated
6 radishes, coarsely grated
1 red capsicum (pepper), chopped
4 spring onions (scallions), sliced
15 g ($^1/_2$ oz) chopped flat-leaf (Italian) parsley
250 g (9 oz/1 cup) whole-egg mayonnaise

## method

Remove the hard core from the cabbages and shred the leaves with a sharp knife. Place in a large bowl and add the grated carrot, grated radish, red capsicum, spring onion and parsley.

Add the mayonnaise just before serving, season to taste and toss until well combined.

# tandoori lamb with tomato and onion salsa

serves 4

## ingredients

60 g (2$^{1}/_{4}$ oz/$^{1}/_{4}$ cup) tandoori paste
250 g (9 oz/1 cup) plain yoghurt
1 tablespoon lemon juice
4 racks of lamb with 4–5 cutlets in each

### tomato and onion salsa

6 roma (plum) tomatoes
1 red onion
2 tablespoons lemon juice
1 teaspoon sugar
2 tablespoons olive oil

minted potato salad, to serve (optional)

## method

Mix together the tandoori paste, yoghurt and the lemon juice in a large, non-metallic bowl. Trim any excess fat off the racks of lamb, add to the marinade and turn to coat. Cover and refrigerate for at least 4 hours, or overnight.

To make the tomato and onion salsa, cut the tomatoes into thin wedges, slice the onion very thinly and toss with the lemon juice, sugar and olive oil. Season.

Preheat a kettle or covered barbecue to medium–high indirect heat. Cook the lamb, covered, for 10 minutes, then turn, baste with the marinade and cook for a further 8 minutes. Leave to rest, covered with foil, for 5 minutes. Serve the racks whole or sliced with the tomato salsa. Serve with minted potato salad, if desired.

# bacon and avocado salad

serves 4

## ingredients

8 bacon slices
400 g (14 oz) green beans, topped, tailed
    and halved
300 g ($10^1/_2$ oz) baby English spinach leaves
2 French shallots, finely sliced
2 avocados
$^1/_4$ teaspoon brown sugar
1 garlic clove, crushed
4 tablespoons olive oil
1 tablespoon balsamic vinegar
1 teaspoon sesame oil

## method

Turn on the grill (broiler). Put the bacon on a tray and grill on both sides until it is nice and crisp. Leave to cool, then break into pieces.

Bring a saucepan of water to the boil and cook the beans for 4 minutes. Drain and hold under cold running water for a few seconds to stop them cooking any further.

Put the spinach in a large bowl and add the beans, bacon and shallots. Halve the avocados, then cut into cubes and add to the bowl of salad.

Mix the brown sugar and garlic in a small bowl. Add the rest of the ingredients and whisk everything together to make a dressing. Pour the dressing over the salad, season and toss well.

# barbecue fish with green bean salad

serves 4

## ingredients

**marinade**
3 tablespoons grapeseed oil
2 teaspoons grated lemon zest
2 tablespoons lemon juice
2 teaspoons baharat

**green bean salad**
225 g (8 oz) green beans, trimmed
1 zucchini (courgette)
1 small carrot, peeled
$^1/_2$ red onion, finely sliced into wedges

**salad dressing**
2 tablespoons grapeseed oil
1 tablespoon lemon juice
1 teaspoon honey
$^1/_2$ teaspoon baharat

4 firm white fish fillets (800 g/1 lb 12 oz),
    such as snapper
olive oil
100 g ($3^1/_2$ oz) mixed salad leaves or baby rocket
    (arugula) leaves
lemon wedges, to serve

## method

To make the marinade, combine the oil, lemon zest and juice and the baharat in a non-metallic dish. Coat the fish in the marinade and set aside for 30 minutes.

To make the salad, shred or finely slice the beans. Using a vegetable peeler, cut the zucchini and carrot into fine strips. Put all the ingredients into a large bowl. Combine the salad dressing ingredients and just prior to serving, pour over the salad and toss well.

Preheat a barbecue flat plate or grill plate. Lightly coat with the oil. Cook the fillets for 1 minute on each side to seal, then lower the heat and cook for 2–3 minutes on each side, or until just cooked through. The cooking time will depend on the thickness of the fillets. Brush with the marinade one or two times.

To serve, divide the salad leaves or rocket onto serving plates, pile the bean salad over and top each with a fish fillet. Serve with lemon wedges.

# minted potato salad

serves 4

## ingredients

600 g (1 lb 5 oz) new potatoes, large ones halved
125 g (4$\frac{1}{2}$ oz/$\frac{1}{2}$ cup) plain yoghurt
1 Lebanese (short) cucumber, grated and
   squeezed dry
15 g ($\frac{1}{2}$ oz) finely chopped mint leaves
2 garlic cloves, crushed

## method

Boil or steam the potatoes for 10 minutes, or until they are tender, then leave to cool.

Mix together the yoghurt, cucumber, mint and garlic and toss through the cooled potatoes. Season well and serve.

# lamb kebabs

serves 4

## ingredients

5 garlic cloves, roughly chopped
5 cm (2 in) piece of ginger, roughly chopped
3 green chillies, roughly chopped
1 onion, roughly chopped
3 tablespoons thick natural yoghurt
3 tablespoons coriander (cilantro) leaves
$1/2$ teaspoon ground black pepper
500 g (1 lb 2 oz) minced (ground) lamb
red onion rings, to garnish
lemon wedges, to serve

## method

Combine the garlic, ginger, chilli, onion, yoghurt and coriander leaves in a food processor to form a thick smooth paste. If you don't have a processor, chop the vegetables more finely and use a mortar and pestle. Add the pepper, season with salt, then mix in the lamb. If you are using a mortar and pestle, mix the lamb with the paste in a bowl.

Divide the meat into 16 portions, about 2 tablespoons each. Shape each portion into an oval patty, cover and chill for 20 minutes.

Heat the grill (broiler) to high. Using four metal skewers, thread four meatballs onto each. Grill (broil) for 7 minutes, or until brown on top. Turn over and brown the other side. Check that the meatballs are cooked. Serve with onion rings and lemon wedges.

# insalata caprese

serves 4

## ingredients

3 large vine-ripened tomatoes
250 g (9 oz) bocconcini (fresh baby mozzarella cheese)
12 basil leaves
3 tablespoons extra virgin olive oil
4 basil leaves, roughly torn, extra (optional)

## method

Slice the tomatoes into 1 cm ($^1/_2$ in) slices, to make twelve slices altogether. Slice the bocconcini into twenty-four 1 cm ($^1/_2$ in) slices.

Arrange the tomato slices on a serving plate, alternating them with two slices of bocconcini. Place the basil leaves between the bocconcini slices.

Drizzle with the oil, sprinkle with the basil, if desired, and season well.

# shish kebabs with risoni salad

serves 4

## ingredients

### risoni salad
200 g (7 oz/1 cup) risoni
2 teaspoons extra virgin olive oil
2 teaspoons balsamic vinegar
$^1/_2$ teaspoon grated lemon zest
2 teaspoons lemon juice
40 g (1$^3/_4$ oz) baby rocket (arugula) leaves
1$^1/_2$ tablespoons shredded basil leaves
$^1/_2$ small red onion, finely sliced

### shish kebabs
250 g (9 oz) minced (ground) lamb
250 g (9 oz) minced (ground) veal
1 onion, finely chopped
2 garlic cloves, crushed
1 teaspoon ground allspice
1 teaspoon ground cinnamon
oil, for brushing

## method

To make the risoni salad, bring a saucepan of salted water to the boil. Add the risoni and cook for about 12 minutes, or until tender. Drain, rinse under cold water, then drain again. Put the risoni in a large bowl with the oil, vinegar, lemon zest, lemon juice, rocket, basil and onion. Mix well, season to taste and refrigerate until ready to serve.

To make the shish kebabs, put the lamb, veal, onion, garlic, allspice and cinnamon in a food processor and season. Blend until fine, but not mushy. Divide the mixture into eight equal portions, then roll into long sausage-shaped shish kebabs. Insert a long metal skewer through the middle of each shish kebab, pressing the mixture firmly onto the skewers. Refrigerate for 30 minutes.

Preheat a barbecue grill plate, flat plate or chargrill pan to medium. Brush the hotplate with oil and grill the kebabs for about 8–10 minutes, or until cooked through, turning often. Serve warm with the risoni salad.

# yakitori chicken burger

serves 4

## ingredients

4 boneless, skinless chicken thighs, trimmed
185 ml (6 fl oz/$^3/_4$ cup) yakitori sauce
1 teaspoon cornflour (cornstarch)
oil, for brushing
4 soft hamburger buns, halved
80 g (2$^3/_4$ oz/$^1/_3$ cup) mayonnaise
80 g (2$^3/_4$ oz) mizuna lettuce
1 Lebanese (short) cucumber, ends trimmed and
    shaved into ribbons

## method

Toss the chicken and yakitori sauce together in a bowl until the chicken is well coated, then cover and refrigerate for 4 hours.

Drain the yakitori sauce from the chicken into a saucepan and sprinkle with the cornflour. Stir the cornflour into the marinade, bring the mixture to the boil and simmer, stirring frequently, for 5 minutes, or until thickened, then keep warm.

Brush a chargrill plate with oil and heat it to low–medium direct heat. Cook the chicken for 6–7 minutes on each side, or until cooked through.

Toast the burger buns for about 1 minute on each side, or until they are marked and golden.

Spread some mayonnaise on each bun, cover the base with the lettuce and the cucumber ribbons, and top with the chicken. Spread some of the thickened marinade on top of the chicken, top with the other half of the bun and serve immediately.

# red cabbage salad

serves 4

## ingredients

150 g (5$^1$/$_2$ oz/2$^1$/$_2$ cups) finely shredded red
    cabbage
125 g (4$^1$/$_2$ oz/2 cups) finely shredded
    green cabbage
2 spring onions (scallions), finely chopped
3 tablespoons olive oil

### caraway dressing
2 teaspoons white wine vinegar
$^1$/$_2$ teaspoon French mustard
1 teaspoon caraway seeds

## method

Put the red and green cabbage in a large serving bowl with the
spring onion and mix together well.

Put all the caraway dressing ingredients in a small screw-top
jar and shake well. Pour the dressing over the salad, toss lightly
and serve.

# steak sandwich with balsamic onions and sun-dried tomato and basil cream

serves 4

## ingredients

125 g (4$^1/_2$ oz/$^1/_2$ cup) sour cream
40 g (1$^1/_2$ oz) sun-dried tomatoes, well drained and finely chopped
3 garlic cloves, crushed
2 tablespoons finely chopped basil leaves
2 teaspoons lemon juice
2 red onions
2 tablespoons olive oil
2 tablespoons balsamic vinegar
1 tablespoon soft brown sugar
8 large slices of sourdough bread
400 g (14 oz) piece of fillet steak, cut into 1 cm ($^1/_2$ in) thick slices
55 g (2 oz) baby rocket (arugula) leaves, rinsed and well drained

## method

Preheat the barbecue to medium–high direct heat. Mix the sour cream, sun-dried tomatoes, garlic, basil and lemon juice in a small bowl and season to taste.

Thinly slice the onions, separate the rings and toss with 1 tablespoon of olive oil. Spread the onion across the flat grill plate and cook for 10 minutes, or until softened and starting to brown. Gather the rings into a pile and pour the combined balsamic vinegar and sugar over. Turn the onion to coat in the balsamic mixture, then spread it out a little and cook for a further 2–3 minutes, or until slightly glazed. Remove the onion from the barbecue and toast the bread on the chargrill plate for 30 seconds on each side, or until grill marks appear.

Brush the steaks with a little olive oil and season. Chargrill for 1 minute each side for medium–rare, or 2 minutes for well done.

To serve, put a piece of steak on a slice of toasted bread and top with the onion, a dollop of the sour cream mixture and some rocket leaves. Finish with a second piece of toast.

# piri piri prawns

serves 4

## ingredients

1 kg (2 lb 4 oz) large raw prawns (shrimp), peeled and deveined, leaving the tail intact
4 long red chillies, seeded
185 ml (6 fl oz/$^3$/$_4$ cup) white wine vinegar
2 large garlic cloves, chopped
6–8 small red chillies, chopped
125 ml (4$^1$/$_2$ fl oz/$^1$/$_2$ cup) olive oil
150 g (5$^1$/$_2$ oz) mixed lettuce leaves

## method

To make the sauce, put the long chillies in a saucepan with the vinegar and simmer over medium–high heat for 5 minutes, or until the chillies are soft. Let the mixture cool slightly, then put the chillies and 3 tablespoons of the vinegar in a food processor. Add the garlic and chopped small chillies, and blend until smooth. While the motor is running, gradually add the oil and remaining vinegar to the food processor.

Put the prawns in the marinade, making sure they are well coated, then cover and refrigerate for 30 minutes.

Remove the prawns from the marinade, bring the marinade to the boil and simmer for 5 minutes, or until slightly thickened and reduced.

Preheat the chargrill plate to high and brush with oil. Cook the prawns, basting with the marinade, for 2–3 minutes on each side, or until cooked through. Arrange the lettuce on four plates, top with the prawns and serve immediately with the chilli sauce.

# chargrilled tomato salad

serves 4

## ingredients

8 roma (plum) tomatoes
1$^1/_2$ teaspoons capers, rinsed and drained
4 basil leaves, torn
3 teaspoons olive oil
3 teaspoons balsamic vinegar
1 garlic clove, crushed
$^1/_4$ teaspoon honey

## method

Cut the tomatoes lengthways into quarters and scoop out the seeds. Heat a chargrill pan (griddle) to medium and cook the tomato quarters for 1–2 minutes on each side, or until grill marks appear and the tomatoes have softened. Allow to cool to room temperature and put in a bowl.

Combine the capers, basil, oil, vinegar, garlic and honey in a small bowl and season. Pour the mixture over the tomatoes and toss together. Serve at room temperature with crusty bread and grilled meats.

# lobster with burnt butter sauce and grilled lemon

serves 8

## ingredients

150 g (5$\frac{1}{2}$ oz) butter
3 tablespoons lemon juice
2 tablespoons chopped flat-leaf (Italian) parsley
1 small garlic clove, crushed
8 lobster tails, in the shell
2 lemons, cut into wedges

## method

Melt the butter in a small saucepan over medium heat and cook for 3 minutes, or until it begins to brown. Reduce the heat, and cook the butter for a further 2 minutes, or until dark, golden brown. Remove the pan from the heat, add the lemon juice, parsley and garlic, and season.

Cut the lobster tails lengthways and remove any digestive tract, but leave the meat in the shell. Preheat a barbecue chargrill plate to medium direct heat and brush the exposed lobster meat with lots of the butter mixture. Cook the lobster tails, cut-side down, on the chargrill plate for 6 minutes, then turn over and cook for a further 3–5 minutes, or until the shells turn bright red.

Meanwhile, put the lemon wedges on the hottest part of the chargrill and cook for 1 minute on each side, or until marked and heated through. Arrange the lobster on a serving plate and serve with the grilled lemon wedges and the rest of the warm brown butter as a dipping sauce. Serve with a green salad and some crusty bread to soak up the juices.

# barbecued Asian pork ribs with spring onion rice

serves 4

## ingredients

1 kg (2 lb 4 oz) American-style pork ribs, cut into
  sections of 4–5 ribs
3 tablespoons hoisin sauce
3 tablespoons soy sauce
1 tablespoon Chinese rice wine
2 garlic cloves, chopped
2 tablespoons oil
3 spring onions (scallions), finely chopped
1 tablespoon grated ginger
250 g (9 oz/$1^1/_4$ cups) long-grain rice
600 g (1 lb 5 oz) baby bok choy (pak choy), leaves
  separated

## method

Put the ribs in a non-metallic bowl. Combine the hoisin sauce, soy sauce, rice wine, garlic, 1 tablespoon of the oil, 2 tablespoons of the spring onion and half the ginger. Pour onto the ribs and mix to coat. Marinate for at least 10 minutes.

Bring a large saucepan of water to the boil. Add the rice and cook for 12 minutes, stirring occasionally. Drain well.

Heat the remaining oil in a saucepan over medium–low heat. When the oil is warm, remove the pan from the heat and add the remaining spring onion and ginger. Season with $1/_4$ teaspoon salt, stirring. Stir this mixture through the rice.

Preheat a chargrill pan or barbecue plate and brush with oil. Remove the ribs from the marinade with tongs and reserve the marinade. Cook the ribs, in batches, if necessary, for 8–10 minutes on each side, or until cooked through.

Pour the reserved marinade into a saucepan. If there is not much liquid, add 4 tablespoons of water. Boil for 2 minutes, then add the bok choy, stirring to coat. Cook, covered, for 1–2 minutes, or until just wilted. Serve the ribs with the rice and bok choy, and drizzle with the marinade.

# three-bean salad

serves 4

## ingredients

100 g (3$^1/_2$ oz) green beans, trimmed and cut into
   4 cm (1$^1/_2$ in) lengths
200 g (7 oz) frozen broad (fava) beans, defrosted
310 g (10$^1/_2$ oz) tinned butter beans, rinsed and
   drained
310 g (10$^1/_2$ oz) tinned red kidney beans, rinsed
   and drained
1 small red onion, finely sliced
2 tablespoons chopped flat-leaf (Italian) parsley
2 tablespoons ready-made French dressing

## method

Bring a small saucepan of lightly salted water to the boil. Add the green beans and broad beans. Cook for 1 minute, then drain. Refresh under cold water, then drain again.

Put the green beans and broad beans in a serving bowl with the tinned beans, onion and parsley. Pour the dressing over and toss well.

# warm Mediterranean lamb salad

serves 4

## ingredients

500 g (1 lb 2 oz) lamb backstraps or loin fillets
125 ml (4 fl oz/$^1/_2$ cup) olive oil
2 garlic cloves, crushed
2 teaspoons thyme leaves
1 teaspoon ground black pepper
3 small red capsicums (peppers)
5 slender eggplants (aubergines), thickly sliced
   on the diagonal
2 tablespoons olive tapenade
100 g (3$^1/_2$ oz) semi-dried (sun-blushed)
   tomatoes, sliced
1 Lebanese (short) cucumber, seeded and
   chopped
150 g (5$^1/_2$ oz) green beans, trimmed and
   blanched
150 g (5$^1/_2$ oz) Niçoise or Ligurian olives
100 g (3$^1/_2$ oz) baby rocket (arugula) leaves

### dressing

2 garlic cloves, crushed
2 tablespoons extra virgin olive oil
1 tablespoon lemon juice

## method

Put the lamb in a non-metallic bowl. Combine half the oil with the garlic, thyme and pepper, then pour over the lamb and toss to coat. Set aside.

Heat the grill (broiler) to high. Cut the capsicums into large flat pieces, discarding the seeds and membrane. Arrange skin side up on the grill tray and grill until the skin blackens and blisters. Leave to cool in a plastic bag, then peel away the skin and cut the flesh into thirds.

Meanwhile, preheat a barbecue chargrill plate or chargrill pan to high. Toss the eggplant in the remaining oil to coat, then grill for 2–3 minutes on each side, or until golden.

Cook the lamb on the hot chargrill plate for about 4 minutes on each side for medium–rare, or until done to your liking. Remove from the heat, cover with foil and leave for 5 minutes.

Thinly slice the lamb across the grain and toss in a bowl with the capsicum, eggplant, tapenade, tomato, cucumber, beans and olives. Add the rocket. Put the dressing ingredients in a screw-top jar and shake well. Pour over the lamb salad, season and toss to combine.

# Lebanese chicken

serves 4–6

## ingredients

250 g (9 oz/1 cup) Greek-style yoghurt
2 teaspoons soft brown sugar
4 garlic cloves, crushed
3 teaspoons ground cumin
1$^1$/$_2$ teaspoons ground coriander
7 g ($^1$/$_4$ oz) chopped flat-leaf (Italian) parsley
3 tablespoons lemon juice
1 x 1.8 kg (4 lb) whole chicken, cut into
    10 serving pieces
cooking oil spray

## method

Put the yoghurt, brown sugar, garlic, cumin, coriander, chopped parsley and lemon juice in a large non-metallic bowl and mix together.

Add the chicken pieces to the marinade and turn to coat. Cover and refrigerate for at least 2 hours, or overnight.

Lightly spray the barbecue plates with oil, then preheat the barbecue to medium heat. Remove the chicken pieces from the marinade and season. Cook the chicken pieces on the flat plate, turning them frequently, for 20–30 minutes, or until they are cooked through.

# tabbouleh

serves 6

## ingredients

130 g ($4^3/_4$ oz/$^3/_4$ cup) burghul
3 ripe tomatoes
1 telegraph (long) cucumber
4 spring onions (scallions), sliced
120 g ($4^1/_4$ oz/4 cups) chopped flat-leaf (Italian)
   parsley
25 g (1 oz) chopped mint

### dressing

4 tablespoons lemon juice
3 tablespoons olive oil
1 tablespoon extra virgin olive oil

## method

Place the burghul in a bowl, cover with 500 ml (17 fl oz/2 cups) water and leave for $1^1/_2$ hours.

Cut the tomatoes in half, squeeze to remove any excess seeds and cut into 1 cm ($^1/_2$ in) cubes. Cut the cucumber in half lengthways, remove the seeds with a teaspoon and cut the flesh into 1 cm ($^1/_2$ in) cubes.

To make the dressing, place the lemon juice and $1^1/_2$ teaspoons salt in a bowl and whisk until well combined. Season well and slowly whisk in the olive oil and extra virgin olive oil.

Drain the burghul and squeeze out any excess water. Spread the burghul out on a tea towel (dish towel) and leave to dry for about 30 minutes.

Put the burghul in a salad bowl, add the tomato, cucumber, spring onion, parsley and mint, and toss to combine.

Pour the dressing over the salad and toss until evenly coated.

# marinated prawns with mango chilli salsa

serves 4–6

## ingredients

**lemon dill marinade**
4 tablespoons lemon juice
4 tablespoons olive oil
1 teaspoon sea salt
3 tablespoons chopped dill

1 kg (2 lb 4 oz) raw prawns (shrimp), peeled and
    deveined, leaving the tail intact
150 g (5$\frac{1}{2}$ oz) rocket (arugula)

**mango chilli salsa**
450 g (1 lb/1$\frac{1}{2}$ cups) diced fresh or tinned mango
1 red onion, finely diced
1 small red chilli, seeded and finely chopped
1 tablespoon grated lemon zest

## method

Combine the lemon dill marinade ingredients in a large
non-metallic bowl and mix well. Add the prawns, toss well,
then cover and refrigerate for 1 hour.

Preheat the barbecue flat plate to high. Just before serving,
put the mango chilli salsa ingredients in a bowl, mix well and
set aside.

Drain the prawns from the marinade and cook them on the
flat plate for about 2–4 minutes, turning once, or until they have
changed colour but are still soft and fleshy to touch. Remove
from the heat and allow to cool slightly.

Arrange a bed of rocket on individual serving plates. Add a
generous scoop of salsa, then the prawns. Season to taste and
serve immediately.

# lamb loin chops with artichoke and olive stuffing

serves 4

## ingredients

8 lamb loin chops, with tails

**stuffing**

75 g (2$^1/_2$ oz/1 cup) coarse fresh breadcrumbs,
   made from an Italian bread such as ciabatta
12 pitted black olives, roughly chopped
8 marinated artichoke quarters, roughly chopped
   (reserve 1 tablespoon of the marinade)
2 tablespoons chopped flat-leaf (Italian) parsley
$^1/_2$ teaspoon finely grated lemon zest

## method

Preheat the barbecue grill plate to high. To make the stuffing, put the breadcrumbs, olives, artichoke and reserved artichoke marinade in a bowl with the parsley and lemon zest. Mix lightly to combine.

Unroll the tails from the lamb chops and fill them with the stuffing. Roll the tails up to enclose the stuffing, then secure with a toothpick.

Season, then place on the hotplate and cook for about 5–7 minutes on each side, or until cooked to your liking—the cooking time will vary according to thickness of your chops. Serve warm.

# salade niçoise

serves 4

## ingredients

8 small salad potatoes (about 600 g/1 lb 5 oz)
180 g (6 oz) small green beans, topped, tailed
    and halved
1 tablespoon olive oil
400 g (14 oz) tuna steak, cubed
1 garlic clove, crushed
1 teaspoon dijon mustard
2 tablespoons white wine vinegar
125 ml (4 fl oz/$^1$/$_2$ cup) olive oil, extra
4 handfuls green lettuce leaves
12 cherry tomatoes, halved
90 g (3$^1$/$_4$ oz) black olives
2 tablespoons capers, drained
4 hard-boiled eggs, cut into wedges
8 anchovies, halved
lemon wedges, to serve

## method

Cook the potatoes in boiling salted water for about 10 minutes, or until they are just tender. Drain, cut into wedges, then put in a bowl.

Cook the beans in boiling salted water for 3 minutes, then drain and hold under cold running water for 1 minute. Add to the potatoes.

Heat the olive oil in a frying pan over high heat and cook the tuna cubes for about 3 minutes, or until browned on all sides. Add to the potatoes and beans.

Whisk together the garlic, mustard and vinegar, then add the extra oil in a thin, steady stream, whisking until smooth. Season well.

Cover the base of a large bowl with the lettuce leaves. Scatter the potatoes, beans, tuna, tomatoes, olives and capers over the leaves and drizzle with the dressing. Decorate with the egg wedges and anchovies. Squeeze some lemon juice over the salad.

# eggplant, tahini and mint salad

serves 4

## ingredients

**tahini dressing**
3 tablespoons tahini
2 teaspoons olive oil
1 garlic clove, crushed
2 tablespoons lemon juice

1 large eggplant (aubergine), thinly sliced
2 tablespoons olive oil
1 garlic clove, crushed
1 large handful mint leaves, roughly chopped
3 tablespoons chopped flat-leaf (Italian) parsley
2 tablespoons Greek-style yoghurt
$1/_4$ teaspoon mild smoked paprika

## method

Put all the tahini dressing ingredients in a food processor with 125 ml (4 fl oz/$^1/_2$ cup) of warm water. Blend until well combined and set aside.

Preheat a barbecue grill plate, flat plate or chargrill pan to medium. Put the eggplant slices in a large bowl, add the oil and garlic, then toss well to coat. Cook the eggplant for about 3 minutes, or until grill marks appear, turning once. Put in a large bowl and allow to cool.

Toss the mint, parsley and tahini dressing through the eggplant slices, mixing well. Serve at room temperature, dolloped with yoghurt and sprinkled with the paprika.

# beef teriyaki with cucumber salad

serves 4

## ingredients

4 beef fillet steaks (about 180 g/6 oz each)
4 tablespoons soy sauce
2 tablespoons mirin
1 tablespoon sake (optional)
1 garlic clove, crushed
1 teaspoon grated fresh ginger
oil, for brushing
1 teaspoon sugar
1 teaspoon toasted sesame seeds

### cucumber salad

1 large Lebanese (short) cucumber, peeled, seeded and diced
$1/2$ red capsicum (pepper), diced
2 spring onions (scallions), sliced thinly on the diagonal
2 teaspoons sugar
1 tablespoon rice wine vinegar

## method

Put the beef steaks side by side in a large dish. Combine the soy sauce, mirin, sake, garlic and ginger and pour over the steaks, turning to coat. Cover and refrigerate for at least 30 minutes, turning once or twice.

To make the cucumber salad, toss the cucumber, capsicum and spring onion in a bowl. Put the sugar and rice wine vinegar in a saucepan with 3 tablespoons of water and stir over medium heat. Increase the heat and simmer for 3–4 minutes, or until thickened. Pour over the cucumber salad. Stir to combine and leave to cool.

Heat a barbecue hotplate to high and brush with a little oil. Drain the beef fillets, reserving the marinade. Cook for 4 minutes on each side, or until done to your liking. Remove from the heat, cover with foil and rest in a warm place for 5–10 minutes.

Put the sugar and the reserved marinade in a saucepan and heat, stirring, until the sugar has dissolved. Bring to the boil and simmer for 2 minutes. Keep warm.

Slice each fillet into 1 cm ($1/2$ in) strips and arrange on four serving plates. Spoon some of the marinade and cucumber salad over the top and sprinkle with the sesame seeds.

# chargrilled baby octopus

serves 4

## ingredients

2 kg (4 lb 8 oz) baby octopus
375 ml (13 fl oz/1$^1$/$_2$ cups) red wine
3 tablespoons balsamic vinegar
2 tablespoons soy sauce
125 ml (4 fl oz/$^1$/$_2$ cup) sweet chilli sauce
50 g (1$^3$/$_4$ oz/1 cup) Thai basil leaves, to serve

## method

Using a small knife, carefully cut between the head and tentacles of the octopus, just below the eyes. Grasp the body of the octopus and push the beak out and up through the centre of the tentacles with your finger. Cut the eyes from the head of the octopus by slicing a small disc off with a sharp knife. Discard the eye section. To clean the octopus head, carefully slit through one side, avoiding the ink sac and scrape out any gut from inside. Rinse under running water to remove any remaining grit.

Put the octopus, red wine and balsamic vinegar in a large, non-aluminium saucepan and bring to the boil. Reduce the heat and simmer for 15 minutes, or until just tender. Drain and transfer to a bowl. Add the soy sauce and sweet chilli sauce.

Heat a barbecue chargrill (griddle) to high and cook the octopus until it is sticky and slightly charred. Serve on a bed of Thai basil leaves.

# beef with mustard seed butter

serves 4

## ingredients

### mustard seed butter
1 tablespoon vegetable oil
1 tablespoon mustard seeds
1 garlic clove, crushed
$^1/_2$ onion, diced
$^1/_2$ teaspoon Hungarian paprika
$^1/_2$ teaspoon salt
2 tablespoons chopped flat-leaf (Italian) parsley
2 teaspoons seeded mustard
90 g ($3^1/_4$ oz) butter, softened

### marinade
2 garlic cloves, crushed
30 ml (1 fl oz) oyster sauce
1–2 tablespoons worcestershire sauce
1 tablespoon balsamic vinegar
1 tablespoon tomato sauce (ketchup)

4 x 200 g (7 oz) sirloin steaks
green salad, to serve

## method

To make the mustard seed butter, heat the oil in a small heavy-based saucepan and add the mustard seeds. Heat for about 1 minute, or until they start to crackle. Add the garlic and onion and stir for about 5 minutes, or until softened and transparent. Cool slightly, then add to a bowl with the remaining ingredients and combine well.

Place the butter mixture onto a rectangle of foil in a long sausage shape about 2 cm ($^3/_4$ in) in diameter. Roll the foil around the butter, twisting the ends, then refrigerate.

To make the marinade, combine the garlic, oyster sauce, worcestershire, balsamic vinegar and tomato sauce in a non-metallic dish. Add the steaks, cover and marinate for at least 2 hours.

Barbecue or chargrill the steaks for 4 minutes on each side for medium, or until cooked to your liking. Serve topped with a slice of mustard seed butter and a green salad.

# garlic and mint lamb skewers with almond couscous and yoghurt sauce

serves 4

## ingredients

8 lamb fillets, trimmed and cut into 2.5 cm
  (1 in) cubes
2 tablespoons olive oil
4 tablespoons lemon juice
2 garlic cloves, crushed
2 teaspoons dried mint leaves

### yoghurt sauce
250 g (9 oz/1 cup) Greek-style yoghurt
1 garlic clove, crushed

### almond couscous
370 g (13 oz/2 cups) instant couscous
1 tablespoon olive oil
500 ml (17 fl oz/2 cups) chicken stock
40 g (1$^1$/$_2$ oz) butter
2 teaspoons ras el hanout
35 g (1$^1$/$_4$ oz/$^1$/$_4$ cup) currants, soaked in warm
  water for 10 minutes
60 g (2$^1$/$_4$ oz/$^1$/$_2$ cup) slivered almonds, toasted
25 g (1 oz) chopped mint leaves

## method

Put the lamb in a non-metallic bowl with the olive oil, lemon juice, garlic and mint. Stir until well coated and season. Cover and refrigerate for at least 4 hours, or overnight.

To make the yoghurt sauce, mix the yoghurt and garlic in a small bowl, then refrigerate it until needed.

Put the couscous in a heatproof bowl, drizzle it with the olive oil and season well with salt. Bring the chicken stock to the boil and pour over the couscous, then cover the bowl and leave for 10 minutes to absorb the stock. Add the butter and fluff it through with a fork until melted and the grains are separated. Stir in the ras el hanout, currants, almonds and mint, and season to taste.

Soak eight wooden skewers in cold water for 1 hour, then thread the lamb on and season well. Preheat the barbecue to medium–high direct heat and grill the skewers for about 3–4 minutes on each side, or until cooked to your liking. Serve the skewers on a bed of couscous with the yoghurt sauce.

# chargrilled vegetables with mint and feta pesto

serves 4

## ingredients

1 fennel bulb
12 spring onions (scallions)
150 g (5$\frac{1}{2}$ oz) green beans, trimmed
4 small zucchini (courgettes), quartered
   lengthways
2 tablespoons olive oil

### mint and feta pesto

80 g (2$\frac{3}{4}$ oz) mint, leaves picked
100 g (3$\frac{1}{2}$ oz) feta cheese, crumbled
1 tablespoon lemon juice
125 ml (4 fl oz/$\frac{1}{2}$ cup) extra virgin olive oil

## method

Trim the base of the fennel bulb, remove the outer layer and cut the bulb into quarters lengthways. Cut out and discard the inner core, then slice the fennel into long pieces. Trim the spring onions, leaving about 7 cm (2$\frac{3}{4}$ in) of the green stem on top, and remove the outer layer from around the white base. Lay all the vegetables in a shallow non-metallic dish, drizzle with the oil and toss to coat.

Preheat a barbecue grill plate or chargrill pan to medium. Grill all the vegetables, turning occasionally, until tender and charred — the beans and spring onions should take about 5–7 minutes, the fennel may take up to 10 minutes. Transfer to a serving platter and allow to cool slightly.

Meanwhile, to make the mint and feta pesto, put the mint, feta and lemon juice in a food processor and blend until roughly chopped. With the motor running, add the oil in a thin stream and blend until incorporated. Season.

Serve the vegetables hot or at room temperature, with the mint and feta pesto on the side, or dolloped over the top.

# caesar salad

serves 4

## ingredients

1$\frac{1}{2}$ cos (romaine) lettuces
16 thin slices baguette
310 ml (10$\frac{3}{4}$ fl oz/1$\frac{1}{4}$ cups) olive oil
6 bacon slices, chopped
1 egg yolk
1 garlic clove
4 anchovy fillets
1 tablespoon lemon juice
worcestershire sauce, to taste
parmesan cheese, to serve

## method

Tear the cos lettuce into pieces and put them in a large bowl. Preheat the grill (broiler).

Brush the slices of baguette on both sides with some of the oil and grill until golden brown. Allow to cool.

Fry the bacon in a frying pan over medium heat until browned. Sprinkle over the bowl of lettuce.

Put the egg yolk, garlic and anchovies in a blender and process for 1 minute, then with the motor still running, add the remaining oil in a steady stream through the top hole. The oil and egg should thicken immediately and form mayonnaise. Add the lemon juice and worcestershire sauce, stir well and season.

Using a potato peeler, make some parmesan curls by running the peeler along one edge of the cheese.

Pour the dressing over the lettuce, add the parmesan curls and toss well. Divide the salad among four bowls and arrange the slices of toasted baguette on each one.

# tuna burgers with herbed mayonnaise

serves 4

## ingredients

4 garlic cloves, crushed
2 egg yolks
250 ml (9 fl oz/1 cup) light olive oil
3 tablespoons chopped flat-leaf (Italian) parsley
1 tablespoon chopped dill
2 teaspoons dijon mustard
1 tablespoon lemon juice
1 tablespoon red wine vinegar
1 tablespoon baby capers in brine, drained
4 anchovy fillets in oil, drained
4 x 150 g (5$^1/_2$ oz) tuna steaks
2 tablespoons olive oil
2 red onions, thinly sliced
4 large round bread rolls, halved and buttered
100 g (3$^1/_2$ oz) mixed lettuce leaves

## method

Put the garlic and egg yolks in a food processor and process for 10 seconds. With the motor running, add the oil in a thin, slow stream. When the mixture starts to thicken, start pouring the oil a little faster until all of the oil has been added and the mixture is thick and creamy. Add the parsley, dill, mustard, lemon juice, vinegar, capers and anchovies, and process until the mixture is smooth. Refrigerate until needed.

Preheat the chargrill plate to high direct heat. Brush the tuna steaks with 1 tablespoon of olive oil and cook for 2 minutes on each side, or until almost cooked through. Add the remaining olive oil to the onion, toss to separate and coat the rings, and cook on the flat plate for 2 minutes, or until the onion is soft and caramelized. Toast the rolls, buttered-side down, on the chargrill plate for 1 minute, or until they are marked.

Put some lettuce, a tuna steak, some of the onion and a dollop of herbed mayonnaise on one half of each roll. Season and top with the other half of the roll.

# vine-wrapped blue-eye with dill and lemon butter

serves 4

## ingredients

8 fresh or preserved vine leaves
2 tablespoons chopped dill
60 g (2$^1$/$_4$ oz) butter, softened
4 x 200 g (7 oz) blue-eye fillets
1 tablespoon lemon juice
oil, for brushing

## method

If you are using fresh vine leaves, bring a saucepan of water to the boil and blanch the leaves in batches for 30 seconds. Pat dry on crumpled paper towels. If you are using preserved vine leaves, simply rinse and dry them. Place 2 leaves on a work surface, slightly overlapping them. Repeat with the remaining leaves.

Combine the dill and butter in a small bowl and divide into four portions. Put each portion in the centre of each set of overlapping vine leaves. Rest a piece of fish on top of the butter, drizzle with the lemon juice and season.

Wrap the fish in the vine leaves by bringing the edge closest to you over the fish, folding in the sides (if the leaves are wide enough) as you go, rolling up very firmly. Put the parcels on a plate, then cover and refrigerate for 30 minutes.

Preheat a barbecue flat plate to medium. Brush the hotplate with oil and grill the fish for 6–8 minutes, or until cooked through, turning once.

# grilled chicken with capsicum couscous

serves 4

## ingredients

200 g (7 oz/1 cup) instant couscous
1 tablespoon olive oil
1 onion, finely chopped
2 zucchini (courgettes), sliced
$^1/_2$ red or yellow chargrilled capsicum (pepper),
    chopped
12 semi-dried (sun-blushed) tomatoes, chopped
$^1/_2$ tablespoon grated orange zest
250 ml (9 oz/1 cup) orange juice
a large handful chopped mint
8 boneless chicken thighs or 4 chicken breasts,
    skin on
2 tablespoons butter, softened

## method

Preheat the grill (broiler). Bring 500 ml (17 fl oz/2 cups) water to the boil in a saucepan. Add the couscous, then remove from the heat and leave to stand for 10 minutes.

Heat the oil in a frying pan and fry the onion and zucchini until lightly browned. Add the capsicum and semi-dried tomatoes, then stir in the couscous. Stir in the orange zest, one-third of the orange juice and the mint.

Put the chicken in a large shallow baking dish in a single layer and dot with the butter. Sprinkle with the remaining orange juice and season well. Grill the chicken for 8–10 minutes, turning over halfway through, or until browned and crisp.

Serve the chicken on the couscous with any juices poured over it.

# sumac-crusted lamb fillets with baba ghanoush

serves 4

## ingredients

2 tablespoons olive oil

750 g (1 lb 10 oz) small new potatoes

2–3 garlic cloves, crushed

3 tablespoons lemon juice

1 red capsicum (pepper), seeded and quartered
   lengthways

4 lamb backstraps (about 200 g/7 oz each)

1 tablespoon sumac

3 tablespoons finely chopped flat-leaf (Italian)
   parsley

250 g (9 oz) baba ghanoush

## method

Heat the oil in a large saucepan. Add the potatoes and garlic, and cook, turning frequently, for 3–5 minutes. When golden, add the lemon juice and reduce the heat to medium–low. Simmer, covered, for 15–20 minutes, or until tender. Remove from the heat and season well.

Meanwhile, heat a barbecue chargrill plate to high and brush with oil. Cook the capsicum skin-side down for 1–2 minutes, or until the skin starts to blister and turn black. Cook the other side for 1–2 minutes. Place in a plastic bag and set aside.

Coat the lamb with sumac. Cook on the chargrill plate for 4–5 minutes on each side, or until cooked to your liking. Remove from the heat, cover with foil and rest.

Remove the skin from the capsicum and slice the quarters into thin strips.

Stir the parsley through the potatoes. Divide the baba ghanoush among four plates. Cut the lamb into 1 cm ($1/2$ in) slices on the diagonal and arrange on top of the baba ghanoush with the capsicum strips. Serve with the potatoes and a green salad.

# fattoush with fried haloumi

serves 4

## ingredients

2 Lebanese (short) cucumbers
4 pitta breads
1 garlic clove, crushed
2 tablespoons lemon juice
5 tablespoons olive oil
4 spring onions (scallions), sliced
4 tomatoes, diced
2 green capsicums (peppers), diced
150 g (5$^1$/$_4$ oz) flat-leaf (Italian) parsley, chopped
2 tablespoons mint, chopped
2 tablespoons oregano, chopped
sumac (optional)
1 kg (2 lb 4 oz) haloumi cheese, cut into 8 slices

## method

Preheat the grill (broiler). Peel the cucumber, cut into quarters lengthways, then cut each piece into thick slices. Put in a sieve and sprinkle with a little salt to drain off any excess liquid.

Split each pitta bread in half and toast on both sides. When the bread is crisp, break into small pieces.

Mix the garlic, lemon juice and 4 tablespoons of the oil. Rinse and drain the cucumber.

Put the cucumber, spring onion, tomato, green capsicum, parsley, mint and oregano in a large bowl. Add the dressing and toss together well.

Heat the remaining oil in a non-stick frying pan and fry the haloumi cheese on both sides until browned. Scatter the bread over the salad and fold it through.

Serve the fattoush with the slices of haloumi on top. Sprinkle with a little sumac.

# lime and coriander chargrilled chicken

serves 4

## ingredients

3 teaspoons finely grated fresh ginger
25 g (1 oz) chopped coriander (cilantro) leaves
1$\frac{1}{2}$ teaspoons grated lime zest
4 tablespoons lime juice
4 boneless, skinless chicken breasts
    (about 750 g/1lb 10 oz), trimmed
250 g (9 oz/1$\frac{1}{4}$ cups) jasmine rice
2 tablespoons oil
3 zucchini (courgettes), cut into wedges
4 large flat mushrooms, stalks trimmed

## method

Combine the ginger, coriander, lime zest and 2 tablespoons of the lime juice. Spread 2 teaspoons of the herb mixture over each fillet and season well. Marinate for 1 hour. Combine the remaining herb mixture with the remaining lime juice in a screwtop jar. Set aside until needed.

Bring a large saucepan of water tothe boil. Add the rice and cook for 12 minutes, stirring occasionally. Drain well.

Meanwhile, heat a barbecue plate to medium and lightly brush with oil. Brush the zucchini and mushrooms with the remaining oil. Place the chicken on the chargrill plate and cook on each side for 4–5 minutes, or until cooked through. Add the vegetables during the last 5 minutes of cooking, and turn frequently until browned on the outside and just softened. Cover with foil until ready to serve.

Divide the rice among four serving bowls. Cut the chicken fillets into long thick strips, then arrange on top of the rice. Shake the dressing well and drizzle over the chicken and serve with the chargrilled vegetables.

# spicy crab with Singapore-style pepper sauce

serves 4–6

## ingredients

2 kg (4 lb 8 oz) blue crabs
150 g (5¹/₂ oz) butter
2 tablespoons finely chopped garlic
1 tablespoon finely chopped fresh ginger
1 small red chilli, seeded and finely chopped
3 tablespoons ground black pepper
2 tablespoons dark soy sauce
2 tablespoons oyster sauce
1 tablespoon palm sugar or soft brown sugar
1 spring onion (scallion), green part only, sliced
    thinly on the diagonal
steamed rice, to serve

## method

To prepare the crabs pull back the apron and remove the top shell from each crab (it should come off easily and in one piece). Remove the intestine and the grey feathery gills, then use a large sharp knife to cut the crab in half lengthways, leaving the legs attached. Crack the thick part of the legs with the back of a heavy knife or crab crackers to allow the flavours to seep in and to make it easier to extract the meat.

Heat the barbecue flat plate or chargrill plate to medium–high direct heat. Cook the crab pieces on the barbecue for about 5–8 minutes on each side, or until they have turned orange and are cooked through. Heat a wok over medium heat (you'll need to do this on the stovetop if you don't have a special wok burner on your barbecue), and stir-fry the butter, garlic, ginger, chilli and pepper together for 30 seconds or until they are fragrant. Add the combined soy and oyster sauces and sugar to the wok, and simmer the sauce for another minute or until it becomes glossy.

Toss the cooked crab in the sauce until it is completely coated, then arrange it on a serving dish, sprinkle with the spring onion and serve with steamed rice.

# barbecued Asian-style seafood

serves 6

## ingredients

500 g (1 lb 2 oz) prawns (shrimp), peeled and
    deveined, tails intact
300 g (10$^1$/$_2$ oz) scallop meat
500 g (1 lb 2 oz) baby squid, cleaned, tubes cut
    into quarters
500 g (1 lb 2 oz) baby octopus, cleaned
250 ml (9 fl oz/1 cup) sweet chilli sauce
1 tablespoon fish sauce
2 tablespoons lime juice
3 tablespoons peanut oil
steamed rice and lime wedges, to serve

## method

Put the prawns, scallops, squid and octopus in a shallow non-metallic bowl. In a separate bowl, combine the sweet chilli sauce, fish sauce, lime juice and 1 tablespoon of the peanut oil. Pour the mixture over the seafood and mix gently to coat. Allow to marinate for an hour. Drain the seafood well and reserve the marinade.

Heat the remaining oil on a barbecue flatplate. Cook the seafood, in batches if necessary, over high heat for 3–5 minutes, or until tender. Drizzle each batch with a little of the leftover marinade during cooking. Serve on a bed of steamed rice with wedges of lime.

# nibbles

shake off the conventions of cutlery and dig into
**bite-sized snacks** and dips,
**wraps** and sandwiches, and **burgers** and **pies**.
Food that's laid-back, unfussy with
**minimal work** involved—
perfect for when all you're doing is lounging around.

# guacamole

**serves 4–6**

### ingredients

2 ripe avocados, mashed
2$\frac{1}{2}$ tablespoons lime juice
3 spring onions (scallions), finely sliced
15 g ($\frac{1}{2}$ oz) chopped coriander (cilantro) leaves
1 teaspoon finely chopped red chilli

### method

Combine the avocado, lime juice, spring onion, coriander and chilli, and season the mixture to taste. Cover the guacamole with plastic wrap, resting the plastic directly on the surface of the mixture, and refrigerate until needed.

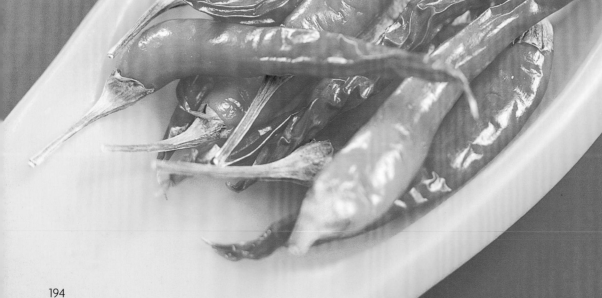

# crunchy wedges

makes 48

## ingredients

6 floury or all-purpose potatoes
1 tablespoon oil
25 g (1 oz/$^1$/$_4$ cup) dry breadcrumbs
2 teaspoons chopped chives
1 teaspoon celery salt
$^1$/$_4$ teaspoon garlic powder
$^1$/$_2$ teaspoon chopped rosemary

## method

Preheat the oven to 200°C (400°F/ Gas 6). Cut the potatoes into eight wedges each and toss in the oil.

Combine the breadcrumbs, chives, celery salt, garlic powder and rosemary in a bowl. Add the wedges and coat well. Place on greased baking trays and bake for 40 minutes, or until crisp and golden.

# layered Mexican dip

**makes 7 cups**

## ingredients

450 g (1 lb) tinned refried beans
35 g ($1^1/_4$ oz) taco seasoning mix
300 g ($10^1/_2$ oz) sour cream
2 cups ready-made guacamole
200 g (7 oz) ready-made salsa sauce
    (medium heat)
60 g ($2^1/_4$ oz/$^1/_2$ cup) grated cheddar cheese
1 tablespoon chopped coriander (cilantro)

## method

Combine the beans and the seasoning mix together in a bowl.

Spread the bean mixture over the base of a serving plate, leaving a border to place the corn chips. Spread with the sour cream, then guacamole, then salsa, layering so you can see each separate layer. Sprinkle with the cheese and coriander.

# bacon and potato skewers

makes 8

## ingredients

16 new potatoes
8 bacon slices
olive oil, for brushing

### tarragon cream
125 g ($4^1/_2$ oz/$^1/_2$ cup) whole-egg mayonnaise
3 anchovy fillets, finely chopped
$^1/_2$ teaspoon dijon mustard
1 tablespoon chopped tarragon leaves

## method

Soak eight bamboo skewers in cold water for 30 minutes. Meanwhile, put the potatoes in a saucepan of lightly salted water. Bring to the boil, then reduce the heat and simmer for about 10 minutes, or until tender when pierced with a sharp knife. Drain well and leave to cool, then cut the potatoes in half lengthways.

Heat the grill (broiler) to high. Cut the bacon widthways into four strips. Wrap a piece of bacon around each potato half and thread 4 pieces onto each skewer. Brush the bacon and potatoes with a little oil and grill for 3–4 minutes, then turn the skewers and grill for another 3–4 minutes, or until the potatoes and bacon are browned on both sides and the bacon is cooked through.

Put the tarragon cream ingredients in a small bowl and stir in about 1 tablespoon of hot water. Mix together well. Drizzle over the skewers and serve warm.

# curried nuts

makes 4$^1/_2$ cups

## ingredients

500 g (1 lb 2 oz) mixed nuts (almonds, brazil nuts,
    pecans, macadamias, cashew nuts)
1 egg white
2 tablespoons curry powder
1 teaspoon ground cumin

## method

Preheat the oven to 150°C (300°F/Gas 2). Spread the nuts in a single layer on a baking tray and roast for 10 minutes.

Whisk the egg white until frothy, then add the nuts, curry powder, cumin and 1 teaspoon salt. Toss together and return to the oven for a further 10–15 minutes, then allow to cool.

# cheese pinwheel scones

makes 10

## ingredients

250 g (9 oz/2 cups) plain (all-purpose) flour
1 tablespoon baking powder
$^1/_8$ teaspoon cayenne pepper
30 g (1 oz) unsalted butter, chilled and diced
185 ml (6 fl oz/$^3/_4$ cup) milk

### filling

40 g (1$^1/_2$ oz/1/4 cup) goat's cheese, crumbled
40 g (1$^1/_2$ oz/$^1/_2$ cup) grated parmesan cheese
40 g (1$^1/_2$ oz/$^1/_3$ cup) grated mature cheddar
  cheese
2 tablespoons chopped flat-leaf (Italian) parsley

## method

Preheat the oven to 220°C (425°F/Gas 7). Grease or line a baking tray.

Sift the flour, baking powder, a pinch of salt and cayenne into a large mixing bowl. Using your fingertips, rub in the butter until the mixture resembles breadcrumbs. Add the milk and, using a flat-bladed knife, mix to form a soft dough. Add a little extra flour if the dough is too sticky.

Turn the dough out onto a floured work surface and roll out to form a 20 x 25 cm (8 x 10 in) rectangle. Sprinkle the goat's cheese over the surface, then sprinkle over the parmesan, cheddar and parsley. Starting from the long side, roll the dough into a cylinder. Cut the cylinder into 10 equal 2 cm ($^3/_4$ in) thick slices. Transfer the slices to a baking tray, spacing them 2 cm ($^3/_4$ in) apart.

Bake for 10–12 minutes, or until golden and cooked through. Cool on a wire rack. Serve warm.

# bruschetta

**serves 8**

## ingredients

**classic Tuscan**

6 ripe tomatoes

15 g ($^1/_2$ oz) basil, shredded

1 garlic clove, finely chopped

2 tablespoons extra virgin olive oil

**mushroom and parsley**

2 tablespoons olive oil

200 g (7 oz) small button mushrooms, quartered

1 tablespoon lemon juice

50 g ($1^3/_4$ oz) goat's cheese, crumbled

1 tablespoon finely chopped flat-leaf (Italian) parsley

1 teaspoon chopped thyme

16 slices crusty white Italian-style bread, cut into 1 cm ($^1/_2$ in) slices

4 garlic cloves, halved

3 tablespoons olive oil

## method

To make the classic Tuscan topping, score a cross in the base of each tomato and place in a bowl of boiling water for 10 seconds, then plunge into cold water. Peel the skin away from the cross. Cut in half and scoop out the seeds with a teaspoon. Finely dice the flesh, then combine with the basil, garlic and oil.

To make the mushroom and parsley topping, heat the oil in a frying pan and cook the mushrooms over medium heat for 5 minutes, or until just tender. Remove from the heat and transfer to a small bowl. Stir in the lemon juice, goat's cheese, parsley and thyme.

Toast the bread and, while still hot, rub with the cut side of a garlic clove. Drizzle oil over each slice of bread, then season. Divide the toppings among the bread slices.

# taramasalata

makes 1$^{1}/_{2}$ cups

## ingredients

5 slices of white bread, crusts removed
4 tablespoons milk
100 g (3$^{1}/_{2}$ oz) tarama (grey mullet roe)
1 egg yolk
$^{1}/_{2}$ small onion, grated
1 garlic clove, crushed
2 tablespoons lemon juice
4 tablespoons olive oil
bread, to serve

## fish substitution

smoked cod's roe

## method

Soak the bread in the milk for 10 minutes. Press in a strainer to extract any excess milk, then mix the bread in a food processor with the tarama, egg yolk, onion and garlic for 30 seconds, or until smooth. Mix in 1 tablespoon of the lemon juice.

With the motor running, slowly pour in the olive oil until the mixture is smooth. Add the remaining lemon juice and a pinch of white pepper. If the dip tastes too salty, add another piece of bread and blend it together. Serve the dip with bread.

# fried whitebait

serves 4

## ingredients

500 g (1 lb 2 oz) whitebait
2 teaspoons sea salt
2 tablespoons plain (all-purpose) flour
1¹/₂ tablespoons cornflour (cornstarch)
2 teaspoons finely chopped flat-leaf (Italian)
    parsley
vegetable oil, for deep-frying
lemon wedges, to serve

## method

Combine the whitebait and sea salt in a bowl and mix well. Cover and refrigerate until needed.

Combine the sifted flours and parsley in a bowl and season well with freshly ground black pepper. Fill a deep-fat fryer or large saucepan one-third full of oil and heat to 180°C (350°F), or until a cube of white bread dropped into the oil browns in 15 seconds. Toss a third of the whitebait in the flour mixture, shake off the excess flour, and deep-fry for 1¹/₂ minutes, or until pale and crisp. Drain well on crumpled paper towels. Repeat with the remaining whitebait.

Just before serving, reheat the oil to 190°C (375°C), or until a cube of white bread browns in 10 seconds, and fry the whitebait a second time, in batches, for 1 minute each batch, or until lightly browned. Drain on crumpled paper towels and salt lightly. Serve hot with lemon wedges.

# bean enchiladas

serves 4

## ingredients

1 tablespoon light olive oil
1 onion, finely sliced
3 garlic cloves, crushed
1 bird's eye chilli, finely chopped
2 teaspoons ground cumin
125 ml (4 fl oz/$^1/_2$ cup) vegetable stock
3 tomatoes, peeled, seeded and chopped
1 tablespoon tomato paste (concentrated purée)
860 g (1 lb 14 oz) tinned three-bean mix
2 tablespoons chopped coriander (cilantro)
    leaves
8 flour tortillas
1 small avocado, peeled and chopped
125 g (4$^1/_2$ oz/$^1/_2$ cup) light sour cream
10 g ($^1/_4$ oz/$^1/_2$ cup) coriander (cilantro) sprigs
115 g (4 oz/2 cups) shredded lettuce

## method

Heat the oil in a deep frying pan over medium heat. Add the onion and cook for 3–4 minutes, or until soft. Add the garlic and chilli and cook for a further 30 seconds. Add the cumin, vegetable stock, tomato and tomato paste and cook for 6–8 minutes, or until the mixture is thick and pulpy. Season.

Preheat the oven to 170ºC (325ºF/Gas 3). Drain and rinse the beans. Add the beans to the sauce and cook for 5 minutes to heat through, then add the chopped coriander.

Meanwhile, wrap the tortillas in foil and warm in the oven for 3–4 minutes.

Place a tortilla on a plate and spread with $^1/_4$ cup of the bean mixture. Top with some avocado, sour cream, coriander sprigs and lettuce. Roll the enchiladas up, tucking in the ends. Cut each one in half to serve.

# barbecued honey chicken wings

serves 4

## ingredients

12 chicken wings
4 tablespoons soy sauce
3 tablespoons sherry
3 tablespoons oil
1 garlic clove, crushed
3 tablespoons honey

## method

Rinse the chicken wings, then pat dry with paper towels. Tuck the wing tips into the underside.

Put the chicken wings in a shallow non-metallic dish. Whisk together the soy sauce, sherry, oil and garlic, then pour over the chicken wings, lightly tossing. Cover with plastic wrap, then refrigerate for 2 hours.

Heat the honey in a small saucepan over medium heat until it has a brushing consistency.

Lightly grease a barbecue or chargrill pan and heat it up. Lift the chicken out of the marinade and add it to the hot pan. Cook the chicken wings for 12 minutes, or until tender and cooked through, turning occasionally. Brush the wings with the warmed honey and cook for a further 2 minutes.

# spinach and feta triangles

makes 8

## ingredients

1 kg (2 lb 4 oz) English spinach leaves
3 tablespoons olive oil
1 onion, chopped
10 spring onions (scallions), sliced
20 g ($^3/_4$ oz) chopped flat-leaf (Italian) parsley
1 tablespoon chopped dill
large pinch of ground nutmeg
35 g ($1^1/_4$ oz/$^1/_3$ cup) grated parmesan cheese
150 g ($5^1/_2$ oz) crumbled feta cheese
90 g ($3^1/_4$ oz) ricotta cheese
4 eggs, lightly beaten
40 g ($1^1/_2$ oz) butter, melted
1 tablespoon olive oil, extra
12 sheets filo pastry

## method

Trim any stems from the spinach. Wash the leaves, roughly chop and place in a large saucepan with a little water clinging to the leaves. Cover and cook over low heat for 5 minutes, or until the leaves have wilted. Drain well and allow to cool slightly before squeezing to remove the excess water.

Heat the oil in a heavy-based frying pan. Add the onion and cook over low heat for 10 minutes, or until tender and golden. Add the spring onion and cook for a further 3 minutes. Remove from the heat. Stir in the spinach, parsley, dill, nutmeg, parmesan, feta, ricotta and egg. Season well.

Preheat the oven to 180°C (350°F/Gas 4). Grease two baking trays. Combine the butter with the extra oil. Work with three sheets of pastry at a time, covering the rest with a damp tea towel (dish towel). Brush each sheet with butter mixture and lay them on top of each other. Halve lengthways.

Place 4 tablespoons of filling on an angle at the end of each strip. Fold the pastry to enclose the filling and form a triangle. Continue folding the triangle over until you reach the end. Brush with the remaining butter mixture and bake for 20 minutes, or until golden brown.

# mini leek pies

makes 32

## ingredients

60 g ($2^{1}/_{4}$ oz) butter
2 tablespoons olive oil
1 onion, finely chopped
3 leeks, finely sliced
1 garlic clove, chopped
1 tablespoon plain (all-purpose) flour
2 tablespoons sour cream
100 g ($3^{1}/_{2}$ oz/1 cup) grated parmesan cheese
1 teaspoon chopped thyme
4 sheets frozen puff pastry, thawed
1 egg, lightly beaten

## method

Heat the butter and oil in a large frying pan over medium heat. Add the onion and cook, stirring occasionally, for 2 minutes. Add the leek and garlic and cook for 5 minutes, or until the leek is softened and lightly coloured. Add the flour and stir into the mixture for 1 minute. Add the sour cream and stir until slightly thickened. Transfer to a bowl and add the parmesan and thyme. Season and allow to cool.

Preheat the oven to 200ºC (400ºF/ Gas 6). Place a lightly greased baking tray in the oven to heat. Using a 6 cm ($2^{1}/_{2}$in) cutter, cut the pastry into 64 circles. Place 2 heaped teaspoons of filling on half the pastry circles, leaving a small border. Lightly brush the edges with egg, then place a pastry circle on top of each. Seal the edges well with a fork. Lightly brush the tops with egg.

Place the pies on the heated tray and bake for 25 minutes, or until the pies are puffed and golden.

# battered savaloys

makes 8

## ingredients

8 savaloys or frankfurts
plain (all-purpose) flour, for dusting
oil, for deep-frying
tomato sauce (ketchup), to serve

### batter

30 g (1 oz/$^1$/$_4$ cup) self-raising flour
2 tablespoons plain (all-purpose) flour
$^1$/$_4$ teaspoon bicarbonate of soda (baking soda)
1 egg, lightly beaten

## method

Insert wooden skewers through the centre of the savaloys lengthways, leaving about 8 cm (3$^1$/$_4$ in) protruding at one end for a handle. Dust savaloys lightly with flour.

To make the batter, place the flours, soda, 125 ml (4 fl oz/ $^1$/$_2$ cup) water and egg in a food processor or blender. Process the mixture for 10 seconds or until all the ingredients are combined and the mixture is free of lumps. Transfer the mixture to a bowl.

Heat the oil to hot in a deep heavy-based saucepan. Holding the end of the skewers, dip the savaloys one or two at a time into the batter. Use a spoon, if necessary, to coat the savaloys completely. Drain off the excess batter.

Holding the skewer ends, gently lower the battered savaloys into the oil. Hold for a few seconds until the savaloys float unaided. Cook for 1 minute, or until lightly golden and crisp. Carefully remove from the oil with tongs or a slotted spoon and drain on paper towels. Repeat the process with the remaining savaloys. Re-dip each cooked savaloy in the remaining batter and repeat the cooking process. Serve with tomato sauce.

# sausage rolls

makes 8

## ingredients

150 g (4$^3$/$_4$ oz) minced (ground) sausage meat
150 g (4$^3$/$_4$ oz) lean minced (ground) beef
1 small onion, finely chopped or grated
2 eggs
1–2 garlic cloves, crushed
1 tablespoon barbecue sauce
3 teaspoons worcestershire sauce
40 g (1$^1$/$_3$ oz/$^1$/$_2$ cup) fresh breadcrumbs
2–3 tablespoons finely chopped flat-leaf (Italian)
    parsley
2 sheets ready-rolled frozen puff pastry, thawed
tomato or chilli sauce, to serve

## method

Preheat the oven to 180°C (350°F/Gas 4). Line 2 baking trays with non-stick baking paper.

Using your hands, mix together the sausage and beef, onion, 1 egg, garlic, sauces, breadcrumbs, parsley and season.

Cut the pastry sheets in half and brush lightly with some of the remaining beaten egg. Divide the beef mixture into 4 equal portions and place 1 portion in a long sausage shape down the centre of each sheet.

Roll the pastry over the mixture and press the edges to seal, leaving the ends open. Use a sharp knife to cut the sausage rolls in half, then place on the trays, seam side down, ensuring there is enough room for them to spread. Brush with egg and lightly score the tops diagonally with a sharp knife. Bake for 35 minutes, or until crisp and golden. Serve with tomato or chilli sauce.

# chipolatas with sage and pancetta and fresh tomato salsa

serves 4

## ingredients

16 chipolata sausages
16 sage leaves
8 thin slices pancetta, cut in half
oil, for brushing

**fresh tomato salsa**
4 roma (plum) tomatoes, cut into 1 cm ($^1/_2$ in)
    cubes
1 tablespoon extra virgin olive oil
1 teaspoon balsamic vinegar
1 garlic clove, very thinly sliced
1 tablespoon chopped mint leaves
1 teaspoon chopped sage leaves

## method

Soak eight bamboo skewers in cold water for 30 minutes.

Meanwhile, put the chipolatas in a saucepan and cover with cold water. Bring to the boil, remove from the heat and drain.

Preheat a barbecue grill plate or flat plate to low. Put a sage leaf along a chipolata and wrap half a slice of pancetta around it. Repeat with the remaining sausages.

Thread 4 chipolatas onto a skewer about a quarter of the way in from one end of the sausages. Push a second skewer up through the other end of the chipolatas so they are suspended between two skewers. Repeat with the remaining sausages.

Lightly brush the hotplate with oil and cook the chipolatas for about 8 minutes, or until browned on both sides and cooked through, turning once.

Meanwhile, put all the tomato salsa ingredients together in a bowl, season and mix together well. Arrange the skewers on a serving plate and spoon some salsa over the top.

# baked potatoes filled with salad

serves 4

## ingredients

4 large baking potatoes (about 365 g/
  12$^1/_2$ oz each)
4 prosciutto slices
310 g (10$^1/_2$ oz) tinned corn kernels, drained
2 celery stalks, sliced
100 g (3$^1/_2$ oz) baby English spinach leaves

### dressing
2$^1/_2$ tablespoons tomato juice
1$^1/_2$ tablespoons red wine vinegar
2 tablespoons olive oil

## method

Preheat the oven to 200°C (400°F/Gas 6). Thoroughly scrub the skins of the potatoes and prick them several times. Transfer to a roasting tin and bake, uncovered, for 1 hour, or until tender when pierced with a sharp knife.

Meanwhile, whisk all the dressing ingredients together in a small bowl. Season and set aside.

Put a frying pan over high heat. Add the prosciutto and dry-fry for a few minutes on both sides, or until crispy. Break the prosciutto into small pieces and set aside.

Sit the potatoes on a chopping board and make two deep incisions crossways over the top so they open out into quarters — be careful not to cut all the way through.

Put the corn, celery and spinach in a large bowl, pour over two-thirds of the dressing and toss well. Sit the potatoes on four serving plates and spoon a little dressing into each potato. Spoon the salad mixture into each potato, letting it spill over a little. Top with prosciutto and serve at once.

# empanadas

makes about 15

## ingredients

2 eggs
40 g (1$^1$/$_4$ oz) stuffed green olives, chopped
95 g (3 oz) ham, finely chopped
30 g (1 oz/$^1$/$_4$ cup) grated cheddar cheese
3 sheets ready-rolled puff pastry, thawed
1 egg yolk, lightly beaten

## method

Place the eggs in a small saucepan, cover with water and bring to the boil. Boil for 10 minutes, then drain and cool for 5 minutes in cold water. Peel and chop.

Preheat the oven to 220°C (425°F/Gas 7). Lightly grease two baking trays. Combine the egg, olives, ham and cheddar in a large bowl.

Cut about five 10 cm (4 in) rounds from each pastry sheet. Spoon a tablespoon of the filling into the centre of each round, fold the pastry over and crimp the edges to seal.

Place the pastries on the trays, about 2 cm ($^3$/$_4$ in) apart. Brush with the egg yolk and bake in the centre or top half of the oven for 15 minutes, or until well browned and puffed. Swap the trays around after 10 minutes and cover loosely with foil if the empanadas start to brown too much. Serve hot.

# Thai fish cakes

serves 4–6

## ingredients

450 g (1 lb) skinned firm white fish fillets, such as
    cod or hake
45 g (1$^1$/$_2$ oz/$^1$/$_4$ cup) rice flour
1 tablespoon fish sauce
1 egg, lightly beaten
3 tablespoons coriander (cilantro) leaves
3 teaspoons red curry paste
1–2 teaspoons chopped red chillies (optional)
100 g (3$^1$/$_2$ oz) green beans, very thinly sliced
2 spring onions (scallions), finely chopped
oil, for frying
sweet chilli sauce, to serve
chopped peanuts and finely diced cucumber
    (optional), to garnish

## method

Roughly chop the fish into chunks, then process in a food
processor for 20 seconds, or until smooth.

Add the rice flour, fish sauce, egg, coriander leaves, curry
paste and chillies, if using. Process for 10 seconds, or until
well combined, then transfer to a large bowl. Alternatively,
finely chop and blend by hand. Mix in the green beans and
spring onion. With wet hands, form 2 tablespoons of mixture
at a time into flattish patties.

Heat the oil in a heavy-based frying pan over medium heat.
Cook four fish cakes at a time until golden brown on both
sides. Drain on crumpled paper towels, then serve with sweet
chilli sauce. Garnish the sauce with a sprinkle of chopped
peanuts and finely diced cucumber.

# prawn cocktails

serves 6

## ingredients

250 g (9 oz/1 cup) whole-egg mayonnaise
3 tablespoons tomato sauce
2 teaspoons worcestershire sauce
$^1/_2$ teaspoon lemon juice
1 drop of Tabasco sauce

1 kg (2 lb 4 oz) cooked medium prawns (shrimp)

lettuce leaves, lemon wedges and sliced bread,
    to serve

## method

For the cocktail sauce, mix all the ingredients together in a bowl and season.

Peel the prawns, leaving some with their tails intact to use as a garnish. Remove the tails from the rest. Gently pull out the dark vein from each prawn back, starting at the head end. Add the prawns without tails to the sauce and mix to coat.

Arrange lettuce in serving dishes or bowls. Spoon some prawns into each dish. Garnish with the reserved prawns and drizzle with some dressing. Serve with lemon wedges and bread.

# deep-fried calamari in chickpea batter with parsley salad

serves 4

## ingredients

### deep-fried calamari

150 g (5$^1/_2$ oz) besan (chickpea flour)
1$^1/_2$ teaspoons smoked paprika
1$^1/_2$ teaspoons ground cumin
$^1/_2$ teaspoon baking powder
250 ml (9 fl oz/1 cup) soda water
oil, for deep-frying
6 cleaned squid hoods, cut into rings about
    8 mm ($^1/_2$ in) wide

### parsley salad

$^1/_4$ preserved lemon, rinsed, pith and flesh
    removed
3 tablespoons lemon juice
3 tablespoons extra virgin olive oil
1 garlic clove, finely chopped
20 g ($^3/_4$ oz) flat-leaf (Italian) parsley
harissa, to serve (optional)

## method

To make the batter, sift the besan, paprika, cumin and baking powder into a bowl, add $^1/_4$ teaspoon pepper, mix together and make a well in the centre. Gradually add the soda water, whisking until smooth. Season with salt. Cover, then leave for 30 minutes.

Cut the lemon zest into very thin slivers. To make the dressing, whisk the lemon juice, extra virgin olive oil and garlic together in a bowl.

Fill a large heavy-based saucepan or wok one-third full of oil and heat until a cube of bread dropped into the oil browns in 15 seconds.

Dip the squid into the batter, allowing any excess to drip away. Cook in batches for 30–60 seconds, or until pale gold and crisp. Drain well on crumpled paper towels and keep warm.

Add the parsley and lemon slivers to the dressing, tossing to coat the parsley leaves. Divide the leaves among four bowls or plates. Top with the squid rings and serve with harissa.

# falafel with rocket and tahini yoghurt dressing

serves 4

## ingredients

### falafel
250 g (9 oz) dried chickpeas
1 onion, finely chopped
2 garlic cloves, crushed
5 large handfuls flat-leaf (Italian) parsley
4 large handfuls coriander (cilantro) leaves
2 teaspoons ground coriander
1 teaspoon ground cumin
$^1/_2$ teaspoon baking powder

### tahini yoghurt dressing
3 tablespoons Greek-style yoghurt
1 tablespoon tahini paste
1 garlic clove, crushed
1 tablespoon lemon juice
3 tablespoons extra virgin olive oil

vegetable oil, for frying
125 g ($4^1/_2$ oz) rocket (arugula) leaves, to serve

## method

Put the dried chickpeas into a bowl and add enough cold water to cover them by about 12 cm ($4^1/_2$ in) and leave to soak overnight.

Drain the chickpeas well and transfer to a food processor. Process until coarsely ground. Add the remaining falafel ingredients and process until smooth and a vibrant green colour. Leave to infuse for 30 minutes.

To make the tahini dressing, put all the ingredients in a bowl and whisk together until smooth. Season to taste and set aside until required.

Using slightly wet hands, shape the falafel mixture into 24 ovals (about the size of an egg). Heat 5 cm (2 in) of vegetable oil in a wok or deep saucepan and fry the falafel in batches for 2–3 minutes, or until dark brown. Drain on paper towel and keep warm in a low oven while cooking the remaining mixture.

Arrange the rocket leaves on serving plates, top with the falafel and drizzle over the tahini dressing. Serve immediately.

# sausage and sweet potato wraps

serves 4

## ingredients

1 tablespoon olive oil

400 g (14 oz) orange sweet potato, peeled
   and thinly sliced

1 large zucchini (courgette), cut lengthways
   into 4 pieces

4 thick beef sausages

4 pieces lavash bread

75 g ($2^1/_2$ oz/$^1/_3$ cup) ready-made hummus

175 g (6 oz/1 cup) ready-made tabouleh

sweet chilli sauce, to serve

## method

Heat the grill (broiler) and grill tray to medium. Pour the oil into a bowl and season. Add the sweet potato and zucchini, gently toss the vegetables about to coat, then arrange them in a single layer on the preheated grill tray — you will probably need to work in two batches. Grill the vegetables for 5 minutes, then flip them over and cook for another 5 minutes, or until tender. Remove and set aside.

Arrange the sausages on the tray and grill for 10–12 minutes, turning once, until browned all over and cooked through. Set aside to cool for 5 minutes, then cut the sausages in half lengthways.

To assemble the wraps, spread each lavash bread with 1 tablespoon of hummus and 3 tablespoons of tabouleh. Top with the sweet potato, zucchini and the sausage halves, drizzle with sweet chilli sauce, then roll up and serve.

# smoked mozzarella sandwiches

serves 4

## ingredients

8 thick slices ciabatta or other Italian-style bread
butter, for spreading
12 thin slices smoked mozzarella cheese
2 vine-ripened tomatoes, thinly sliced
8 large basil leaves

## method

Preheat a barbecue flat plate or grill plate to medium. Spread each slice of bread with butter, then place 4 slices, buttered-side-down, on a clean, flat surface. Layer the cheese, tomato and basil on top, then add the remaining bread slices, placing them buttered-side-up. Tie the sandwiches together with kitchen string.

Put the sandwiches on the hotplate, pressing them down firmly with a spatula.

Grill for 3 minutes, pressing down firmly during cooking. Turn and cook the sandwiches for another 2 minutes, again pressing down firmly with the spatula, until the bread is golden brown and the filling has heated through.

Remove from the heat and cut each sandwich crossways into three 'fingers'. Arrange on four serving plates and serve hot, sprinkled with sea salt.

# grilled nachos

## ingredients

600 g (1 lb 5 oz) corn chips
4 tomatoes, chopped
1 red onion, finely chopped
3 jalapeño chillies, thinly sliced
2 tablespoons lime juice
4 tablespoons chopped coriander (cilantro)
　　leaves
220 g (7$^3$/$_4$ oz/1$^1$/$_2$ cups) feta cheese, crumbled

## method

Turn on the grill (broiler). Arrange the corn chips on four ovenproof plates.

Scatter the tomato, onion and chilli on top of the corn chips, then drizzle with the lime juice and season with some salt. Scatter the coriander and feta cheese over the top, making sure the corn chips are well covered.

Grill the nachos until they start to brown around the edges and the cheese starts to melt. Serve hot.

# cayenne chicken pieces

serves 6

## ingredients

500 ml (17 fl oz/2 cups) buttermilk
3 garlic cloves, crushed
1 tablespoon finely chopped thyme
1 teaspoon salt
2 kg (4 lb 8 oz) chicken pieces, skin on (about
    12 assorted pieces)
peanut oil, for deep-frying
250 g (9 oz/2 cups) plain (all-purpose) flour
1 tablespoon Hungarian sweet paprika
$1^{1}/_{2}$ tablespoons cayenne pepper
1 tablespoon celery salt
2 tablespoons onion powder
lemon wedges, to serve (optional)

## method

Combine the buttermilk, garlic, thyme and salt in a large bowl. Add the chicken pieces and stir to coat. Cover tightly with plastic wrap and refrigerate for 24 hours, stirring occasionally.

Fill a deep-fryer or large heavy-based saucepan one-third full with peanut oil and heat to 170°C (325°F), or until a cube of bread dropped in the oil browns in 20 seconds. Combine the flour, paprika, cayenne, celery salt and onion powder. Lift the chicken out of the buttermilk but don't shake off the excess. Roll in the flour mixture until thickly coated.

Deep-fry the chicken pieces, a few at a time, for 10–12 minutes, or until deep golden and just cooked through. Drain well on paper towel and rest in a warm oven while cooking the remaining chicken. Serve with lemon wedges, if desired.

# grilled cheesy club sandwich

serves 4

## ingredients

4 bacon slices, halved
125 g (4$^1$/$_2$ oz/$^1$/$_2$ cup) mayonnaise
1 garlic clove, crushed
1 tablespoon lemon juice
12 thin, large slices country-style or
    sourdough bread
2 tomatoes, sliced
10 thin slices swiss or jarlsberg cheese
1 ripe avocado, coarsely mashed

## method

Heat the grill (broiler) to high. Put the bacon on the grill tray and grill for about 2 minutes on each side, or until lightly browned but not crisp.

Meanwhile, mix together the mayonnaise, garlic and lemon juice and season well with freshly ground black pepper. Put 8 bread slices under the grill and toast on one side only for about 1 minute, or until golden. Sit 4 of the slices on a work surface, toasted-side-down. Spread the tops with half the garlic mayonnaise, then add the tomato slices, then a slice of cheese. Put an untoasted slice of bread on top of each, spread with the remaining garlic mayonnaise and sit a bacon slice on top. Spread with the avocado, then top with the remaining slices of grilled bread, placing them toasted-side-up. Press each sandwich down firmly to compact the filling. Arrange 1$^1$/$_2$ slices of cheese on top of each toasted sandwich, allowing the cheese to fall over the sides a little.

Return the sandwiches to the grill and cook for 1 minute, or until the cheese bubbles and browns. Cool slightly, then cut in half diagonally. Serve warm.

# five-spice pork ribs

serves 4

## ingredients

1 kg (2 lb 4 oz) American-style pork ribs
shredded spring onions (scallions) (optional),
    to serve

### marinade
125 ml (4 fl oz/$^1/_2$ cup) tomato sauce (ketchup)
2 tablespoons Chinese rice wine or dry sherry
2 tablespoons light soy sauce
2 tablespoons honey
1 tablespoon sweet chilli sauce
2 teaspoons five-spice powder
2 garlic cloves, crushed

## method

Cut the pork ribs into individual ribs. Combine all the marinade ingredients in a large non-metallic bowl. Add the ribs and toss well to coat evenly. Cover and marinate for several hours, or overnight.

Preheat the oven to 180°C (350°F/Gas 4). Line a large baking tray with foil. Remove excess marinade from the ribs, reserving the remaining marinade. Put the ribs on a rack on the baking tray. Bake for 30 minutes, or until cooked and golden brown. Brush with the reserved marinade 1–2 times during cooking. Serve hot, garnished with spring onions if desired.

# chicken and tzatziki wrap

makes 4

## ingredients

$^1/_2$ telegraph (long) cucumber, seeded and grated
100 g (3$^1/_2$ oz) low-fat natural yoghurt
$^1/_4$ teaspoon lemon juice
1 tablespoon chopped mint
4 boneless, skinless chicken thighs
pinch of paprika
4 sheets lavash or other flat bread
4 large butter lettuce leaves

## method

Sprinkle the grated cucumber with $^1/_2$ teaspoon salt. Leave the cucumber for 10 minutes, then drain and mix with the yoghurt, lemon juice and mint. Season.

Flatten the chicken with a meat mallet or rolling pin, season and sprinkle with the paprika. Grill (broil) the fillets for 5–7 minutes on each side, or until cooked through.

Lay out the lavash breads and place a large butter lettuce leaf on each. Spread each with one-quarter of the tzatziki, then top with a sliced chicken fillet. Roll up, folding one end closed. Wrap in baking paper to serve.

# steak baguette with rocket and mustardy mayo

serves 4

## ingredients

3 tablespoons olive oil, plus extra for frying
1 red onion, sliced
1 teaspoon brown sugar
2 teaspoons balsamic vinegar
1 teaspoon thyme
1 tablespoon dijon mustard
3 tablespoons mayonnaise
100 g (3$^1$/$_2$ oz) rocket (arugula)
500 g (1 lb 2 oz) beef fillet, cut into 4 thin slices
2 thick baguettes, cut in half, or 8 thick slices of bread
2 tomatoes, sliced

## method

Heat 2 tablespoons of oil in a small saucepan. Add the onion and cook very slowly, with the lid on, stirring occasionally, until the onion is soft but not brown. Remove the lid, add the sugar and vinegar and cook for a further 10 minutes, or until the onion is soft and just browned. Remove the pan off the stove and stir in the thyme.

Meanwhile, make the mustardy mayo by mixing together well the mustard and mayonnaise in a small bowl.

Drizzle the rocket leaves with the remaining olive oil and season.

Heat 1 tablespoon of the extra oil in a frying pan over high heat and cook the steaks for 2 minutes on each side, adding more oil if necessary. Season to taste.

To serve, put out the bread, along with separate bowls containing the onion, mustardy mayo, rocket leaves, steak and sliced tomatoes. Let everyone make their own baguette.

# burger with the works

serves 6

## ingredients

750 g (1 lb 10 oz) minced (ground) beef
1 onion, finely chopped
1 egg
40 g (1$^1$/$_2$ oz/$^1$/$_2$ cup) fresh breadcrumbs
2 tablespoons tomato paste (concentrated purée)
1 tablespoon worcestershire sauce
2 tablespoons chopped flat-leaf (Italian) parsley
3 large onions
30 g (1 oz) butter
6 slices cheddar cheese
butter, extra, for cooking
6 eggs, extra
6 bacon slices
6 large hamburger buns, lightly toasted
2 handfuls shredded lettuce
2 tomatoes, thinly sliced
6 large slices beetroot, drained
6 pineapple rings, drained
tomato sauce (ketchup), to serve

## method

Mix together the beef, onion, egg, breadcrumbs, tomato paste, worcestershire sauce and parsley with your hands. Season well. Divide into six portions and shape into burgers. Cover and set aside.

Slice the onions into thin rings. Heat the butter on a barbecue flat plate. Cook the onion, turning often, until well browned. Move the onion to the outer edge of the flat plate to keep warm. Brush the barbecue grill or flat plate liberally with oil.

Cook the burgers for 3–4 minutes each side, or until browned and cooked through. Move to the cooler part of the barbecue or transfer to a plate and keep warm. Place a slice of cheese on each burger.

Heat a small amount of butter on a barbecue flat plate or in a large frying pan. Fry the eggs and bacon until the eggs are cooked through and the bacon is golden and crisp. Fill the hamburger buns with lettuce, tomato, beetroot and pineapple topped with a burger. Pile the onion, egg, bacon and tomato sauce on top of the burger.

# lamb and hummus wraps

serves 4

## ingredients

500 g (1 lb 2 oz) minced (ground) lamb
1 onion, finely chopped
2–3 garlic cloves, chopped
1 tablespoon za'atar, plus extra, for sprinkling
30 g (1 oz/1 cup) coriander (cilantro) leaves
olive oil
4 Lebanese (pitta) breads, to serve
75 g ($2^1/_2$ oz) mixed salad leaves

### hummus

300 g ($10^1/_2$ oz) tinned chickpeas
2 garlic cloves, crushed
1 tablespoon tahini paste
3 tablespoons lemon juice

## method

Put the lamb, onion, garlic, za'atar and coriander leaves in a food processor and blend until smooth. Put into a bowl, cover and refrigerate for 1 hour.

With wet hands, form the meat into eight 12 cm ($4^1/_2$ in) elongated sausage shapes. Heat a barbecue flat plate or grill plate and coat with the oil. Coat the lamb with oil. Cook and turn for 8 minutes, or until evenly browned and cooked through.

Meanwhile, to make the hummus, drain the chickpeas, reserving the liquid and put in a food processor or blender. Add the garlic and tahini. With the motor running, add the lemon juice and 3 tablespoons of the reserved chickpea liquid. Process until smooth. Add a little more lemon juice and reserved liquid, if desired, and season.

Lightly brush one side of the breads with oil and sprinkle with the za'atar. Put the unoiled side on the chargrill or hotplate for 2–3 minutes, or until heated through.

To serve, place the breads on serving plates. Spread over the hummus. Top each with two of the lamb sausages and some salad leaves and roll up firmly.

# pizza margherita

makes 2 large

## ingredients

8 very ripe roma (plum) tomatoes
1 handful basil leaves
4 garlic cloves, crushed
2 tablespoons tomato passata (puréed tomatoes)
    or tomato pasta sauce
100 ml ($3^1/_2$ fl oz) olive oil
2 ready-made pizza bases
400 g (14 oz) fresh mozzarella cheese, chopped

## method

Remove the cores, seeds and juices from the tomatoes, chop the tomatoes roughly, then purée them in a food processor with 8 basil leaves. Stir in the garlic, passata and 2 tablespoons of olive oil and season well.

Put the pizza bases on oiled baking trays. Drizzle each with a little of the olive oil. Spoon the tomato sauce over the base, spreading it up to the rim. Scatter the mozzarella over the top and drizzle with a little more olive oil.

Cook the pizza for 5–12 minutes, or until the base is light brown and crisp and the topping is cooked. Just before serving, drizzle with a little more oil and scatter the remaining basil over the top.

# Lebanese wrap with chargrilled chicken

serves 4

## ingredients

3 large boneless, skinless chicken breasts
1 tablespoon olive oil
4 Lebanese (pitta) breads
200 g (7 oz) hummus
200 g (7 oz) beetroot dip
200 g (7 oz) Greek-style yoghurt
3 garlic cloves, crushed
4 tablespoons chopped flat-leaf (Italian) parsley
10 cos (romaine) lettuce leaves, shredded
1 small red onion, thinly sliced
3 roma (plum) tomatoes, thinly sliced

## method

Place the chicken breasts between two sheets of plastic wrap and slightly flatten them with a mallet or rolling pin.

Preheat a barbecue grill plate, chargrill plate or chargrill pan to medium. Lightly brush the hotplate with oil and grill the chicken for 4 minutes on each side, or until cooked through. Remove from the heat, allow to cool slightly, then slice thinly. Lay the bread rounds on a flat surface and spread evenly with the hummus and the beetroot dip, leaving a 3 cm ($1^1/_4$ in) border. Top with the chicken and drizzle with the combined yoghurt and garlic.

Sprinkle the parsley, lettuce, onion and tomato lengthways along the centre of each round and roll up tightly, tucking in the ends. Wrap tightly in foil and grill the wraps on the hotplate for 1–2 minutes on each side, or until the bread is crispy, pressing down lightly with a spatula during grilling. Unwrap the foil, cut the wraps in half on the diagonal and serve hot.

# meat pies with tomato sauce

makes 8

## ingredients

1 tablespoon oil
2 bacon slices, finely chopped
1 onion, finely chopped
1 garlic clove, crushed
500 g (1 lb 2 oz) minced (ground) beef
2 tablespoons plain (all-purpose) flour
2 teaspoons dry mustard powder
3 tablespoons tomato sauce (ketchup)
1 tablespoon worcestershire sauce
500 ml (17 fl oz/2 cups) beef stock
$^1/_2$ teaspoon dried mixed herbs
4 sheets ready-rolled shortcrust pastry
1 egg yolk, lightly beaten
4 sheets frozen puff pastry, thawed
tomato sauce (ketchup), extra, to serve

## method

Preheat the oven to 180°C (350°F/Gas 4). Heat the oil in a frying pan and add the bacon, onion and garlic. Stir over medium heat for 3 minutes.

Add the beef to the pan and stir over high heat for 3 minutes, or until the meat is browned. Add the flour and mustard powder and stir for 1 minute. Add the tomato and worcestershire sauces, stock and mixed herbs. Bring to the boil, then reduce the heat. Simmer, uncovered, for 5 minutes or until the mixture has reduced and thickened, stirring occasionally. Allow to cool.

Using a plate or bowl as a guide, cut the shortcrust pastry into eight 14 cm (5$^1/_2$ in) diameter circles. Line eight 11 cm (4$^1/_4$ in) pie tins. Divide cooled filling evenly into pastry shells. Brush around pastry rim with the beaten egg yolk.

Using a plate as a guide, cut the puff pastry into eight 12 cm (4$^1/_2$ in) diameter circles. Place over the tops of the pies, press edges to seal, trim pastry edges. Brush the tops with egg yolk. Using a sharp knife, make 2 small slits in the top of each pie. Place the tins on a baking tray. Bake for 15 minutes, or until golden. Serve hot with tomato sauce.

# crispy chicken wings

serves 6

## ingredients

12 chicken wings
3 tablespoons soy sauce
3 tablespoons hoisin sauce
125 g ($4^1/_2$ oz/$^1/_2$ cup) tomato sauce
2 tablespoons honey
1 tablespoon soft brown sugar
1 tablespoon cider vinegar
2 garlic cloves, crushed
$^1/_4$ teaspoon Chinese five-spice powder
2 teaspoons sesame oil

## method

Tuck the chicken wing tips to the underside and place in a non-metallic bowl. Mix together all the remaining ingredients and pour over the wings, tossing to coat. Cover and leave in the fridge for at least 2 hours, turning occasionally. Drain, reserving the marinade.

Cook the wings on a hot, lightly oiled barbecue grill or flat plate for 5 minutes, or until cooked through, brushing with the reserved marinade several times.

# pizzette

makes 4

## ingredients

125 g (4$^1$/$_2$ oz/1 cup) plain (all-purpose) flour
150 g (5$^1$/$_2$ oz/1 cup) wholemeal plain
    (all-purpose) flour
2 teaspoons dry yeast
$^1$/$_2$ teaspoon sugar
$^1$/$_2$ teaspoon salt
2 tablespoons plain yoghurt
2 tablespoons tomato paste (concentrated purée)
1 garlic clove, crushed
1 teaspoon dried oregano
20 g ($^1$/$_2$ oz) lean shaved ham
2 teaspoons grated light mozzarella cheese
chopped rocket (arugula), to serve
extra virgin olive oil, to serve

## method

Sift the plain flour into a bowl, then add the wholemeal plain flour, dry yeast, sugar and salt. Make a well in the centre, add 125 ml (4 fl oz/$^1$/$_2$ cup) water and the yoghurt and mix to a dough. Knead on a lightly floured surface for 5 minutes, or until smooth and elastic. Cover with a tea towel (dish towel) and rest in a warm place for 20–30 minutes, or until doubled in size.

Preheat the oven to 200°C (400°F/Gas 6). Punch the dough down and knead for 30 seconds, then divide into four portions. Roll each portion into a 15 cm (6 in) round and place on a baking tray.

Combine the tomato paste, garlic, oregano and 1 tablespoon water. Spread the paste over each base then top with the ham and mozzarella. Bake for 12–15 minutes, or until crisp and golden on the edges. Just before serving, top with chopped rocket and drizzle with extra virgin olive oil.

# prawn tacos

serves 4

## ingredients

2 firm ripe tomatoes, seeded and diced
2 tablespoons lime juice
$^1/_2$ teaspoon chilli powder
$^1/_2$ teaspoon ground cumin
2 tablespoons oil
1 red onion, diced
4 garlic cloves, crushed
18 raw prawns (shrimp), peeled, deveined and
    roughly chopped
3 tablespoons chopped flat-leaf (Italian) parsley
8 corn taco shells
150 g ($5^1/_2$ oz) shredded iceberg lettuce
1 avocado, diced
125 g ($4^1/_2$ oz/$^1/_2$ cup) sour cream

## method

Preheat the oven to 180°C (350°F/ Gas 4). Combine the tomato, lime juice, chilli powder and cumin.

Heat the oil in a frying pan, add the onion and garlic and cook gently for 3–5 minutes, or until soft. Add the prawns and toss briefly, then stir in the tomato mixture. Cook for a further 3–5 minutes, or until the prawns are pink and cooked. Stir in the parsley.

Meanwhile, heat the taco shells on a baking tray in the oven for 5 minutes.

Place some lettuce in the bottom of each taco shell, then fill with the prawn mixture. Top with some avocado and a dollop of sour cream.

# mini roasted vegetable frittatas

makes 24

## ingredients

4 tablespoons olive oil
3 French shallots, thinly sliced
3 garlic cloves, crushed
4 slender eggplants (aubergines), cut into 5 mm ($^1/_4$ in) slices
2 zucchini (courgettes), cut into 5 mm ($^1/_4$ in) slices
2 red capsicums (peppers), seeded and cut into 2–3 flat pieces
2 tablespoons finely chopped mint
1 handful basil, torn into small pieces
8 eggs
125 ml (4 fl oz/$^1/_2$ cup) pouring (whipping) cream
pinch of ground nutmeg
25 g (1 oz/$^1/_4$ cup) grated parmesan cheese
mint leaves, extra, to garnish

## method

Preheat the oven to 200°C (400°F/Gas 6). Grease 24 x 5 cm (2 in) non-stick tart holes. Heat the oil, shallots and garlic in a saucepan over low heat for 1–2 minutes, or until just soft.

Put the eggplant and zucchini slices on a baking tray and brush both sides with the hot oil. Roast for 10 minutes, then turn and cook for a further 10 minutes, or until golden. Put the capsicum strips, skin side up, under a hot grill (broiler) until the skin blackens and blisters. Cool in a plastic bag, then peel away the skin. Cut into strips, then transfer to a bowl. Remove the vegetables from the oven. Reduce the oven to 180°C (350°F/Gas 4). Cut the vegetables into strips and add to the bowl. Add the mint and basil, season and mix well.

Beat the eggs, cream, nutmeg and parmesan. Season.

Fill each tart hole one-third full of assorted pieces of vegetable mixture. Pour the egg mixture in just short of the top. Distribute the remaining vegetables among the holes, pressing the pieces into the egg. Use the remaining egg mixture to top up the holes. Bake for 15 minutes, or until golden and set. Cool for 5 minutes before turning out onto a wire rack. Top with a mint leaf and serve warm or cold.

# fajitas

serves 4

## ingredients

185 ml (6 fl oz/³/₄ cup) olive oil
2 tablespoons lime juice
4 garlic cloves, chopped
3 red chillies, chopped
2 tablespoons tequila (optional)
1 kg (2 lb 4 oz) rump steak, thinly sliced into strips
1 red and yellow capsicum (pepper), thinly sliced
1 red onion, thinly sliced
8 flour tortillas
guacamole, shredded lettuce, diced tomato and
    sour cream, to serve

## method

Combine the oil, lime juice, garlic, chilli, tequila and some pepper. Add the meat, cover and marinate for several hours or overnight.

Drain the meat and toss with the capsicum and onion.

Just before serving, wrap the tortillas in foil and warm them in a 150°C (300°F/Gas 2) oven for about 5 minutes. Cook the meat and vegetables in batches in a hot heavy-based frying pan until cooked. Put the tortillas on a serving plate and sit in the middle of the table with the tortillas, guacamole, shredded lettuce, diced tomato and sour cream. Let everyone assemble their own fajita.

# lamb pide with garlic and chickpea purée

serves 4

## ingredients

1 tablespoon lemon juice
1 teaspoon ground cumin
1 tablespoon olive oil
4 trimmed lamb fillets
1 bulb of garlic
100 g (3$^1/_2$ oz/$^1/_2$ cup) tinned chickpeas, drained
2 teaspoons lemon juice, extra
1 tablespoon plain yoghurt
4 x 100 g (3$^1/_2$ oz) pieces pide (Turkish/flat bread)
tomato and rocket (arugula) leaves, to serve

## method

Mix the lemon juice, cumin, olive oil and season. Add the lamb fillets and leave to marinate for at least 1 hour.

Preheat the oven to 210°C (415°F/Gas 6–7). Wrap the bulb of garlic in foil, then roast for 20 minutes, or until soft. Cool, then squeeze out the pulp from each clove. Purée the pulp with the chickpeas, extra lemon juice and yoghurt in a food processor— add a little water to achieve a spreading consistency, if needed. Season.

Barbecue the lamb for 3 minutes on each side, or until done to your liking. Grill (broil) or toast the Turkish bread, then slice through the middle and spread with the chickpea spread. Top with thin slices of the lamb, tomato and rocket leaves.

# Mediterranean blt

serves 4

## ingredients

4 small vine-ripened tomatoes, halved
1 head garlic, halved
1 tablespoon extra virgin olive oil
15 g ($^1/_2$ oz) basil leaves
1 loaf Italian woodfired bread
8 slices provolone cheese
8 slices mortadella
100 g ($3^1/_2$ oz) rocket (arugula)
extra virgin olive oil, extra
balsamic vinegar, to serve

## method

Preheat the oven to 200°C (400°F/Gas 6). Place the tomato and garlic in a roasting pan and drizzle with the oil. Sprinkle with sea salt and cracked black pepper and roast for 40 minutes, or until the garlic is soft and the tomatoes are slightly dried. Add the basil leaves and continue cooking for 5 minutes, or until the leaves are crisp. Remove from the oven.

Cut four thick slices from the loaf of woodfired bread and lightly toast on both sides.

Peel the roasted garlic cloves and spread half onto the toast. Top with the provolone, mortadella, rocket, basil and roasted tomatoes. Sprinkle with the remaining roasted garlic, drizzle with extra olive oil and the balsamic vinegar.

# posh nosh

For those of us who **love to cook**, there are few pleasures in life greater than having friends over for dinner. Hosting a dinner party can be an excellent opportunity to dust off the crystal, raid the wine cellar and put together **swish food** to **match**. The key is to have spectacular recipes on hand.

# buckwheat blini with smoked salmon

makes about 40

## ingredients

7 g ($^1/_4$ oz) dried yeast
pinch sugar
250 ml (9 fl oz/1 cup) warm milk
100 g ($3^1/_2$ oz/$^3/_4$ cup) buckwheat flour
60 g ($2^1/_4$ oz/$^1/_2$ cup) plain (all-purpose) flour
2 eggs, separated
20 g ($^3/_4$ oz) butter
4 tablespoons oil
150 g ($5^1/_2$ oz) crème fraîche
300 g ($10^1/_2$ oz) smoked salmon, cut into 2 cm
($^3/_4$ in) strips
50 g ($1^3/_4$ oz) salmon roe
dill sprigs, to garnish

## method

Place the yeast and sugar in a small bowl and gradually stir in the milk. Sift the flours into a large bowl and make a well in the centre. Add the egg yolks and warm milk mixture and whisk until combined and smooth. Cover and stand in a warm place for 45 minutes to prove.

Melt the butter, then stir into the proved dough and season. Place the egg whites in a dry bowl and beat with electric beaters until soft peaks form. Fold one-third of the egg whites into the batter until just mixed. Gently fold in the remaining egg whites until just combined.

Heat 1 tablespoon of the oil in a large frying pan over medium heat. Drop $^1/_2$ tablespoon of batter into the pan for each blini. Cook for 1 minute, or until bubbles form on the surface. Turn over and cook for 30 seconds, or until golden. Repeat to make about 40 blini, adding more oil as needed. Cool completely.

Spread 1 teaspoon of crème fraîche on each blini, then arrange a strip of smoked salmon over it. Spoon $^1/_4$ teaspoon of salmon roe on top. Garnish with a sprig of dill and serve.

# black figs with goat's cheese wrapped in prosciutto

serves 4

## ingredients

8 large black figs
80 g (2³/₄ oz) soft goat's cheese
8 thin slices of prosciutto
2 tablespoons lemon oil
2 tablespoon chopped pistachio nuts

## method

Line a steamer with baking paper and punch with holes. Cut the figs into quarters almost to the base so that they still keep together, then carefully stuff small chunks of goat's cheese into each fig.

Place the stuffed figs in the prepared steamer and cover with a lid. Sit the steamer over a saucepan of boiling water and steam for 5–8 minutes, or until the figs are tender and the cheese is warm, but still holds its shape.

Carefully wrap a slice of prosciutto around each fig, then season well with freshly ground black pepper and drizzle with the lemon oil. Sprinkle the pistachios over the top before serving.

# cheese biscuits

makes about 40

## ingredients

125 g ($4^1/_2$ oz/1 cup) plain (all-purpose) flour
2 tablespoons self-raising flour
1 teaspoon curry powder
125 g ($4^1/_2$ oz) butter
50 g ($1^3/_4$ oz/$^1/_2$ cup) grated parmesan cheese
85 g (3 oz/$^2/_3$ cup) grated cheddar cheese
20 g ($^3/_4$ oz) crumbled blue-vein cheese
1 tablespoon lemon juice
25 g (1 oz/$^1/_4$ cup) finely grated parmesan cheese, extra

## method

Place the flours, curry powder and butter in a food processor. Process until the mixture resembles fine breadcrumbs.

Stir in the cheeses and the lemon juice. Bring the mixture together into a ball.

Roll into a 30 cm (12 in) log. Wrap in plastic wrap and chill for 1 hour. Slice into 5 mm ($^1/_4$ in) slices. Reshape if necessary. Preheat the oven to 200°C (400°F/Gas 6).

Place on a baking paper-lined baking tray, allowing some room for spreading. Sprinkle the tops with parmesan. Bake for 15 minutes, or until the biscuits are golden. Allow to cool on the trays.

# asparagus gremolata

serves 4

## ingredients

50 g (1³/₄ oz) butter
80 g (2³/₄ oz/1 cup) coarse fresh white breadcrumbs
7 g (¹/₈ oz) chopped flat-leaf (Italian) parsley
2 garlic cloves, very finely chopped
3 teaspoons very finely chopped lemon zest
400 g (14 oz) green asparagus, trimmed
1¹/₂ tablespoons virgin olive oil

## method

Melt the butter in a heavy-based frying pan over high heat. Add the breadcrumbs and, using a wooden spoon, stir until the crumbs are golden and crisp. Remove to a plate to cool slightly.

Combine the parsley, garlic and lemon zest in a bowl, add the breadcrumbs, and season to taste.

Bring a large, wide saucepan of water to the boil, add the asparagus and cook for 2–3 minutes, or until just tender when pierced with a fine skewer. Drain well and arrange on a warmed serving plate. Drizzle with the olive oil and sprinkle gremolata over the top. Serve immediately.

# bloody mary oyster shots

serves 12

## ingredients

4 tablespoons vodka
125 ml (4 fl oz/$^1/_2$ cup) tomato juice
1 tablespoon lemon juice
dash of worcestershire sauce
2 drops of Tabasco sauce
pinch of celery salt
12 oysters
1 Lebanese (short) cucumber, peeled, seeded and
    finely julienned

## method

Combine the vodka, tomato juice, lemon juice, worcestershire sauce, Tabasco and celery salt in a jug. Mix well, then refrigerate for 30 minutes, or until chilled.

Just before serving, fill each shot glass about two-thirds full. Drop an oyster in each glass, then top with a teaspoon of julienned cucumber. Crack some black pepper over the top of each shot glass, then serve.

# chicken liver parfait

makes 48

## ingredients

35 g (1¹/₄ oz) butter
2 French shallots, peeled and sliced
500 g (1 lb 2 oz) chicken livers, trimmed
3 tablespoons thick (double/heavy) cream
1 tablespoon cognac or brandy
48 Melba toasts
8 cornichons (baby gherkins), thinly sliced on
    the diagonal

## method

Heat a large frying pan over medium heat. Melt the butter, then add the shallots to the pan and cook, stirring, for 4–5 minutes, or until they are soft and transparent. Use a slotted spoon to transfer them to a food processor.

In the same pan, add the chicken livers and cook in batches over high heat, stirring, for 4–5 minutes, or until seared on the outside but still pink and quite soft on the inside. Add to the food processor along with 2 tablespoons of the pan juices, the cream and cognac, then season. Blend for 4–5 minutes, or until quite smooth. Push through a fine sieve to remove any remaining lumps. Transfer to a bowl or serving dish, put plastic wrap directly on the surface of the mixture and refrigerate for at least 4 hours, or until cold.

To serve, spoon a heaped teaspoon of parfait onto each Melba toast and top with a slice of cornichon.

# artichokes in aromatic vinaigrette

serves 4

## ingredients

2 tablespoons lemon juice
4 large globe artichokes
2 garlic cloves, crushed
1 teaspoon finely chopped oregano
$^1/_2$ teaspoon ground cumin
$^1/_2$ teaspoon ground coriander
pinch of dried chilli flakes
3 teaspoons sherry vinegar
3 tablespoons olive oil

## method

Add the lemon juice to a large bowl of cold water. Trim the artichokes, cutting off the stalks to within 5 cm (2 in) of the base and removing the tough outer leaves. Cut the top quarter of the leaves from each. Slice each artichoke in half from top to base, or into quarters if large. Remove each small, furry choke with a teaspoon, then put the artichokes in the bowl of acidulated water to prevent them from discolouring while you prepare the rest.

Bring a large non-reactive saucepan of water to the boil, add the artichokes and a teaspoon of salt and simmer for 20 minutes, or until tender. The cooking time will depend on the artichoke size. Test by pressing a skewer into the base. If cooked, the artichoke will be soft and give little resistance. Strain, then place the artichokes on their cut side to drain.

Combine the garlic, oregano, cumin, coriander and chilli flakes in a bowl. Season, and blend in the vinegar. Beating constantly, slowly pour in the oil to form an emulsion. This can be done in a small food processor.

Arrange the artichokes in rows on a platter. Pour the vinaigrette over the top and leave to cool completely.

# quail eggs with spiced salts

makes 48

## ingredients

2 teaspoons cumin seeds
48 quail eggs
125 g ($4^1/_2$ oz/$^1/_2$ cup) table salt
$1^1/_2$ teaspoons Chinese five-spice
3 teaspoons celery salt

## method

Toast the cumin seeds in a dry frying pan over low heat for 1–2 minutes, or until fragrant. Cool slightly, then grind until finely crushed into a powder.

Place half the eggs in a large saucepan of water, bring to the boil and cook for $1^1/_2$ minutes for medium-hard boiled eggs. Remove from the pan and rinse under cold water to cool. Repeat with the remaining eggs. Peel when cold—this is easiest done under gently running cold water.

Divide the table salt among three small bowls and add the Chinese five-spice to one, the celery salt to another and the ground cumin to the third. Mix the flavourings into the salt in each bowl.

To serve, pile the eggs into a large bowl and serve each of the salts in a small bowl. Invite your guests to dip their egg into the flavoured salt of their choice.

# vegetable chips

serves 4–6

## ingredients

500 g (1 lb 2 oz) orange sweet potato
500 g (1 lb 2 oz) beetroot
500 g (1 lb 2 oz) parsnip
oil, for deep-frying

## method

Preheat the oven to 180°C (350°F/Gas 4). Run a vegetable peeler along the length of the sweet potato and beetroot to make thin ribbons. Cut the parsnip into thin slices.

Fill a deep, heavy-based saucepan one-third full of oil and heat to 190°C (375°F), or until a cube of bread dropped into the oil browns in 10 seconds. Cook the vegetables in batches for about 30 seconds, or until golden and crisp, turning with tongs, if necessary. Drain on crumpled paper towels and season with salt. Keep warm on a baking tray in the oven and cook the remaining chips.

# stuffed black olives

makes 36

## ingredients

36 pitted jumbo black or large kalamata olives
100 g (3$^1$/$_2$ oz) goat's cheese
1 teaspoon capers, drained and finely chopped
1 garlic clove, crushed
1 tablespoon chopped flat-leaf (Italian) parsley
1$^1$/$_2$ tablespoons plain (all-purpose) flour
2 eggs, lightly beaten
100 g (3$^1$/$_2$ oz/1 cup) dry breadcrumbs
1 tablespoon finely chopped flat-leaf (Italian)
    parsley, extra
oil, for deep-frying

## method

Carefully cut the olives along the open cavity so they are
opened out, but still in one piece.

Mash the goat's cheese, capers, garlic and parsley together in
a small bowl, then season. Push an even amount of the mixture
into the cavity of the olives, then press closed.

Put the flour in one small bowl, the egg in another and combine
the breadcrumbs and extra parsley in a third. Dip each olive
first into the flour, then into the egg and, finally, into the
breadcrumbs. Put the crumbed olives on a plate and refrigerate
for at least 2 hours.

Fill a deep heavy-based saucepan or deep-fryer one-third full of
oil and heat to 180°C (350°F), or until a cube of bread dropped
into the oil browns in 15 seconds. Cook the olives in batches
for 1–2 minutes, or until golden brown all over. Drain on
crumpled paper towels and season. Serve warm or at room
temperature with lemon wedges.

# chilled almond soup

serves 4–6

## ingredients

1 loaf day-old white Italian bread, crust removed
155 g (5$^1$/$_2$ oz/1 cup) whole blanched almonds
3–4 garlic cloves, chopped
125 ml (4 fl oz/$^1$/$_2$ cup) extra virgin olive oil
4 tablespoons sherry vinegar or white wine
    vinegar
375 ml (13 fl oz/1$^1$/$_2$ cups) vegetable stock or
    water
2 tablespoons olive oil
75 g (2$^3$/$_4$ oz) day-old white Italian bread, extra,
    crust removed and cut into 1 cm ($^1$/$_2$ in) cubes
200 g (7 oz) small seedless green grapes

## method

Soak the bread in cold water for 5 minutes, then squeeze to remove any excess moisture. Place the almonds and garlic in a food processor and process until well ground. Add the bread and process to a smooth paste.

With the motor running, add the oil in a slow steady stream until the mixture is the consistency of thick mayonnaise. Slowly add the sherry vinegar and 315 ml (10$^3$/$_4$ fl oz/1$^1$/$_4$ cups) of the stock, or water, until the mixture has reached the desired consistency. Blend for 1 minute. Season with salt, then refrigerate for at least 2 hours. The soup thickens on refrigeration so add more stock or water to reach the desired consistency.

Heat the olive oil in a large frying pan. Add the bread and toss over medium heat for 2–3 minutes, or until evenly golden brown. Drain on crumpled paper towels. Serve the soup very cold garnished with the grapes and bread cubes.

# carrot soup with caraway butter

serves 6

## ingredients

**caraway butter**
1 tablespoon caraway seeds
125 g ($4^1/_2$ oz) butter, softened

1 onion, chopped
1 garlic clove, crushed
750 g (1 lb 10 oz) carrots, chopped
1 litre (35 fl oz/4 cups) vegetable stock
250 ml (9 fl oz/1 cup) orange juice
rye bread, to serve

## method

To make the butter, dry-fry the caraway seeds in a frying pan over medium heat for 3–4 minutes, or until they start to brown and release their aroma. Leave to cool and then grind in a spice grinder or coffee grinder until fine. Beat the butter and caraway together until smooth. Place in a small square of foil, roll into a log and refrigerate for 30 minutes, or until firm.

Put the onion, garlic, carrots, stock and orange juice into a saucepan and bring to the boil. Cover and simmer over a low heat for 25 minutes, or until the carrots are cooked.

Transfer to a blender and blend until smooth. Return to the pan, season to taste and heat through. Cut the butter into 5 mm ($^1/_4$ in) thick slices.

Spoon the soup into bowls, top each with two slices of the butter and serve with some rye bread.

# oysters with ginger and lime

serves 2

## ingredients

12 oysters, shucked, in their shells
$1/2$ teaspoon finely grated fresh ginger
zest and juice of 2 limes
2 teaspoons Thai fish sauce
1 tablespoon chopped coriander (cilantro) leaves
2 teaspoons sugar
lime wedges, to serve

## method

Nestle the opened oysters on a bed of crushed ice or rock salt on a large platter.

Mix the ginger, lime zest and juice, fish sauce, coriander and sugar together. Drizzle a little of the sauce into each oyster shell and serve with lime wedges.

# seafood soup and rouille

serves 4

## ingredients

### rouille

1 cooked roasting (floury) potato, such as russet (idaho), peeled and diced
1 red capsicum (pepper), grilled and peeled
2 garlic cloves, chopped
1 egg yolk
125 ml (4 fl oz/$\frac{1}{2}$ cup) olive oil

1 litre (35 fl oz/4 cups) fish stock
$\frac{1}{2}$ teaspoon saffron threads
4 thyme sprigs
5 cm (2 in) piece orange peel
1 small baguette
olive oil, for brushing
300 g (10$\frac{1}{2}$ oz) salmon fillet, cut into 4 pieces
300 g (10$\frac{1}{2}$ oz) ling fillet, cut into 4 pieces
1 squid tube, cleaned and cut into rings
8 raw king prawns (shrimp), shelled and deveined

## method

To make the rouille, place the potato, capsicum, garlic and egg yolk in a food processor, and process until smooth. With the motor running, gradually add the olive oil until the mixture has the consistency of mayonnaise.

Preheat the oven to 180°C (350°F/Gas 4). Place the stock in a large saucepan and bring to the boil. Add the saffron, thyme and orange peel. Remove from the heat and leave to stand for 10 minutes to allow the flavours to infuse.

Meanwhile, cut the baguette into 1 cm ($\frac{1}{2}$ in) slices, brush with oil and place on a baking tray. Bake for 10 minutes, or until crisp and golden.

Strain the stock and return to the boil, then add the salmon, ling, squid rings and prawns. Remove the stock from the heat and leave for 2 minutes, or until the seafood is cooked. Divide among four warm soup bowls and serve with the rouille and croutons.

# cauliflower soup with smoked salmon croutons

serves 4

## ingredients

### croutons
1 loaf day-old white bread, sliced lengthways
40 g (1$^1$/$_2$ oz) butter, melted
1 garlic clove, crushed
150 g (5$^1$/$_2$ oz) smoked salmon or gravlax
1 tablespoon finely chopped dill

### soup
1 tablespoon oil
1 leek, white part only, chopped
1 garlic clove, chopped
400 g (14 oz) cauliflower, cut into florets
1 potato, chopped
250 ml (9 fl oz/1 cup) chicken stock
250 ml (9 fl oz/1 cup) milk
315 ml (10$^3$/$_4$ fl oz/1$^1$/$_4$ cups) pouring (whipping) cream
1 tablespoon lemon juice
1 tablespoon horseradish cream
1 tablespoon snipped chives

## method

Preheat the oven to 150°C (300°F/Gas 2). Brush three slices of the bread on both sides with the combined butter and garlic, then season with salt. Cut off the crusts, cut each slice into four strips, then transfer the strips to a baking tray, spacing them a little apart. Bake for 30 minutes, or until crisp and golden.

Meanwhile, heat the oil in a large saucepan, add the leek and garlic, and cook over medium heat for 6–8 minutes, or until the leek is soft but not brown. Increase the heat to high, add the cauliflower, potato, stock and milk, and bring just to the boil. Reduce the heat and simmer, covered, for 20 minutes, or until the potato and cauliflower have softened.

Cool the mixture slightly, then transfer to a blender or food processor and purée until smooth. Return to a clean saucepan and add the cream, lemon and horseradish. Reheat gently for 5 minutes, then add the chives.

Cut the salmon into strips the same width as the croutons and lay along the top of each crouton. Sprinkle with the dill. Serve the soup in deep bowls with two long croutons for each person.

# roasted leek and celeriac soup

serves 4

## ingredients

2 tablespoons olive oil
800 g (1 lb 12 oz/about 2 large) leeks, white part
    only, cut into 5 cm (2 in) lengths
1 garlic bulb, unpeeled, halved
800 g (1 lb 12 oz) celeriac, chopped
250 ml (9 fl oz/1 cup) milk
125 ml (4 fl oz/$^1/_2$ cup) thick (double/heavy)
    cream
2 tablespoons snipped chives
slices of toasted baguette, to serve

## method

Preheat the oven to 200°C (400°F/Gas 6). Put the olive oil in a roasting tin and heat in the oven for 5 minutes. Add the leek and garlic bulb halves and season. Shake the roasting tin to coat the vegetables with the oil. Roast for 20–25 minutes, or until the leek is tender. Remove the leek and roast the garlic for a further 10–15 minutes, or until tender when pierced with the tip of a knife.

Meanwhile, put the celeriac and 750 ml (26 fl oz/3 cups) of water in a large saucepan. Cover and bring to the boil, then reduce the heat to medium–low and simmer for 20 minutes, or until tender. Add the roasted leek.

Squeeze or scoop the garlic into the saucepan. Season and mix well. Add the milk.

Remove the saucepan from the heat. Using an immersion blender fitted with the chopping blade, whizz for 45 seconds, or until puréed. Stir through the cream and gently reheat the soup. Check the seasoning and thickness, adding additional milk if the soup is too thick. Sprinkle with the chives and serve topped with slices of toasted baguette.

# potato and anchovy chowder with garlic prawns

serves 4

## ingredients

**garlic prawns**
2 garlic cloves, chopped
1 small red chilli, seeded and chopped
2 tablespoons chopped flat-leaf (Italian) parsley
1 tablespoon olive oil
16 raw prawns (shrimp), peeled and deveined

1 tablespoon olive oil
3 bacon slices, fat trimmed, chopped
1 onion, chopped
2 celery stalks, chopped
2 garlic cloves, chopped
80 g (2$^3$/$_4$ oz) tinned anchovies, drained
1 carrot, chopped
3 all-purpose) potatoes, about 400 g (14 oz),
   roughly chopped
375 ml (13 fl oz/1$^1$/$_2$ cups) chicken stock or
   fish stock
250 ml (9 fl oz/1 cup) milk
125 ml (4 fl oz/$^1$/$_2$ cup) pouring (whipping) cream
3 tablespoons finely chopped flat-leaf (Italian)
   parsley

## method

To make the garlic prawns, put the garlic, chilli and parsley in a food processor and whizz for 15–20 seconds, or until chopped. With the motor running, add the oil and continue whizzing until the mixture forms a rough paste. Transfer to a bowl, add the prawns and toss to coat. Set aside to marinate for 30 minutes.

Heat the oil in a large heavy-based saucepan over medium–low heat. Add the bacon, onion, celery and garlic and cook, stirring, for 2 minutes. Reduce the heat, cover and simmer, stirring occasionally, for 5 minutes.

Drain the anchovies on paper towels and pat dry. Chop and add to the bacon mixture. Add the carrot and potato and stir. Cook for 2 minutes, then add the stock and milk. Bring to the boil, then cover and cook for 15 minutes. Remove the saucepan from the heat. Blend the soup for 20–30 seconds, or until smooth. Add the cream and most of the parsley, reserving some for garnishing. Season well

Heat a frying pan over high heat and add the prawns and marinade. Cook, turning, for 2 minutes, or until cooked through. Place a pile of prawns in the centre of four large soup bowls and ladle the soup around the prawns. Sprinkle with the remaining parsley and serve immediately.

# jerusalem artichoke soup

serves 4

## ingredients

50 g (1³/₄ oz) butter
1 onion, roughly chopped
1 leek, white part only, chopped
1 celery stalk, chopped
2 garlic cloves, chopped
800 g (1 lb 12 oz) jerusalem artichokes, cut into
    5 cm (2 in) pieces
2 potatoes, about 250 g (9 oz), cut into 5 cm
    (2 in) pieces
1 teaspoon freshly grated nutmeg
500 ml (17 fl oz/2 cups) chicken stock or
    vegetable stock
500 ml (17 fl oz/2 cups) milk
2 tablespoons finely snipped chives

## method

Heat the butter in a large heavy-based saucepan over low heat. Add the onion, leek, celery and garlic and cook for 2 minutes. Cover and simmer, stirring occasionally, for 5 minutes. Do not allow the vegetables to brown.

Add the jerusalem artichokes, potato and nutmeg and stir to combine. Cook for 2 minutes, then add the stock and 250 ml (9 fl oz/1 cup) of the milk. Bring to the boil, cover and cook for 20 minutes, or until the vegetables are tender.

Remove the saucepan from the heat. Using an immersion blender fitted with the chopping blade, whizz the soup for 10 seconds, or until roughly puréed. Season well. Stir in the remaining milk and half the chives and gently reheat the soup.

Ladle the soup into four bowls and sprinkle with the remaining chives and some freshly ground black pepper.

# bouillabaisse

serves 6

## ingredients

### rouille

1 small red capsicum (pepper)
1 slice of white bread, crusts removed
1 red chilli
2 garlic cloves
1 egg yolk
4 tablespoons olive oil

### soup

2 tablespoons oil
1 fennel bulb, thinly sliced
1 onion, chopped
750 g (1 lb 10 oz) ripe tomatoes
1.25 litres (44 fl oz/5 cups) fish stock or water
pinch of saffron threads
1 bouquet garni
5 cm (2 in) piece of orange zest
1.5 kg (3 lb 5 oz) monkfish fillets, cut into
    bite-sized pieces
18 black mussels, cleaned

### fish substitution

rascasse, sea bass, snapper, red mullet,
    John Dory, eel (skin on)

## method

To make the rouille, preheat the grill (broiler). Cut the capsicum in half lengthways, remove the seeds and membrane and place, skin side up, under the grill until the skin blackens and blisters. Peel the skin. Chop the capsicum flesh. Soak the bread in 3 tablespoons water, then squeeze dry with your hands. Put the capsicum, bread, chilli, garlic and egg yolk in a mortar and pestle and pound together. Gradually add the oil in a thin stream, pounding until smooth. Cover and refrigerate.

Heat the oil in a large saucepan and cook the fennel and onion for 5 minutes, or until golden.

Score a cross in the base of each tomato. Cover with boiling water for 30 seconds, then plunge into cold water. Drain and peel the skin. Chop the tomatoes, discarding the cores.

Add the tomato to the saucepan and cook for 3 minutes. Stir in the stock, saffron, bouquet garni and orange zest, bring to the boil and boil for 10 minutes. Remove the bouquet garni and orange zest and push the soup through a sieve. Return to the saucepan, season and bring back to the boil. Reduce the heat to a simmer and add the fish and mussels. Cook for 5 minutes, or until the fish is tender and the mussels have opened. Serve the soup with rouille and bread or toast.

# zucchini timbales with lime buttermilk cream

serves 6

## ingredients

**lime buttermilk cream**
150 ml (5 fl oz) pouring (whipping) cream
2$\frac{1}{2}$ tablespoons buttermilk
1 teaspoon finely grated lime zest
white pepper, to taste

40 g (1$\frac{1}{2}$ oz) butter
2 leeks, white part only, thinly sliced
350 g (12 oz) zucchini (courgettes), trimmed
1 small handful mint
1 small handful basil
3 eggs
150 ml (5 fl oz) pouring (whipping) cream
2$\frac{1}{2}$ tablespoons buttermilk
extra basil, to serve

## method

To make the lime buttermilk cream, combine the cream and buttermilk in a glass bowl and set aside at room temperature for 6 hours, or until the mixture has the consistency of custard. Add the lime zest and season. Preheat the oven to 170°C (325°F/Gas 3). Grease six 200 ml (7 fl oz) timbale or dariole moulds.

Melt the butter in a frying pan over low heat and cook the leek for 5 minutes, or until soft.

Add the zucchini to a saucepan of boiling salted water and simmer over medium heat for 8–10 minutes, or until tender. Drain and cut the zucchini into chunks. Transfer the zucchini to a food processor and add the leek, mint and basil. Process for 20 seconds, or until chopped. Add the eggs, cream and buttermilk and process until combined.

Pour the zucchini mixture into the prepared moulds and cover each with a circle of baking paper. Put in a large roasting tin and pour in boiling water to a depth of 4 cm (1$\frac{1}{2}$ in). Bake for 30 minutes, or until firm. Set aside to cool for 5 minutes.

Invert the timbales onto plates and serve warm with the lime buttermilk cream and garnished with extra basil leaves.

# feta, ricotta and prosciutto terrine

serves 10–12

## ingredients

200 g (7 oz) prosciutto, very thinly sliced
2 red capsicums (peppers)
350 g (12 oz/1$^1$/$_3$ cups) ricotta cheese
200 g (7 oz) feta cheese
1$^1$/$_2$ tablespoons lemon juice
2 tablespoons chopped basil
1$^1$/$_2$ teaspoons powdered gelatine
4 tablespoons thick (double/heavy) cream
1 handful basil
rocket (arugula) leaves, to serve

## method

Grease an 18 x 9 x 6 cm (7 x 3$^1$/$_2$ x 2$^1$/$_2$ in) loaf (bar) tin and line the tin with plastic wrap, pressing it into the edges. Reserve 8 prosciutto slices and use the remainder to line the tin.

Preheat the grill (broiler) to high. Grill the capsicums for 6 minutes on each side. Cool in a plastic bag, then peel and discard the skin. Remove the seeds and cut the flesh into strips.

Process the ricotta, feta, lemon juice and chopped basil in a food processor for 20 seconds, or until combined. Season. Chop half of the reserved prosciutto and stir through the cheese mixture.

Put the gelatine in a bowl with 1 tablespoon of cold water and stir until dissolved. Pour the cream into a saucepan, add the gelatine mixture and heat, stirring, for 1 minute. Stir into the ricotta mixture. Spread one-third of the ricotta mixture into the tin and top with half the capsicum strips. Add half the basil leaves in a layer on top of the capsicum. Cover with another third of the ricotta mixture, a final layer of capsicum and the remaining basil. Spread the ricotta mixture over the top. Fold over the ends of the prosciutto and cover with the reserved prosciutto slices. Wrap in plastic wrap and chill overnight. Invert the terrine onto a board. Use a knife to cut into slices.

# individual Italian summer tarts

## serves 4

### ingredients

3 tablespoons olive oil
2 red onions, sliced
1 tablespoon balsamic vinegar
1 teaspoon soft brown sugar
1 tablespoon chopped thyme
1 sheet frozen puff pastry, thawed
170 g (6 oz) marinated quartered artichokes,
   drained
16 black olives, pitted
extra virgin olive oil, to serve
thyme sprigs, to garnish

### method

Heat 2 tablespoons of the oil in a saucepan over low heat.
Add the onion and cook, stirring occasionally, for 15 minutes,
or until soft. Add the vinegar and brown sugar and cook for
15 minutes, or until lightly browned. Remove from the heat,
stir in the chopped thyme and set aside to cool.

Preheat the oven to 220°C (425°F/ Gas 7) and heat a lightly
greased baking tray. Cut four 10 cm (4 in) rounds from the
sheet of puff pastry and spread the onion over them, leaving
a 1.5 cm ($5/8$ in) border.

Place the pastry bases on the hot baking tray and cook in the
top half of the oven for 12–15 minutes, or until the edges are
risen and the pastry is golden brown.

Arrange the artichokes over the onion, then fill the spaces with
olives. Drizzle the tarts with extra virgin olive oil and serve
garnished with thyme.

# caramelized onion quiche

serves 6

## ingredients

### pastry
185 g (6 oz/1$^1$/$_2$ cups) plain (all-purpose) flour
125 g (4$^1$/$_2$ oz) butter, chopped
1 egg yolk

### filling
800 g (1 lb 10 oz) onions, thinly sliced
75 g (2$^1$/$_2$ oz) butter
1 tablespoon soft brown sugar
185 ml (6 fl oz/$^3$/$_4$ cup) sour cream
2 eggs
40 g (1$^1$/$_4$ oz) prosciutto, cut into strips
40 g (1$^1$/$_4$ oz) grated mature cheddar cheese
2 teaspoons thyme leaves

## method

Process the flour and butter until crumbly. Add the egg yolk and 1–2 tablespoons of water. Process in short bursts until the mixture comes together. Add extra water if needed. Turn out and gather into a ball. Cover with plastic wrap and chill for 20 minutes.

Blanch the onion in boiling water for 2 minutes, then drain. Melt the butter in a pan and cook the onion over low heat for 25 minutes, or until soft. Stir in the brown sugar and cook for a further 15 minutes, stirring occasionally to prevent burning. Preheat the oven to 200°C (400°F/Gas 6). Grease a loose-based flan tin measuring 22 cm (8$^3$/$_4$ in) across the base.

Roll out the pastry until large enough to fit the flan tin. Fit the pastry into the tin, trimming off any excess using a sharp knife. Cover with baking paper and fill evenly with baking beads. Bake for 15 minutes. Remove the paper and beads and bake for 5 minutes. Cool slightly.

Lightly beat the sour cream and eggs together. Add the prosciutto, cheese and thyme leaves. Season. Stir in the onion. Fill the pastry shell with the onion mixture. Bake for 40 minutes, or until set. If the pastry starts to darken, cover with a piece of foil.

# goat's cheese galette

serves 6

## ingredients

**pastry**
125 g (4$^1$/$_2$ oz/1 cup) plain (all-purpose) flour
3 tablespoons olive oil
3–4 tablespoons chilled water

**filling**
1 tablespoon olive oil
2 onions, thinly sliced
1 teaspoon thyme leaves
125 g (4 oz) ricotta cheese
100 g (3$^1$/$_2$ oz) goat's cheese
2 tablespoons pitted Niçoise olives
1 egg, lightly beaten
3 tablespoons pouring (whipping) cream

## method

To make the pastry, sift the flour and a pinch of salt into a large bowl and make a well. Add the olive oil and mix with a flat-bladed knife until crumbly. Gradually add the water until the mixture comes together. Remove and pat together to form a disc. Refrigerate for 30 minutes.

To make the filling, heat the olive oil in a frying pan. Add the onion, cover and cook over low heat for 30 minutes. Season and stir in half the thyme. Allow to cool slightly.

Preheat the oven to 180° C (350°F/Gas 4). Lightly flour the work bench and roll out the pastry to a 30 cm (12 in) circle. Evenly spread the onion over the pastry leaving a 2 cm ($^3$/$_4$ in) border. Sprinkle the ricotta and the goat's cheese evenly over the onion. Place the olives over the cheeses, then sprinkle with the remaining thyme. Fold the pastry border in to the edge of the filling, gently pleating as you go.

Combine the egg and cream in a small jug, then carefully pour over the filling. Bake on a heated baking tray on the lower half of the oven for 45 minutes, or until the pastry is golden. Serve warm or at room temperature.

# eggplant stacks

serves 4

## ingredients

1 small eggplant (aubergine), cut into 4 thick
   slices
oil, for brushing
2 vine-ripened tomatoes, quartered
150 g (5¹/₂ oz) rocket (arugula) leaves
150 g (5¹/₂ oz) bocconcini (fresh baby mozzarella)
   cheese, sliced
4 tablespoons virgin olive oil
1 tablespoon white wine vinegar
1 garlic clove, crushed
6 kalamata olives, pitted and finely chopped
2 tablespoons finely chopped basil leaves

## method

Heat the grill (broiler) to high. Brush the eggplant slices with oil. Place on the grill tray, season and grill for about 10 minutes, or until lightly browned and almost cooked through, turning once during cooking.

Add the tomato to the grill tray, lightly brush with oil and season. Grill for a further 2 minutes, then remove the tomato and eggplant from the heat and allow to cool.

To assemble the stacks, arrange the rocket leaves on four serving plates. Add an eggplant slice, and top each with some tomato and bocconcini.

In a small bowl, whisk together the oil, vinegar and garlic. Add the olives and season to taste. Spoon over the stacks, sprinkle with the basil and serve warm.

# fresh salmon and dill quiche

serves 4–6

## ingredients

185 g (6 oz/1$^1$/$_2$ cups) plain (all-purpose) flour
125 g (4$^1$/$_2$ oz) cold butter, chopped
1 teaspoon icing (confectioners') sugar

### filling

2 eggs
1 egg yolk
250 ml (9 fl oz/1 cup) pouring (whipping) cream
1 teaspoon finely grated lemon zest
2 tablespoons finely chopped spring onion
  (scallion)
500 g (1 lb 2 oz) fresh salmon fillet, bones and
  skin removed and cut into bite-sized chunks
1 tablespoon chopped dill

## method

Process the flour, butter and icing sugar for about 15 seconds until crumbly. Add 1–2 tablespoons of water. Process in short bursts until the mixture just comes together. Add a little extra water if needed. Turn out onto a floured surface and gather into a ball. Cover the pastry with plastic wrap and refrigerate for 15 minutes.

Roll the pastry between 2 sheets of baking paper until it is large enough to fit a loose-based flan tin measuring 22 cm (8$^3$/$_4$ in) across the base. Fit the pastry into the tin and trim off any excess using a knife. Place the lined flan tin in the fridge for 15 minutes. Preheat the oven to 180°C (350°F/Gas 4).

To make the filling, lightly beat the eggs and egg yolk until combined. Add the cream, lemon zest and spring onion and season. Cover and set aside.

Prick the base of the pastry with a fork. Cover with baking paper and fill with baking beads or rice. Bake for 15 minutes, or until golden. Remove the paper and beads or rice and arrange the salmon chunks over the base. Scatter the dill over the salmon, then pour over the egg mixture. Bake for 40 minutes, or until the salmon is cooked and the filling has set.

# country-style pork and juniper terrine

serves 12

## ingredients

500 g (1 lb 2 oz) bacon slices
500 g (1 lb 2 oz) pork belly, diced
500 g (1 lb 2 oz) lean pork, diced
1 small onion, finely chopped
2 garlic cloves, crushed
4 tablespoons dry white wine
2 tablespoons brandy
1 tablespoon chopped thyme
2 tablespoons chopped flat-leaf (Italian) parsley
$^1/_2$ teaspoon ground nutmeg
8 juniper berries, crushed
baguette and salad leaves, to serve

## method

Cut the eye piece of the bacon slices and set aside. Use the long thin strips of bacon to line the base and sides of a 1 litre (35 fl oz/4 cup) capacity loaf (bar) tin.

Put the pork belly, lean pork and chopped bacon into a food processor and process until coarsely minced. Transfer to a bowl and mix in all the remaining ingredients except the baguette and salad leaves. Cover and set aside for 1 hour.

Preheat the oven to 150°C (300°F/Gas 2). Spoon the pork mixture into the prepared tin and smooth the top. Arrange the reserved eye bacon pieces over the top and cover the loaf tin with foil. Transfer to a roasting pan. Pour in enough boiling water to come halfway up the sides of the tin, transfer to the oven and cook for 1 hour. Remove the foil and cook for a further 30 minutes.

Remove the terrine from the oven carefully so as not to spill any meat juices and leave to cool. Remove the tin from the roasting pan. Place a piece of baking paper over the terrine, top with a heavy weight and refrigerate overnight.

Unmould the terrine, wipe or scrape off any excess fat and cut into thin slices. Serve with a baguette and salad leaves.

# gravlax

**serves 12**

## ingredients

55 g (2 oz/$^1$/$_4$ cup) sugar
2 tablespoons coarse sea salt
1 teaspoon crushed black peppercorns
2.5 kg (5 lb 8 oz) good-quality salmon, filleted,
    skin on
1 tablespoon vodka or brandy
2 tablespoons very finely chopped dill
2 tablespoons chopped dill, extra

**mustard sauce**
125 ml (4 fl oz/$^1$/$_2$ cup) olive oil
2 tablespoons dijon mustard
1$^1$/$_2$ tablespoons cider vinegar
2 teaspoons chopped dill
1 teaspoon caster (superfine) sugar

## method

Combine the sugar, salt and peppercorns in a small dish.

Remove any pinbones from the salmon with tweezers or your fingers. Pat dry with paper towels and lay a fillet skin-side down in a shallow tray. Sprinkle the fish with half the vodka, rub half the sugar mixture into the flesh, then sprinkle with 2 tablespoons of the dill. Sprinkle the flesh side of the other salmon fillet with the remaining vodka and then rub the remaining sugar mixture into the flesh. Lay it flesh-side down on top of the other fillet. Cover with plastic wrap, place a heavy board on top and weigh the board down with three heavy tins so that the salmon is being flattened. Refrigerate for 24 hours, carefully turning it over after 12 hours.

For the mustard sauce, whisk all the ingredients together.

Uncover the salmon and lay both fillets on a board. Brush off all the dill and seasoning using a stiff pastry brush. Sprinkle with the extra dill and press it onto the flesh, shaking off any excess. Serve whole or thinly sliced on an angle towards the tail, with the mustard sauce.

# tagliatelle with mushrooms and saffron cream

serves 4

## ingredients

15 g ($^1/_2$ oz) dried porcini mushrooms
30 g (1 oz) butter
250 g (9 oz) swiss brown mushrooms, sliced
150 g ($5^1/_2$ oz) shiitake mushrooms, sliced
3 bulb spring onions (scallions), sliced
2 garlic cloves, crushed
125 ml (4 fl oz/$^1/_2$ cup) dry white wine

### saffron cream
$^1/_2$ teaspoon saffron threads
$^1/_4$ teaspoon cayenne pepper
300 ml ($10^1/_2$ fl oz) thick (double/heavy) cream
400 g (14 oz) fresh tagliatelle
2 tablespoons roughly snipped chives
grated parmesan cheese, to serve

## method

Soak the porcini mushrooms in 3 tablespoons of water for 30 minutes. Remove from the liquid and slice, reserving the liquid.

In a large heavy-based frying pan, melt the butter over medium heat until foaming, then add all the mushrooms, spring onions and garlic, stirring, for 5 minutes. Add the white wine, reserved mushroom liquid, saffron threads, cayenne pepper and cream. Reduce the heat to low and simmer for 7 minutes, or until the sauce thickens slightly, stirring occasionally. Season to taste.

In a large saucepan, bring salted water to the boil and cook the pasta for 5–6 minutes, or until *al dente*. Strain the pasta in a colander.

Toss the pasta through the sauce and serve in bowls. Sprinkle each bowl with chopped chives and ground pepper. Serve with parmesan cheese.

# angel hair pasta with garlic, scallops and rocket

serves 4

## ingredients

20 large scallops with roe
250 g (9 oz) angel hair pasta
150 ml (5 fl oz) extra virgin olive oil
2 garlic cloves, finely chopped
3 tablespoons white wine
1 tablespoon lemon juice
100 g (3$^{1}/_{2}$ oz) baby rocket (arugula) leaves
25 g (1 oz) chopped coriander (cilantro) leaves

## method

Trim any veins, membrane or hard white muscle from the scallops. Pat dry with paper towels. Bring a large saucepan of water to the boil, add the pasta and cook until *al dente*. Drain the pasta well and toss with 1 tablespoon oil.

Meanwhile, heat 1 tablespoon of oil in a frying pan, add the garlic and cook for a few seconds, or until fragrant. Do not brown. Add the combined wine and lemon juice, and remove from the heat.

Heat a chargrill plate over high heat and brush with a little oil. Season the scallops and cook for 1 minute each side, or until just cooked. Gently reheat the garlic mixture, add the rocket and stir over medium heat for 1–2 minutes, or until wilted. Toss through the pasta then add the remaining oil and half the coriander, and mix well. Divide the pasta among four serving bowls, arrange the scallops over the top and garnish with the remaining coriander.

# pasta with seared prawns

serves 2

## ingredients

8 raw jumbo prawns (shrimp)
2 tablespoons olive oil
100 g (3$^1$/$_2$ oz) unsalted butter, chopped
1$^1$/$_2$ tablespoons drained baby capers
250 g (9 oz) angel hair pasta
3 tablespoons lemon juice
1 teaspoon grated lemon zest
1–2 small fresh red chillies, seeded and thinly
    sliced
15 g ($^1$/$_2$ oz) chopped flat-leaf (Italian) parsley
lemon wedges, to serve

## method

Remove the heads from the prawns. Slice them down the back without cutting right through, then open them out, leaving the tails and shells intact. Rinse under cold water and pull out the vein. Pat dry, then season lightly.

Heat the oil and half the butter in a large frying pan, add the capers and cook for 1 minute. Remove from the pan and set aside. Add the prawns and cook, cut side down first, for 2–3 minutes each side, or until pink and cooked. Remove and keep warm.

Cook the pasta in a saucepan of boiling water until *al dente*. Drain, reserving 1–2 tablespoons of the cooking liquid.

Melt the remaining butter in the frying pan, add the lemon juice and zest, capers and chilli and stir until fragrant. Add the pasta and parsley and toss until the pasta is coated with the butter. If needed, add some of the reserved cooking liquid to moisten the pasta. Season.

Divide the pasta among serving bowls, top with the prawns and serve with lemon wedges.

# creamy seafood ravioli

serves 4

## ingredients

### pasta
250 g (9 oz/2 cups) plain (all-purpose) flour
3 eggs
1 tablespoon olive oil
1 egg yolk, extra

### filling
50 g (1¾ oz) butter, softened
3 garlic cloves, finely chopped
2 tablespoons finely chopped flat-leaf (Italian)
    parsley
100 g (3½ oz) scallops, cleaned and finely
    chopped
100 g (3½ oz) raw prawn (shrimp) meat, finely
    chopped

### sauce
75 g (2½ oz) butter
3 tablespoons plain (all-purpose) flour
375 ml (13 fl oz/1½ cups) milk
300 ml (10½ fl oz) pouring (whipping) cream
125 ml (4 fl oz/½ cup) white wine
50 g (1¾ oz/½ cup) grated parmesan cheese
2 tablespoons chopped flat-leaf (Italian) parsley

## method

To make the pasta, sift the flour and a pinch of salt into a bowl and make a well in the centre. Whisk the eggs, oil and 1 tablespoon water in a jug, then add gradually to the flour and mix to a firm dough. Gather into a ball. Knead on a lightly floured surface for 5 minutes, or until smooth. Transfer to an oiled bowl, cover with plastic wrap and set aside for 30 minutes.

To make the filling, mix together the softened butter, chopped garlic, parsley, scallops and prawn meat. Set aside.

Roll out a quarter of the pasta dough at a time until very thin. Place 1 teaspoonful of filling at 5 cm (2 in) intervals down one side of each strip. Whisk the extra egg yolk with 3 tablespoons of water. Brush along one side of the dough and between the filling. Fold the dough over the filling. Repeat with the remaining filling and dough. Press the edges of the dough together to seal. Cut between the mounds with a knife. Cook, in batches, in a large saucepan of boiling salted water for 6 minutes. Drain well.

To make the sauce, melt the butter in a saucepan, add the flour and cook over low heat for 2 minutes. Remove from the heat and stir in the milk, cream and wine. Cook until the sauce thickens. Bring to the boil and simmer for 5 minutes. Add the parmesan and parsley. Remove from the heat, add to the ravioli and toss.

# risotto nero

serves 6

## ingredients

1 litre (35 fl oz/4 cups) fish stock
100 g (3¹/₂ oz) butter
1 red onion, finely chopped
2 squid, cleaned, heads discarded, tentacles set
    aside and bodies finely chopped
2 garlic cloves, crushed
350 g (12 oz) risotto rice
3 sachets of squid or cuttlefish ink, or the ink sacs
    from the squid
150 ml (5 fl oz) white wine
2 teaspoons olive oil

## method

Pour the stock into a saucepan, bring to the boil, then keep at a low simmer.

Heat the butter in a large, wide heavy-based saucepan and cook the onion until softened but not browned. Increase the heat and add the chopped squid. Cook for 4 minutes, or until the squid turns opaque. Add the garlic and stir briefly. Add the rice and reduce the heat to low. Season and stir briefly to thoroughly coat the rice.

Squeeze out the ink from the sachets and add to the rice with the wine. Increase the heat and stir until all the liquid has been absorbed.

Stir in a ladleful of the simmering stock and cook over medium heat, stirring continuously. When the stock has been absorbed, stir in another ladleful. Continue for about 20 minutes, or until all the stock has been added and the rice is *al dente*. You may not need to use all the stock, or you may need a little extra—every risotto will be slightly different.

Heat the olive oil in a frying pan and fry the squid tentacles quickly, they should turn opaque and brown a little. Garnish the risotto with the tentacles and serve immediately.

# fresh vegetable lasagne with rocket

serves 4

## ingredients

**balsamic syrup**
4 tablespoons balsamic vinegar
1½ tablespoons brown sugar

16 asparagus spears, trimmed and cut into
   5 cm (2 in) lengths
150 g (5½ oz/1 cup) fresh or frozen peas
2 large zucchini (courgettes), cut into thin ribbons
2 fresh lasagne sheets
100 g (3½ oz) rocket (arugula) leaves
30 g (1 oz) basil, torn
2 tablespoons extra virgin olive oil
250 g (9 oz) low-fat ricotta cheese
150 g (9 oz) semi-dried tomatoes
parmesan cheese shavings, to garnish

## method

Stir the vinegar and brown sugar in a small saucepan over medium heat until the sugar dissolves. Reduce the heat and simmer for 3–4 minutes, or until the sauce becomes syrupy. Remove from the heat.

Bring a large saucepan of salted water to the boil. Blanch the asparagus, peas and zucchini in separate batches until just tender, refreshing each batch in cold water. Return the cooking liquid to the boil. Cook the lasagne sheets in the boiling water for 1–2 minutes, or until *al dente*. Refresh in cold water and drain well. Cut each sheet in half lengthways.

Toss the vegetables and the rocket with the basil and olive oil. Season.

To assemble, place one strip of pasta on a serving plate—one-third on the centre of the plate and two-thirds overhanging one side. Place a small amount of the salad on the centre one-third, topped with some ricotta and tomato. Season and fold over one-third of the lasagne sheet. Top with a layer of salad, ricotta and tomato. Fold back the final layer of pasta and garnish with salad and tomato. Repeat with the remaining pasta, salad, ricotta and tomato to make four. Drizzle with the balsamic syrup and garnish with parmesan cheese.

# risotto Milanese

serves 4

## ingredients

200 ml (7 fl oz) dry white vermouth or white wine
large pinch of saffron strands
1.5 litres (52 fl oz/6 cups) chicken stock
100 g (3$\frac{1}{2}$ oz) butter
75 g (2$\frac{1}{2}$ oz) beef marrow
1 large onion, finely chopped
1 garlic clove, crushed
350 g (12 oz) risotto rice
150 g (5$\frac{1}{2}$ oz) parmesan cheese, grated

## method

Put the vermouth or wine in a bowl, add the saffron and leave to soak for 10 minutes. Heat the chicken stock in a saucepan and maintain at a low simmer.

Melt the butter and beef marrow in a deep heavy-based frying pan and gently cook the onion and garlic until soft but not browned. Add the rice and reduce the heat to low. Season and stir to coat the grains of rice in the butter and marrow.

Add the vermouth and saffron to the rice and increase the heat to medium. Cook, stirring, until all the liquid has been absorbed.

Stir in a ladleful of the stock and cook at a fast simmer, stirring constantly. When the stock has been absorbed, stir in another ladleful. Continue for about 20 minutes, or until the rice is *al dente*. Add a little more stock or water if you need to—every risotto will use a different amount.

Stir in 100 g (3$\frac{1}{2}$ oz) of the parmesan and sprinkle the rest over the top to serve.

# seafood risotto

serves 4

## ingredients

1.75 litres (59 fl oz/7 cups) fish stock
2 tablespoons olive oil
2 onions, finely chopped
2 garlic cloves, finely chopped
1 celery stalk, finely chopped
440 g (15$^1$/$_2$ oz/2 cups) risotto rice
8–10 black mussels, cleaned
150 g (5$^1$/$_2$ oz) blue-eye fillet, cubed
8 prawns (shrimp), peeled and deveined, tails
    intact
2 tablespoons chopped flat-leaf (Italian) parsley
1 tablespoon chopped oregano
1 tablespoon chopped thyme

## method

Pour the stock into a saucepan and bring to the boil. Reduce the heat until just simmering, then cover.

Heat the olive oil in a saucepan over medium heat. Add the onion, garlic and celery and cook for 2–3 minutes. Add 2 tablespoons of water, cover with a lid and cook for about 5 minutes, or until the vegetables soften. Add the rice and cook, stirring, for 3–4 minutes, or until the rice grains are well coated. Gradually add 125 ml (4 fl oz/$^1$/$_2$ cup) of the hot stock to the rice, stirring over low heat, until all the stock has been absorbed. Repeat, adding 125 ml (4 fl oz/$^1$/$_2$ cup) of stock each time until the rice is just tender.

Meanwhile, bring 3 tablespoons of water to the boil in a large saucepan. Add the mussels, cover with a lid and cook for 4–5 minutes, shaking the pan occasionally, until the mussels have opened. Drain and discard any unopened ones.

Add the fish, prawns and the remaining hot stock to the rice and stir well. Cook for 5–10 minutes, or until the seafood is just cooked and the rice is tender and creamy. Remove from the heat, add the mussels, cover and set aside for 5 minutes. Stir the parsley, oregano and thyme through the risotto. Season.

# pea and asparagus saffron risotto

serves 4

## ingredients

450 g (1 lb) fresh peas (in the pod), or 235 g
    (8$^1/_2$ oz/1$^1/_2$ cups) frozen peas
175 g (6 oz) asparagus
pinch of saffron threads
2 tablespoons olive oil
1 onion, finely chopped
440 g (15$^1/_2$ oz/2 cups) risotto rice
1.5 litres (52 fl oz/6 cups) vegetable stock
30 g (1 oz) parmesan cheese, finely grated

## method

Shell the peas into a heatproof bowl. Trim the woody ends from the asparagus, and cut the stalks into 3 cm (1$^1/_4$ in) lengths. Add to the bowl, and cover with boiling water. Stand for 3 minutes, then drain and set aside until needed. Put 3 tablespoons of boiling water into a small bowl, and add the saffron threads. Set aside until required.

Heat the oil in a large, heavy-based saucepan. Add the onion and cook over medium heat for 5 minutes, until soft and transparent. Add the rice and cook, stirring, for 1 minute.

Meanwhile, put the stock into a smaller saucepan. Cover and bring to the boil, then reduce the heat to low and simmer.

Add 4 tablespoons of the hot stock to the rice, stirring. When it has absorbed into the rice, add a further 4 tablespoons of the hot stock. Keep adding stock, stirring between each addition, until the rice is tender. This will take about 25 minutes. Add the saffron and the liquid about halfway through adding the stock.

About 5 minutes before the rice is ready, add the peas and asparagus to the rice. Remove from the heat, stir in the parmesan and season.

# salmon carpaccio

serves 4

## ingredients

3 vine-ripened tomatoes
1 tablespoon baby capers, rinsed and drained
1 tablespoon chopped dill
500 g (1 lb 2 oz) sashimi salmon
1 tablespoon extra virgin olive oil
1 tablespoon lime juice
ciabatta bread, to serve

## method

Cut a cross in the base of the tomatoes. Place in a bowl and cover with boiling water. Leave to stand for 2–3 minutes, or until the skin blisters. Drain, plunge into cold water, then drain and peel. Cut the tomatoes in half, scoop out the seeds with a teaspoon and dice the flesh. Place in a bowl and stir in the capers and dill.

Using a very sharp knife, carefully slice the salmon into paper-thin slices, cutting across the grain. Divide the salmon equally among four plates, arranging in a single layer.

Place a mound of the tomato mixture in the centre of each plate. Whisk together the olive oil and lime juice, and season with salt. Drizzle over the tomato and salmon, and season with black pepper. Serve immediately with ciabatta bread.

# squid and scallops with chermoula dressing

serves 4

## ingredients

8 baby squid, cleaned and rinsed
200 g (7 oz) scallops, without roe
2 tablespoons oil
150 g (5$^1/_2$ oz) rocket (arugula), trimmed
3 ripe roma (plum) tomatoes, chopped
2 oranges, peeled and segmented

### chermoula dressing

4 large handfuls coriander (cilantro), finely
    chopped
2$^1/_2$ large handfuls flat-leaf (Italian) parsley,
    chopped
2 teaspoons ground cumin
1 teaspoon ground paprika
3 tablespoons lime juice
3 tablespoons olive oil

## method

Put the squid in a bowl of water with $^1/_4$ teaspoon of salt. Mix well, then chill for 30 minutes. Drain well, then cut the tubes into long thin strips and the tentacles into pieces. Rinse the scallops and pat dry with paper towels.

Heat the oil in a large deep frying pan. Cook the squid in batches over high heat for 1 minute, or until they turn white. Remove and drain. Fry the scallops in small batches over high heat for 1 minute on each side, until golden.

Arrange the rocket on a large platter, then top with the seafood, tomato and orange segments. Quickly whisk the chermoula dressing ingredients together in a non-metallic bowl, pour over the seafood and serve.

# tequila and lime grilled prawns

**serves 4**

## ingredients

32 raw large prawns (shrimp)
125 ml (4 fl oz/$^1/_2$ cup) lime juice
3 tablespoons tequila
2 small red chillies, finely chopped
3 tablespoons chopped coriander (cilantro)
2 tablespoons olive oil
2 garlic cloves, crushed

**green tomato salsa**
1 green tomato, seeded and diced
2 tablespoons finely chopped red onion
2 green chillies, seeded and finely diced
25 g (1 oz) chopped coriander (cilantro)
1 garlic clove, chopped
1 tablespoon olive oil
1 avocado
1 tablespoon lime juice

## method

Soak eight wooden skewers in cold water for 30 minutes. Peel and devein the prawns, leaving the tails intact. Thread four prawns onto each skewer. Lay out the skewers in a single layer in a non-metallic dish.

Combine the lime juice, tequila, chilli, coriander, oil and garlic in a small jug, then pour over the prawns. Cover and marinate in the fridge for 30 minutes.

To make the salsa, mix together the tomato, onion, chilli, coriander, garlic and olive oil, then season. Cover and refrigerate until needed.

Cook the skewers on a hot, lightly oiled chargrill pan or barbecue hotplate for 3–5 minutes, or until pink and cooked through, brushing with the marinade during cooking to keep the prawns moist.

Before serving, halve the avocado, remove the stone, cut the flesh into 1 cm ($^1/_2$ in) dice, then gently mix the avocado into the salsa, stirring in the lime juice at the same time. Season to taste, then serve with the prawns.

# steamed snapper with Asian flavours

serves 2

## ingredients

1 whole snapper, weighing about 800 g (1 lb 12 oz),
    scaled, fins removed and gutted
3 lemon grass stems, white part only
1 handful coriander (cilantro) leaves
3 cm (1$^1/_4$ in) piece fresh ginger, peeled and cut
    into thin matchsticks
1 large garlic clove, peeled and cut into
    thin slivers
2 tablespoons soy sauce
3 tablespoons oil
1 tablespoon fish sauce
1 small red chilli, seeded and finely diced
stir-fried Asian greens, to serve

### fish substitution
coral trout, sea bass, red emperor

## method

Score the fish with diagonal cuts on both sides. Cut each lemon grass stem into three and lightly squash each piece with the end of the handle of a large knife. Put half of the lemon grass in the middle of a large piece of foil and lay the fish on top. Put the remaining lemon grass and half the coriander inside the cavity of the fish.

Mix the ginger, garlic, soy sauce, oil, fish sauce and chilli together in a bowl. Drizzle the mixture over the fish and scatter the remaining coriander leaves over.

Enclose the fish in the foil and place in a bamboo or metal steamer over a large saucepan of simmering water. Steam for 25 minutes, or until the flesh of the fish is opaque and white. Transfer the foil package to a large serving plate and open at the table. Serve the fish with stir-fried Asian greens.

# John Dory with tarator sauce

serves 6

## ingredients

**tarator sauce**
140 g (5 oz/1 cup) hazelnuts
2 slices of white bread, crusts removed
2 garlic cloves, roughly crushed
150 ml (5 fl oz) olive oil, plus a little extra for
    cooking
3 tablespoons lemon juice

800 g (1 lb 12 oz) skinless John Dory fillets
lemon wedges, to serve

**fish substitution**
groper, snapper, halibut, cod, sea bass

## method

To make the tarator sauce, put the hazelnuts in a food processor and grind finely. Briefly soak the bread in a small bowl of water. Squeeze dry, tear into pieces and add to the food processor bowl along with the garlic. Process briefly to combine. Mix the oil and lemon juice together and, with the processor motor running, gradually pour it into the bread and nut mixture. Season, then scoop the sauce into a serving bowl.

Heat a frying pan or chargrill pan until hot. Brush with a little oil and cook the fillets for 3 minutes on each side, or until the flesh is opaque and flakes easily. You may need to cook the fish in two batches; if so, keep the first batch warm, covered with foil, in a low oven. Serve the fish fillets with the tarator sauce and lemon wedges.

# lobster thermidor

serves 2

## ingredients

1 cooked lobster
85 g (3 oz) butter
4 spring onions (scallions), finely chopped
$1^1/_2$ tablespoons plain (all-purpose) flour
$^1/_2$ teaspoon mustard powder
2 tablespoons white wine or sherry
250 ml (9 fl oz/1 cup) milk
3 tablespoons pouring (whipping) cream
1 tablespoon chopped flat-leaf (Italian) parsley
65 g ($2^1/_4$ oz/$^1/_2$ cup) grated gruyère cheese
lemon wedges, to serve

## method

Using a sharp knife, cut the lobster in half lengthways through the shell. Lift the meat from the tail and body. Remove the cream-coloured vein and soft body matter and discard. Cut the meat into 2 cm ($^3/_4$ in) pieces, cover and refrigerate. Wash the head and shell halves, then drain and pat dry.

Heat 60 g ($2^1/_4$ oz) of the butter in a frying pan, add the spring onion and stir for 2 minutes. Stir in the flour and mustard and cook for 1 minute, or until pale and foaming. Remove from the heat and gradually stir in the wine and milk. Return to the heat and stir constantly until the mixture boils and thickens. Reduce the heat and simmer for 1 minute. Stir in the cream, parsley and lobster meat, then season with salt and pepper. Stir over low heat until the lobster is heated through.

Spoon the mixture into the lobster shells, sprinkle with cheese and dot with the remaining butter. Place under a hot griller (broiler) and cook for 2 minutes, or until lightly browned. Serve with salad and some wedges of lemon.

# involtini of swordfish

serves 4

## ingredients

1 kg (2 lb 4 oz) swordfish, skin removed, cut into
   four 5 cm (2 in) pieces
3 lemons
4 tablespoons olive oil
1 small onion, chopped
3 garlic cloves, chopped
2 tablespoons chopped capers
2 tablespoons chopped pitted Kalamata olives
35 g (1¼ oz/⅓ cup) finely grated parmesan
   cheese
120 g (4¼ oz/1½ cups) fresh breadcrumbs
2 tablespoons chopped flat-leaf (Italian) parsley
1 egg, lightly beaten
24 fresh bay leaves
2 small white onions, quartered and separated
   into pieces
2 tablespoons lemon juice, extra

## method

Cut each swordfish piece horizontally into four slices to give you 16 slices in total. Place each piece between two pieces of plastic wrap and roll gently with a rolling pin to flatten without tearing. Cut each piece in half to give 32 pieces.

Peel the lemons with a vegetable peeler. Cut the peel into 24 even pieces. Squeeze the lemons to give 3 tablespoons of juice.

Heat 2 tablespoons olive oil in a pan, add the onion and garlic, and cook over medium heat for 2 minutes. Place in a bowl with the capers, olives, parmesan, breadcrumbs and parsley. Season, add the egg and mix to bind.

Divide the stuffing among the fish pieces and, with oiled hands, roll up to form parcels. Thread four rolls onto each of eight skewers alternating with the bay leaves, lemon peel and onion.

Mix the remaining oil with the lemon juice in a bowl. Cook the skewers on a hot flat plate for 3–4 minutes each side, basting with the oil and lemon mixture. Serve with a little extra lemon juice drizzled over the top.

# lobster mornay

serves 2

## ingredients

1 cooked lobster
315 ml (10 fl oz/1$^1$/$_4$ cups) milk
1 slice of onion
1 bay leaf
6 black peppercorns
30 g (1 oz) butter
2 tablespoons plain (all-purpose) flour
2 tablespoons pouring (whipping) cream
pinch of nutmeg
60 g (2$^1$/$_4$ oz) cheddar cheese, grated
pinch of paprika, to garnish

## method

Using a sharp knife, cut the lobster in half lengthways through the shell. Lift the meat from the tail and body. Remove the cream-coloured vein and soft body matter and discard. Cut the meat into 2 cm ($^3$/$_4$ in) pieces, cover and refrigerate. Wash the head and shell halves, then drain and pat dry. Set aside.

Heat the milk, onion, bay leaf and peppercorns in a small saucepan. Bring to the boil. Remove from the heat, cover and leave for 15 minutes. Strain.

Melt the butter in a large pan, stir in the flour and cook for 1 minute, or until pale and foaming. Remove from the heat and gradually stir in the milk. Return to the heat and stir constantly until the mixture boils and thickens. Reduce the heat and simmer for 1 minute. Stir in the cream. Season with the nutmeg and salt and pepper, to taste.

Fold the lobster meat through the sauce. Stir over low heat until the lobster is heated through. Spoon the mixture into the shells and sprinkle with cheese. Heat the grill (broiler) and place the lobster under the grill for 2 minutes, or until the cheese is melted. Sprinkle with paprika.

# rainbow trout with salmon roe butter

serves 4

## ingredients

4 rainbow trout, cleaned and scaled
1 large lime or lemon, finely sliced
12 lemon thyme sprigs
olive oil, for brushing

### salmon roe butter
50 g (1$^3$/$_4$ oz) butter, softened
1 teaspoon lime or lemon juice
$^1$/$_2$ teaspoon chopped tarragon
$^1$/$_2$ teaspoon snipped chives
1 tablespoon salmon roe

## method

Preheat a barbecue flat plate to medium. Rinse each trout in cold water and pat dry inside and out with paper towels. Fill each trout cavity with slices of lime or lemon, put 3 lemon thyme sprigs in each and season.

Lightly brush the hotplate and the trout with oil. Barbecue the trout for about 4 minutes, then turn and grill for a further 4 minutes, or until cooked through.

To make the salmon roe butter, beat the butter until smooth and stir in the lime or lemon juice, tarragon and chives. Gently fold in the salmon roe and season with freshly ground pepper.

Arrange the trout on four serving plates. Put a generous dollop of the salmon roe butter on each trout and serve immediately.

# fisherman's pie

serves 4

## ingredients

800 g (1 lb 10 oz) white fish fillets
375 ml (13 fl oz/1$^1$/$_2$ cups) milk
1 onion, roughly chopped
2 cloves
50 g (1$^3$/$_4$ oz) butter
2 tablespoons plain (all-purpose) flour
pinch of ground nutmeg
2 tablespoons chopped flat-leaf (Italian) parsley
155 g (5$^1$/$_2$ oz/1 cup) peas
750 g (1 lb 10 oz) potatoes, quartered
2 tablespoons hot milk
3 tablespoons grated cheddar cheese

## method

Place the fish fillets in a frying pan and cover with the milk. Add the onion and cloves and bring to the boil. Reduce the heat and simmer for about 5 minutes, or until the fish is cooked; the flesh should be opaque and flake easily with a fork.

Preheat the oven to 180°C (350°F/Gas 4). Remove the fish from the pan, reserving the milk and onion. Discard the cloves. Allow the fish to cool then remove any skin and bones and flake into bite-sized pieces with a fork.

Heat half of the butter in a saucepan, stir in the flour and cook, stirring, for 1 minute. Remove from the heat, add the reserved milk mixture and stir until smooth. Return to the heat and cook, stirring, until the sauce begins to bubble. Cook for a further minute. Remove from the heat, allow to cool slightly, then add the nutmeg, parsley and peas. Season well and fold in the fish. Spoon into a 1.25 litre (44 fl oz/5 cup) capacity baking dish.

Cook the potatoes in a saucepan of boiling water until tender. Drain and add the milk and remaining butter. Mash until smooth. Add the cheese.

Spoon the potato mixture into a piping bag and pipe over the filling. Bake for 30 minutes, or until heated through.

# cajun swordfish

serves 4

## ingredients

1 tablespoon garlic powder
1 tablespoon onion powder
2 teaspoons white pepper
2 teaspoons cracked black pepper
2 teaspoons dried thyme
2 teaspoons dried oregano
1 teaspoon cayenne pepper
4 swordfish steaks
oil, for cooking
lime wedges, Greek-style yoghurt, and mixed
    salad leaves, to serve

**fish substitution**
tuna, mahi mahi, kingfish, striped marlin

## method

Mix all the dried spices and herbs in a bowl. Pat the swordfish steaks dry with paper towels, then coat both sides of each steak in the spice mixture, shaking off any excess.

Heat a barbecue flatplate and drizzle with a little oil. Cook the swordfish steaks for 3–5 minutes on each side. Serve with wedges of lime, a dollop of yoghurt and a salad.

# fresh seafood salad with green chilli, galangal and lime dressing

serves 4

## ingredients

### dressing
4 thin slices of young galangal, chopped
1 long green chilli, deseeded and finely sliced
1 garlic clove, crushed
2 tablespoons lime juice
1 tablespoon rice vinegar
1 tablespoon fish sauce
1$^1/_2$ tablespoons mirin
1 teaspoon sugar
3 tablespoons vegetable oil

### seafood salad
250 g (9 oz) piece sashimi-grade salmon fillet
250 g (9 oz) squid tubes, scored and cut into
   5 cm (2 in) pieces
8 scallops, shelled
8 raw king prawns (shrimp), peeled and deveined,
   tails intact
1 large avocado, chopped into dice
150 g (5$^1/_2$ oz) snow peas (mangetout), trimmed
   and cut lengthways into thin strips
60 g (2$^1/_4$ oz) bean sprouts, trimmed
$^1/_2$ small red onion, finely sliced
150 g (5$^1/_2$ oz) baby Asian greens

## method

In a mortar and pestle, pound the galangal until broken down into smaller pieces. Add the green chilli and garlic and pound until a paste forms. Remove and put into a small bowl with the remaining dressing ingredients and whisk until combined.

Heat 2 tablespoons of oil in a large frying pan over medium–high heat. Sear the salmon fillet for 1 minute on each side. Remove, cover and set aside.

In the remaining oil, cook the squid tubes, scallops and prawns separately until cooked. Remove and cover. Drizzle 2 tablespoons of the dressing over the seafood.

Combine the vegetables with the seafood. Break large pieces of the salmon from the fillet, allowing 2–3 pieces per person. Divide the salmon and remaining seafood over the salad ingredients. Drizzle with the remaining dressing.

# salmon fillets with lemon hollandaise sauce

serves 4

## ingredients

**lemon hollandaise sauce**
175 g (6 oz) butter
4 egg yolks
2 tablespoons lemon juice

2 tablespoons olive oil
4 salmon fillets with skin on

## method

Melt the butter in a small saucepan over low heat. Skim any froth from the surface and discard. Leave to cool. Whisk the yolks and 2 tablespoons water in a separate small saucepan for 30 seconds, or until pale and foamy. Place the saucepan over very low heat and whisk the egg mixture for 2–3 minutes, or until it is frothy and the whisk leaves a trail behind it as you whisk. Remove from the heat.

Add the cooled butter to the eggs, a little at a time, whisking well after each addition. Avoid using the milky whey from the base of the saucepan. Stir in the lemon juice and season.

Heat the oil in a large non-stick frying pan over high heat and cook the salmon fillets skin side down for 2 minutes. Turn over and cook for 2 minutes, or until cooked to your liking. Serve with the sauce and vegetables of your choice.

# scallops with sesame bok choy

serves 4

## ingredients

24 large scallops with corals
2 tablespoons light soy sauce
1 tablespoon fish sauce
1 tablespoon honey
1 tablespoon kecap manis
grated zest and juice of 1 lime
2 teaspoons grated fresh ginger
lime wedges, to serve

### sesame bok choy
1 tablespoon sesame oil
1 tablespoon sesame seeds
1 garlic clove, crushed
8 baby bok choy (pak choi), halved lengthways

## method

Rinse the scallops, remove the dark vein and dry with paper towels. Mix the soy and fish sauce, honey, kecap manis, lime zest and juice and ginger. Pour over the scallops, cover and refrigerate for 15 minutes. Drain, reserving the marinade.

To make the sesame bok choy, pour the oil onto a hot barbecue flat plate and add the sesame seeds and garlic. Cook, stirring, for 1 minute, or until the seeds are golden. Arrange the bok choy in a single layer on the hot plate and pour over the reserved marinade. Cook for 3–4 minutes, turning once, until tender. Remove and keep warm.

Wipe clean the flat plate, brush with oil and reheat. Add the scallops and cook, turning, for about 2 minutes, or until they become opaque. Serve on top of the bok choy, with the lime wedges.

# peppered tuna steaks with wasabi dressing

serves 4

## ingredients

4 x 250 g (9 oz) fresh tuna steaks
3 tablespoons soy sauce
3 tablespoons cracked black pepper
350 g (12 oz) young asparagus, trimmed and
    blanched
2 red onions, quartered
2 tablespoons olive oil

### wasabi dressing

50 g (1¾ oz) Greek-style yoghurt
3 tablespoons whole-egg mayonnaise
1 tablespoon lemon juice
2 teaspoons wasabi paste
1 tablespoon finely chopped dill

## method

Preheat a barbecue grill plate, flat plate or chargrill pan to high. Toss the tuna steaks in the soy sauce, then coat liberally with the black pepper, pressing in well. Cover and refrigerate until ready to cook.

In a small bowl, combine the wasabi dressing ingredients and mix together well. Set aside until needed.

Toss the asparagus and onion in a bowl with the oil until coated all over. Grill them on the hotplate for about 5 minutes, or until the onion starts to brown. Remove from the heat and keep warm.

Put the tuna on the hotplate and cook for 3–5 minutes, turning once, or until the outside is browned and crisp—the tuna should still be a little pink in the middle. The exact cooking time will vary depending on the thickness of your tuna steaks. Slice the tuna into thick strips.

Arrange the asparagus and onion on four serving plates, top with the tuna slices and drizzle with a little wasabi dressing. Serve any remaining dressing on the side.

# poached atlantic salmon

serves 8–10

## ingredients

2 litres (70 fl oz/8 cups) white wine
3 tablespoons white wine vinegar
2 onions
10 whole cloves
4 carrots, chopped
1 lemon, cut in quarters
2 bay leaves
4 sprigs flat-leaf (Italian) parsley
1 teaspoon whole black peppercorns
2.5 kg (4 lb 8 oz) Atlantic salmon, cleaned and
   scaled

### dill mayonnaise

1 egg, at room temperature
1 egg yolk, at room temperature, extra
1 tablespoon lemon juice
1 teaspoon white wine vinegar
375 ml (12 fl oz/1$^1$/$_2$ cups) light olive oil
1–2 tablespoons chopped dill

## method

Put the wine, wine vinegar and 2.5 litres (85 fl oz/10 cups) of water in a large heavy-based saucepan.

Stud the onions with the cloves. Add to the pan with the carrot, lemon, bay leaves, parsley and peppercorns. Bring to the boil, reduce the heat and simmer for 30–35 minutes. Cool. Strain into a fish kettle that will hold the salmon.

Place the whole fish in the fish kettle and cover. Bring to the boil, reduce the heat and poach gently for 10–15 minutes, until the fish flakes when tested in the thickest part. Remove from the heat and cool the fish in the liquid.

Process the egg, extra yolk, juice and vinegar in a food processor for 10 seconds, or until blended. With the motor running, add the oil in a thin, steady stream, blending until all the oil is added and the mayonnaise is thick and creamy—it should be thick enough to form peaks. Transfer to a bowl and stir in the dill, and season.

Remove the cold fish from the liquid, place on a work surface or serving platter and peel back the skin. Serve garnished with watercress and lemon slices. Serve with the mayonnaise.

# veal scaloppine with white wine and parsley

serves 4

## ingredients

4 x 170 g (6 oz) veal escalopes
30 g (1 oz) butter
3 tablespoons dry white wine or dry Marsala
100 ml (31/2 fl oz) thick (double/heavy) cream
1 tablespoon wholegrain mustard
2 tablespoons chopped flat-leaf (Italian) parsley

## method

Place the veal escalopes between two sheets of plastic wrap and either press down hard with the heel of your hand until flattened, or flatten with a rolling pin or mallet. Heat the butter in a frying pan and cook the escalopes in batches for 1 minute each side, or until just cooked. Remove and cover.

Add the wine to the pan, bring to the boil and cook for 1–2 minutes, or until reduced by half. Then add the cream, bring to the boil and reduce by half again. Stir in the mustard and 1 tablespoon parsley until just combined. Return the veal to the pan to warm through and coat in the sauce. Serve the veal with a little sauce and sprinkle with the remaining parsley. Serve with potatoes and a green salad, if desired.

# herbed lamb cutlets with preserved lemon couscous

serves 4

## ingredients

2 tablespoons finely chopped thyme leaves
2 teaspoons freshly ground black pepper
12 French-trimmed lamb cutlets
3 tablespoons virgin olive oil
2 tablespoons soy sauce
2 garlic cloves, crushed
oil, for brushing
preserved lemon couscous
1 tablespoon olive oil
185 g (6$^1$/$_2$ oz/1 cup) couscous
2 tablespoons thinly sliced preserved lemon zest

## method

Sprinkle the thyme and pepper onto a plate. Use the mixture to coat both sides of each lamb cutlet, pressing it in well.

In a shallow non-metallic dish, whisk the oil, soy sauce and garlic until combined. Add the lamb cutlets, then cover and refrigerate for 20 minutes, turning once.

Preheat a barbecue grill plate or chargrill pan until very hot. Meanwhile, make the preserved lemon couscous. Bring 375 ml (13 fl oz/1$^1$/$_2$ cups) of water to the boil in a saucepan. Add the oil, then stir in the couscous and preserved lemon. Remove from the heat, cover and leave for 5 minutes. Just before serving, fluff up the couscous with a fork.

Shake the excess marinade off the cutlets and set them slightly apart on the barbecue hotplate. Grill for 1–2 minutes on each side, or until cooked to your liking. Serve the cutlets hot, on a bed of preserved lemon couscous.

# glazed spatchcocks

serves 4

## ingredients

4 spatchcocks (poussin), rinsed and patted dry
    with paper towels
1 lemon, cut into wedges
8 garlic cloves, halved
3 tablespoons plum sauce
3 tablespoons oyster sauce
1 tablespoon honey
4 small red chillies, seeded and finely chopped
steamed rice and green beans, to serve

## method

Preheat the oven to 200°C (400°F/Gas 6). Fill the cavity of each spatchcock with the lemon and garlic, then tie the legs together with string.

Place the spatchcocks on a rack, then put the rack in a roasting tin and pour in enough water to cover the base of the tin. Cover loosely with foil and bake for 30 minutes. Remove the foil.

Combine the plum sauce, oyster sauce, honey and chilli and brush over the spatchcocks. Return to the oven and cook, uncovered, for 40 minutes, or until golden brown and the juices run clear when pierced with a knife. Brush occasionally with the marinade during cooking. Serve with steamed rice and green beans.

# chicken braised with ginger and star anise

serves 4

## ingredients

1 teaspoon sichuan peppercorns
2 tablespoons peanut oil
3 cm x 2 cm (11/4 in x 3/4 in) piece fresh ginger, julienned
2 garlic cloves, chopped
1 kg (2 lb 4 oz) boneless, skinless chicken thigh fillets, cut in half
4 tablespoons Chinese rice wine
1 tablespoon honey
3 tablespoons light soy sauce
1 star anise
steamed rice, to serve

## method

Heat a wok over medium heat, add the peppercorns and cook, stirring to prevent burning, for 2–4 minutes, or until fragrant. Remove and lightly crush with the back of a knife.

Reheat the wok, add the oil and swirl to coat. Add the ginger and garlic, and cook over low heat for 1–2 minutes, or until slightly golden. Add the chicken, increase the heat to medium and cook for 3 minutes, or until browned all over.

Add the peppercorns, wine, honey, soy sauce and star anise to the wok, reduce the heat to low and simmer, covered, for 20 minutes, or until the chicken is tender. Serve with steamed rice.

# beef wellington

serves 6–8

## ingredients

1.25 kg (2 lb 12 oz) piece of beef fillet or rib eye,
    trimmed
1 tablespoon oil
125 g (4$^1/_2$ oz) pâté
60 g (2$^1/_4$ oz) button mushrooms, sliced
375 g (13 oz) block ready-made puff pastry,
    thawed
1 egg, lightly beaten
1 sheet frozen puff pastry, thawed
green beans, to serve
rosemary, to garnish

## method

To help the beef keep its shape, tie it four or five times along its length, then rub with pepper. Heat the oil over high heat in a large, heavy-based frying pan, then cook the meat until it is browned all over. Remove the beef from the pan and allow to cool, then cut off the string. Smear the pâté over the top and sides of the beef, then use this as glue to stick the mushrooms on.

Roll the block of pastry out on a lightly floured surface until it is big enough. Then sit the beef on the pastry, brush the edges with egg and bring the edges up until you have a parcel of beef. Use some more of the beaten egg to seal the parcel, then neatly fold in the ends. Lift the beef onto a greased baking tray so the seam is underneath.

Cut shapes from the sheet of pastry. Use the egg to stick the shapes on, then brush all over the Wellington with the egg. Cut a few slits in the top to allow the steam to escape. Cook in a 210°C (415°F/Gas 6–7) oven for 45 minutes for rare, 1 hour for medium or 1$^1/_2$ hours for well done. Rest for 10 minutes, then slice and serve. Serve with green beans and garnish with the rosemary.

# parmesan and rosemary crusted veal chops

serves 4

## ingredients

4 veal chops
150 g (5 oz) fresh white breadcrumbs
75 g (2$^1$/$_2$ oz) grated parmesan cheese
1 tablespoon finely chopped rosemary
2 eggs, lightly beaten, seasoned
3 tablespoons olive oil
60 g (2$^1$/$_4$ oz) butter
4 garlic cloves

## method

Trim the chops of excess fat and sinew and flatten to 1 cm ($^1$/$_2$ in) thickness. Pat the meat dry with paper towels. Combine the breadcrumbs, parmesan and rosemary in a shallow bowl.

Dip each chop in the beaten egg, draining off the excess. Press both sides of the chops firmly in the crumbs.

Heat the oil and butter in a heavy-based frying pan over low heat, add the garlic and cook until golden. Discard the garlic.

Increase the heat to medium, add the chops to the pan and cook for 4–5 minutes on each side, depending on the thickness of the chops, until golden and crisp. Transfer to a warm serving dish and season.

# roast leg of lamb with spring vegetables

serves 6

## ingredients

1 x 2 kg (4 lb 8 oz) leg of lamb
3 rosemary sprigs
6 garlic cloves, unpeeled
500 g (1 lb 2 oz) small potatoes, halved
250 g (9 oz) baby carrots
6 small leeks
250 g (9 oz) small zucchinis (courgettes)
1¹/₂ tablespoons plain (all-purpose) flour
150 ml (5 fl oz) red wine
150 ml (5 fl oz) brown stock

## method

Preheat the oven to 200°C (400°F/Gas 6). Rub the lamb all over with salt and pepper. Put the lamb in a roasting tin, lay the rosemary sprigs on top and scatter the garlic around the lamb. Roast for 20 minutes, then turn the lamb over. Add the potatoes to the roasting tin and toss in the lamb fat, then return to the oven for a further 15 minutes. Turn the lamb again and cook for a further 15 minutes.

Add the baby carrots and leeks to the tin, toss with the potatoes in the lamb fat and turn the lamb again. Roast for a further 15 minutes, then add the zucchini. Toss all the vegetables in the lamb fat and turn the leg of lamb again. Roast for a further 15 minutes, then lift the lamb out of the roasting tin to rest. Remove the vegetables and garlic from the tin and keep warm.

To make the gravy, spoon the fat from the surface of the meat juices. Place the roasting tin over medium heat on the stovetop and stir in the flour to make a roux. Cook, stirring, for 2 minutes, then gradually stir in the wine and stock. Boil the gravy for 2 minutes, then strain into a serving jug.

Carve the lamb and serve with the vegetables, garlic and gravy.

# pork with bacon and baby apples

serves 6

## ingredients

1.5 kg (3 lb 5 oz) rolled pork loin roast
6 bacon slices
600 ml (21 fl oz) apple juice
12 baby red apples or 3 small ripe red apples,
    halved but not cored
red cabbage and baby potatoes, to serve

## method

Preheat a kettle or covered barbecue to medium indirect heat. Remove the string from around the pork loin, then the skin. Sprinkle the pork with freshly ground black pepper and wrap the bacon slices around the loin to cover it. Sit the pork on a rack in a large roasting tin and pour on 375 ml (13 fl oz/ $1^1/_2$ cups) of the apple juice.

Place the roasting tin on the barbecue grill, lower the lid and cook the pork for 15–20 minutes, checking that the apple juice isn't evaporating too quickly from the roasting tin. Reduce the heat to low, baste the pork with the roasting juices and cook for a further 20 minutes, basting and adding more apple juice as needed.

Add the apples to the pork and coat with the roasting tin juices. Baste the pork again, add more apple juice to the roasting tin if needed, and cook for a further 40 minutes, or until the juices run clear when tested with a skewer in the thickest part. Remove the pork from the heat, transfer to a plate with the apples and cover with foil. Leave for 10 minutes.

Serve the pork with the apples and pan juices, and some sautéed red cabbage and boiled baby potatoes.

# roast chicken with rosemary

serves 4

## ingredients

2 rosemary sprigs
3 garlic cloves
1 teaspoon balsamic vinegar
1.5 kg (3 lb 5 oz) whole chicken
2 tablespoons extra virgin olive oil
2 tablespoons olive oil
125 ml (4 fl oz/$^1/_2$ cup) chicken stock

## method

Preheat the oven to 200°C (400°F/Gas 6). Put one rosemary sprig, the garlic and balsamic vinegar inside the cavity of the chicken. Add a large pinch of salt and a few grinds of black pepper. Truss the legs together.

Rub the extra virgin olive oil over the chicken skin. Pour the olive oil into a roasting tin and put the chicken in the tin, breast up. Place the second sprig of rosemary on top.

Transfer to the oven and roast for 1 hour, turning the chicken and basting with the pan juices every 15 minutes.

Put the chicken on a warm serving plate and discard the rosemary sprig. Spoon off the fat from the roasting tin and place it over high heat on the stovetop. Add the chicken stock and deglaze the pan. Boil until reduced and thickened. Taste for salt and pepper, then pour into a sauceboat to accompany the chicken. Serve with roast rosemary potatoes.

# fillet steaks with pink peppercorn sauce

serves 4

## ingredients

60 g ($2^1/_4$ oz) butter
1 tablespoon oil
4 fillet steaks, rump or New York cut, trimmed
125 ml (4 fl oz/$^1/_2$ cup) white wine
2 tablespoons brandy
125 ml (4 fl oz/$^1/_2$ cup) beef stock
2 tablespoons pink peppercorns in brine, drained
    and rinsed
125 ml (4 fl oz/$^1/_2$ cup) pouring (whipping) cream

## method

Heat the butter and oil in a large frying pan, and cook the steaks over high heat for 3–4 minutes each side, or until cooked to your liking. Remove from the pan, cover and keep warm.

Add the wine and brandy to the pan, and simmer for 4 minutes, or until reduced by half. Add the beef stock and reduce by half again; you should have just over 125 ml (4 fl oz/$^1/_2$ cup) sauce. Meanwhile, roughly chop half the peppercorns.

Stir in all the peppercorns and the cream, and cook gently until the sauce has thickened slightly. Place the steaks on four warmed serving plates and spoon the sauce over the top. Serve with a green salad.

# roast sirloin with mustard pepper crust and hasselback potatoes

serves 6–8

## ingredients

90 g (3$^1$/$_4$ oz/$^1$/$_3$ cup) dijon mustard
2 tablespoons light soy sauce
2 tablespoons plain (all-purpose) flour
3 tablespoons olive oil
3 teaspoons chopped thyme leaves
4 garlic cloves, crushed
2.5 kg (5 lb 8 oz) piece of sirloin, trimmed but
   with the fat still on top
6 all-purpose potatoes
40 g (1$^1$/$_2$ oz) butter, melted
1 onion, roughly diced
1 large carrot, roughly diced
2 celery stalks, roughly chopped
250 ml (9 fl oz/1 cup) red wine
500 ml (17 fl oz/2 cups) beef stock
2 bay leaves
2 teaspoons cornflour (cornstarch)

## method

Mix the mustard, soy sauce, flour, 2 tablespoons of oil,
2 teaspoons of thyme, two of the crushed garlic cloves and
1 tablespoon of cracked black pepper in a bowl. Coat the sirloin
with the mustard mixture and refrigerate for 1 hour.

To make the hasselback potatoes, boil the potatoes in their
skins for 10–12 minutes, or until just cooked. Peel and cut in
half lengthways. Make small even slices across the top of the
potato, cutting only two-thirds of the way down. Brush each
one liberally with butter and season.

Heat the remaining olive oil in a large saucepan, add the onion,
carrot, celery and remaining garlic, and cook for 5 minutes.
Pour in the red wine, cook for a further 5 minutes, then add the
beef stock, the bay leaves and the remaining thyme. Mix the
cornflour with 1 tablespoon water until smooth and add to the
pan. Simmer over low heat for 20 minutes, then strain.

Preheat a covered barbecue to medium indirect heat, put the
sirloin in the middle of the barbecue and arrange the potatoes
arround it. Replace the cover and cook for 45 minutes. Remove
the sirloin, leave it to rest, covered, for 10 minutes before
carving. Serve with the potatoes and red wine sauce.

# saltimbocca

serves 4

## ingredients

8 small veal escalopes
8 slices prosciutto
8 sage leaves
2 tablespoons olive oil
60 g ($2^1/_4$ oz) butter
185 ml (6 fl oz/$^3/_4$ cup) dry Marsala or
   dry white wine

## method

Place the veal between two sheets of greaseproof paper and pound with a meat mallet or rolling pin until they are 5 mm ($^1/_4$ in) thick. Make sure you pound them evenly. Peel off the paper and season lightly. Cut the prosciutto slices to the same size as the veal. Cover each piece of veal with a slice of prosciutto and place a sage leaf in the centre. Secure the sage leaf with a cocktail stick.

Heat the olive oil and half the butter in a large frying pan. Add the veal in batches and fry, prosciutto side up, over medium heat for 3–4 minutes, or until the veal is just cooked through. Briefly flip the saltimbocca over and fry the prosciutto side. Transfer each batch to a warm plate as it is done.

Pour off the oil from the pan and add the Marsala or wine. Bring to the boil and cook over high heat until reduced by half, scraping up the bits from the bottom of the pan. Add the remaining butter and, when it has melted, season the sauce. Remove the cocktail sticks and spoon the sauce over the veal to serve.

# spiced duck breast with peach and chilli salad

serves 4

## ingredients

6 ripe peaches
1 lime plus 1 tablespoon lime juice, extra
1 tablespoon extra virgin olive oil
1 small red chilli, seeded and finely sliced
2 tablespoons chopped mint leaves
4 duck breasts
2 teaspoons ground coriander
lime wedges

## method

Dip the peaches into a saucepan of boiling water for 5 seconds then plunge them into iced water. Remove the skins, which should slip off easily. Cut each peach in half, remove the stone, then cut each half into eight wedges. Peel the lime, removing all the pith, and separate the lime sections by carefully cutting each piece away from the membrane.

Toss the peach slices with the lime segments, extra lime juice, olive oil, chilli and mint, and season with a little pepper.

Trim the duck breasts of fat and sinew, and sprinkle each breast with the ground coriander.

Preheat a barbecue flat plate to medium direct heat and cook the duck on the flat plate for 4 minutes or until the skin is golden, then turn and cook for another 4 minutes. Turn the breasts over again and cook them for a further 1 minute to make the skin crispy, then leave to rest in a warm place for 10 minutes.

Slice each breast into four pieces on the diagonal and serve with the peach salad and lime wedges.

# osso buco with gremolata

serves 4

## ingredients

2 tablespoons olive oil
1 onion, finely chopped
1 garlic clove, crushed
1 kg (2 lb 4 oz) veal shin slices (osso buco)
2 tablespoons plain (all-purpose) flour
400 g (14 oz) tinned tomatoes, roughly chopped
250 ml (9 fl oz/1 cup) white wine
250 ml (9 fl oz/1 cup) chicken stock

### gremolata

2 tablespoons finely chopped flat-leaf (Italian)
   parsley
2 teaspoons grated lemon zest
1 teaspoon finely chopped garlic

## method

Heat 1 tablespoon oil in a large shallow flameproof casserole dish. Add the onion and cook over low heat until soft and golden. Add the garlic. Cook for 1 minute, then remove from the dish.

Heat the remaining oil and brown the veal in batches, then remove. Return the onion to the casserole and stir in the flour. Cook for 30 seconds and remove from the heat. Slowly stir in the tomatoes, wine and stock, combining well with the flour. Return the veal to the casserole.

Return to the heat and bring to the boil, stirring. Cover and reduce the heat to low so that the casserole is just simmering. Cook for $2^1/_2$ hours, or until the meat is very tender and almost falling off the bones.

To make the gremolata, combine the parsley, lemon zest and garlic in a bowl. When the osso buco is ready, sprinkle the gremolata over the top and serve with risotto or plain rice.

# rack of lamb with herb crust

serves 4

## ingredients

2 x 6-chop racks of lamb trimmed and bones
    cleaned (ask your butcher to do this)
1 tablespoon oil
80 g (2³/₄ oz/1 cup) fresh breadcrumbs
3 garlic cloves
3 tablespoons finely chopped fresh flat-leaf
    (Italian) parsley
¹/₂ tablespoon fresh thyme leaves
¹/₂ teaspoon finely grated lemon zest
60 g (2¹/₄ oz) butter, softened
250 ml (9 fl oz/1 cup) beef stock
1 garlic clove, extra, finely chopped
1 thyme sprig

## method

Preheat the oven to 250°C (500°F/Gas 10). Score the fat on racks in a diamond pattern. Rub the rack with a little of the oil and season.

Heat the oil in a frying pan over high heat, add the lamb and brown for 4–5 minutes. Remove and set aside.

In a large bowl, mix the breadcrumbs, garlic, parsley, thyme and lemon zest. Season, then mix in the butter to form a paste.

Firmly press a layer of breadcrumb mixture over the fat on the racks, leaving the bones and base clean. Bake in a baking dish for 12 minutes for medium-rare.

Add the beef stock, extra garlic and thyme sprig to the roasting pan juices, scraping the pan. Return this liquid to the original frying pan and simmer over high heat for 5–8 minutes, until the sauce is reduced. Strain and serve on the side.

# stuffed chicken breast with tomato, goat's cheese and asparagus

serves 4

## ingredients

4 large boneless, skinless chicken breasts
100 g (3$^1$/$_2$ oz) semi-dried tomatoes
100 g (3$^1$/$_2$ oz) goat's cheese, sliced
200 g (7 oz) asparagus spears, trimmed, halved and blanched
50 g (1$^3$/$_4$ oz) butter
375 ml (13 fl oz/1$^1$/$_2$ cups) chicken stock
2 zucchini (courgettes), cut into 5 cm (2 in) batons
250 ml (9 fl oz/1 cup) pouring (whipping) cream
8 spring onions (scallions), thinly sliced

## method

Pound each chicken breast between two sheets of plastic wrap with a mallet or rolling pin until 1 cm ($^1$/$_2$ in) thick. Divide the tomato, goat's cheese and 155 g (5$^1$/$_2$ oz) of the asparagus pieces among the breasts. Roll up tightly lengthways, securing along the seam with toothpicks.

Heat the butter in a large frying pan over medium heat. Add the chicken, then brown on all sides. Pour in the stock, then reduce the heat to low. Cook, covered, for 10 minutes, or until the chicken is cooked through. Remove the chicken and keep warm.

Meanwhile, bring a saucepan of lightly salted water to the boil. Add the zucchini and remaining asparagus and cook for 2 minutes, or until just tender. Remove from the pan. Whisk the cream into the frying pan. Add the spring onion and simmer over medium–low heat for 4 minutes, or until reduced and thickened. To serve, cut each chicken roll in half on the diagonal and place on serving plates. Spoon on the sauce and serve with the greens.

# veal parmigiana

**serves 4**

## ingredients

3 tablespoons olive oil
1 garlic clove, crushed
pinch of cayenne pepper
pinch of caster (superfine) sugar
400 g (14 oz) tinned crushed tomatoes
3 teaspoons chopped oregano
40 g ($1^1/_2$ oz/$^1/_3$ cup) plain (all-purpose) flour
2 eggs
65 g ($2^1/_4$ oz/$^2/_3$ cup) dry breadcrumbs
4 large veal cutlets, well trimmed
100 g ($3^1/_2$ oz) mozzarella cheese, thinly sliced
35 g ($1^1/_4$ oz/$^1/_3$ cup) grated parmesan cheese

## method

Preheat the oven to 190°C (375°F/Gas 5). Heat 1 tablespoon of the oil in a small saucepan over medium heat, add the garlic and cook for 30 seconds. Add the cayenne, sugar, tomato and half the oregano and cook, stirring occasionally, for 20 minutes, or until thickened. Season well.

Place the flour in a wide shallow bowl and season well. Beat the eggs with 2 tablespoons of water in another bowl. Mix the breadcrumbs with the remaining oregano, season and place in a third bowl.

Pound the cutlets between two sheets of plastic wrap until flattened to 5 mm ($^1/_4$ in) thick. Coat in the seasoned flour, shaking off the excess, then dip both sides in the egg mixture and then coat in the breadcrumbs. Heat the remaining oil in a large frying pan. Add the cutlets in two batches and brown over medium–high heat for 2 minutes on each side. Transfer to a shallow baking dish large enough to fit them side by side.

Spread the sauce over each cutlet. Cover with the mozzarella and sprinkle with the parmesan. Bake for 20 minutes, or until the cheeses have melted and browned. Serve.

# veal marsala

serves 4

## ingredients

4 pieces (500 g/1 lb 2 oz) veal schnitzel
plain (all-purpose) flour, seasoned
50 g (1³/₄ oz) butter
1 tablespoon oil
185 ml (6 fl oz/³/₄ cup) dry Marsala
3 teaspoons cream
30 g (1 oz) butter, chopped, extra

## method

Using a meat mallet or the heel of your hand, flatten the schnitzel pieces to 5 mm ($^1/_4$ in) thick. Dust the veal in the flour, shaking off any excess.

Heat the butter and oil in a large frying pan and cook the veal over medium–high heat for 1–2 minutes on each side, or until almost cooked through. Remove and keep warm.

Add the Marsala to the pan and bring to the boil, scraping the base of the pan to loosen any sediment. Reduce the heat and simmer for 1–2 minutes, or until slightly reduced. Add the cream and simmer for 2 minutes, then whisk in the extra butter until the sauce thickens slightly. Return the veal to the pan and simmer for 1 minute, or until the meat is warmed through. Serve immediately. Delicious with a creamy garlic mash and a tossed green salad.

# rib eye of beef with spice rub, parsnip mash and merlot reduction

serves 4

## ingredients

### spice rub
1 tablespoon olive oil
1 tablespoon ground coriander
2 teaspoons ground cumin
2 teaspoons smoked paprika
2 teaspoons soft brown sugar
1 teaspoon garlic powder
1 teaspoon salt
$^1/_2$ teaspoon ground black pepper

### merlot reduction
250 ml (9 fl oz/1 cup) beef stock
250 ml (9 fl oz/1 cup) merlot
1 teaspoon caster (superfine) sugar

4 x 280 g (10 oz) rib eye of beef, bone on (beef cutlets from a rack)
450 g (1 lb) parsnips, peeled and chopped
50 g ($1^3/_4$ oz) butter
3 tablespoons thick (double/heavy) cream
1 tablespoon olive oil

## method

Mix all the spice rub ingredients together and rub well into both sides of beef. Cover and allow to rest for 30 minutes.

In a small saucepan, add the stock, merlot and sugar and bring to the boil over a high heat. Reduce the heat to medium and reduce the sauce by a third. Season to taste.

Put the parsnips in a saucepan, cover with water and bring to the boil. Cook for 15 minutes, or until soft. Drain and purée in a food processor with the butter, cream, and salt and pepper, until smooth and creamy.

In a large heavy-based frying pan, heat the olive oil over medium–high heat and sear the beef for 4 minutes on each side for medium–rare, or until cooked to your liking. Remove from the pan and rest for 5 minutes in a warm place.

Spoon a dollop of parsnip purée onto a warmed plate, top with a spiced rib eye and ladle sauce over the beef and around the plate.

# slow-cooked lamb roast

serves 4–6

## ingredients

2 kg (4 lb 8 oz) leg of lamb, deboned
2 tablespoons olive oil
1 teaspoon grated lemon zest
1 tablespoon lemon juice
2 tablespoons dijon mustard
2 tablespoons chopped oregano
4 garlic cloves, crushed
60 g (2$^1$/$_4$ oz) feta cheese
750 ml (26 fl oz/3 cups) chicken stock

## method

Preheat the oven to 160°C (315°F/Gas 2–3). Lay the leg of lamb out flat, skin side down. Combine the oil, lemon zest and juice, mustard, oregano and garlic and spread half of this mixture over the lamb. Crumble the feta over the top. Roll up the lamb tightly and secure with skewers and string.

Place the lamb, skin side down, on a rack and put the rack in a roasting tin. Pour the stock into the tin, then cover loosely with foil and steam for 1 hour 30 minutes.

Remove the foil, turn the lamb skin side up and spread with the remaining mustard mixture. Cook the lamb, uncovered, for 1 hour (for medium), or until cooked the way you like it.

Remove the lamb from the oven, re-cover with the foil, and rest for 15 minutes. Slice and drizzle with the pan juices. Serve with potato mash and steamed greens.

# turkey pot roast

serves 6

## ingredients

1 kg (2 lb 4 oz) frozen turkey breast roll
2 tablespoons oil
20 g ($^3/_4$ oz) butter
1 onion, cut into wedges
125 ml (4 fl oz/$^1/_2$ cup) chicken stock
125 ml (4 fl oz/$^1/_2$ cup) white wine
300 g (10$^1/_2$ oz) sweet potato, cut into 3 cm
    (1$^1/_4$ in) pieces
2 zucchini (courgette), cut into 2 cm ($^3/_4$ in) slices
150 g (5$^1/_2$ oz/$^1/_2$ cup) redcurrant jelly
1 tablespoon cornflour (cornstarch)
1 tablespoon water

## method

Preheat the oven to 180°C (350°F/Gas Mark 4). Thaw the
turkey according to the label. Remove the elasticised string
from the turkey, and tie up securely with string, at regular
intervals, to retain its shape.

Heat the oil and butter in a frying pan. Add the turkey and
brown all over on a high heat. Transfer to a 2 litre (70 fl oz/
8 cup) capacity casserole dish.

Place the onion wedges around the turkey. Pour the stock and
wine over. Cover the casserole dish and bake for 40 minutes.
Add the sweet potato and bake for 10 minutes. Add the
zucchini and bake for a further 20 minutes.

Transfer the turkey and vegetables to a plate and keep warm.
Strain the liquid into a small saucepan. Add the redcurrant jelly
and stir to combine.

Combine the cornflour and water and stir until smooth.
Gradually add to the pan, stirring, until the mixture boils and
thickens. Slice the turkey and serve with the vegetables
and sauce.

# beef fillet with caramelized onion and horseradish cream

serves 4

## ingredients

2 tablespoons olive oil
2 garlic cloves, crushed
5 thyme sprigs, plus extra, to serve
1.25 kg (2 lb 12 oz) piece beef fillet

### caramelized onion

$1^1/_2$ tablespoons olive oil
3 red onions, thinly sliced
1 tablespoon soft brown sugar

### horseradish cream

125 ml (4 fl oz/$^1/_2$ cup) thick (double/heavy)
   cream
75 g ($2^3/_4$ oz/$^1/_4$ cup) ready-made horseradish
   sauce
1 garlic clove, crushed
1 tablespoon lemon juice

## method

Mix together the oil, garlic and thyme, and season. Brush the mixture all over the beef, ensuring it is thoroughly coated.

Preheat a kettle or covered barbecue to medium indirect heat. Put the beef in a baking dish and place it on the rack in the middle of the barbecue. Lower the lid and cook for 40 minutes for medium–rare. Remove the beef from the heat, cover loosely with foil and leave to rest until ready to serve.

Heat the oil in a saucepan over medium heat. Add the onions and cook for 2–3 minutes, or until slightly softened. Reduce the heat to low and cook the onions for a further 15 minutes, stirring occasionally, until they start to caramelize. Stir in the sugar and cook for a further 5 minutes, or until caramelized.

Put the horseradish cream ingredients in a small bowl. Mix well, season to taste and refrigerate until needed.

Once the beef has rested, cut it into 1 cm ($^1/_2$ in) thick slices. Arrange the beef on four serving plates and top with the horseradish cream and caramelized onion. Scatter with some thyme sprigs and serve with steamed potatoes.

# fragrant dry beef curry

serves 4

## ingredients

**curry paste**
2 tablespoons cumin seeds
2 tablespoons coriander seeds
3 green cardamom pods
2 teaspoons white peppercorns
2 teaspoons grated fresh ginger
4 garlic cloves, crushed
2 red onions, roughly chopped
4 long red chillies
2 large handfuls coriander (cilantro) leaves,
    chopped

3 tablespoons olive oil
1 kg (2 lb 4 oz) chuck steak, cut into 3 cm
    (1$^1/_4$ in) pieces
400 g (14 oz) tinned chopped tomatoes
2 tablespoons tomato paste (concentrated purée)
300 ml (10$^1/_2$ fl oz) beef stock
200 g (7 oz) plain yoghurt
2 large handfuls coriander (cilantro) leaves,
    chopped
basmati rice, naan bread and pappadams,
    to serve

## method

In a heavy-based saucepan over medium heat, lightly toast the cumin, coriander, cardamom and peppercorns until fragrant. Cool and crush using a mortar and pestle or spice mill.

Blend all the curry paste ingredients in a food processor until a smooth paste forms.

Heat 2 tablespoons of the oil in a large heavy-based saucepan. Brown the beef in batches over medium heat. Remove from the saucepan.

In the same saucepan, heat the remaining olive oil and fry the curry paste, stirring, for 3 minutes, or until fragrant.

Return the beef to the saucepan and add the chopped tomatoes, tomato paste, and stock. Reduce the heat to low, stir and cover with the lid. Simmer for 1 hour, stirring occasionally.

Remove the lid from the saucepan, stir and simmer for a further 30 minutes, or until the beef is tender and the sauce has reduced by half. Season to taste.

Add the yoghurt and coriander just before serving. Serve with basmati rice, naan bread and pappadams.

# slow-cooked lamb shanks

serves 4

## ingredients

2 tablespoons olive oil
8 French trimmed lamb shanks
1 onion, chopped
2 garlic cloves, crushed
3 dried mace blades or $1^1/_2$ teaspoons ground
    mace
2 teaspoons garam masala
500 ml (17 fl oz/2 cups) tomato pasta sauce
375 ml (13 fl oz/$1^1/_2$ cups) beef stock
1 tablespoon thyme
mashed potato, to serve

## method

Preheat the oven to 150°C (300°F/Gas 2). Heat the oil in a large roasting pan or flameproof casserole dish and cook the lamb in batches for 5 minutes, or until browned all over. Remove from the pan and set aside. Add the onion and garlic to the pan and cook over medium heat for 3 minutes, or until soft. Stir in the mace and garam masala and cook for 30 seconds, or until fragrant.

Return the lamb to the pan with the pasta sauce and stock and bring to a boil. Cover tightly with a lid or foil.

Roast in the oven, covered, for about 4 hours, turning twice during cooking. Serve the lamb sprinkled with the thyme and accompanied by mashed potato.

# marinated lamb with Moroccan spiced carrot salad

serves 4

## ingredients

### Lamb marinade

15 g ($^1/_2$ oz) finely chopped flat-leaf (Italian)
  parsley
20 g ($^3/_4$ oz) finely chopped coriander (cilantro)
  leaves
4 garlic cloves, crushed
1 tablespoon paprika
1 teaspoon dried thyme
125 ml (4 fl oz/$^1/_2$ cup) olive oil
3 tablespoons lemon juice
2 teaspoons ground cumin

4 x 250 g (9 oz) lamb rumps or pieces
  of tenderloin, trimmed

### Carrot salad

4 carrots, peeled, trimmed and halved
  on the diagonal
4 tablespoons olive oil
2 teaspoons ground cumin
95 g ($3^1/_4$ oz/$^1/_2$ cup) Kalamata olives, pitted
  and halved lengthways
1 small handful flat-leaf (Italian) parsley
1 teaspoon harissa
2 tablespoons extra virgin olive oil
1 tablespoon red wine vinegar

## method

Mix the parsley, coriander, garlic, paprika, thyme, oil, lemon juice and $1^1/_2$ teaspoons cumin together in a non-metallic dish. Score diagonal lines in the fat on the lamb pieces with a sharp knife, then put them in the marinade, turning so they are evenly coated. Cover and refrigerate for at least 2 hours or overnight.

To make the spiced carrot salad, preheat the flat plate to low. Bring a saucepan of salted water to the boil and blanch the carrots for 3 minutes, or until they just begin to soften. Drain, pat dry with paper towels, then toss them with 2 tablespoons of the olive oil and 1 teaspoon of the cumin. Cook the carrots for 25 minutes, turning them once so they are cooked through and golden all over.

While the carrots are still warm, cut them into thin diagonal slices and toss them with the olives and parsley. Mix the harissa with 1 tablespoon of water, add the extra virgin olive oil, red wine vinegar, remaining olive oil and remaining cumin, and whisk it together. Pour the dressing over the salad and season to taste with salt and pepper.

Increase the heat under the flat plate to medium direct heat.

# niçoise salad with fresh tuna

serves 4

## ingredients

### dressing
6 anchovy fillets, drained
2 tablespoons red wine vinegar
1 large garlic clove, crushed
125 ml (4 fl oz/$^1/_2$ cup) olive oil

750 g (1 lb 10 oz) new potatoes
1 cos (romaine) lettuce, shredded
1 Lebanese (short) cucumber, cut into 1 cm
    ($^1/_2$ in) slices on the diagonal
$^1/_2$ red capsicum (pepper), thinly sliced
200 g (7 oz) green beans, trimmed and blanched
2 tomatoes, each cut into 8 wedges
1 small red onion, cut into thin wedges
200 g (7 oz) Niçoise or Ligurian olives
$2^1/_2$ handfuls basil leaves, torn
olive oil, for brushing
600 g (1 lb 5 oz) fresh tuna steaks
3 hard-boiled eggs, quartered

## method

To make the dressing, put the anchovies, vinegar and garlic in a food processor and blend until the anchovies are finely chopped. With the motor running, slowly add the oil and blend until combined.

Bring a large saucepan of water to the boil. Add the potatoes and cook for about 10 minutes, or until tender. Drain well, allow to cool a little, then peel and cut into 1 cm ($^1/_2$ in) slices. Put the potato in a large bowl with the lettuce, cucumber, capsicum, beans, tomato, onion, olives and basil. Pour the dressing over and gently toss until combined.

Preheat a barbecue grill plate or chargrill pan to high. Brush the hotplate with oil and cook the tuna for 2 minutes on each side—it should still be a little pink in the middle. Slice the tuna into 2 cm ($^3/_4$ in) cubes.

Arrange the salad on four serving plates and top with the tuna and egg quarters. Season.

# crab salad with green mango and coconut

serves 4

## ingredients

### dressing

2 garlic cloves, peeled
1 small red chilli
$1^1/_2$ tablespoons dried shrimp
$1^1/_2$ tablespoons fish sauce
2 tablespoons lime juice
2 teaspoons palm sugar or soft brown sugar

4 tablespoons shredded coconut
200 g (7 oz/2 cups) shredded green mango
1 small handful mint leaves
1 small handful coriander (cilantro) leaves
2 kaffir (makrut) lime leaves, shredded
$1^1/_2$ teaspoons thinly shredded pickled ginger
350 g (12 oz) fresh crab meat
4 small squares banana leaves (optional)
50 g ($1^3/_4$ oz/$^1/_3$ cup) chopped toasted unsalted
   peanuts
4 lime wedges

## method

Preheat the oven to 180°C (350°F/Gas 4). To make the dressing, pound the garlic, chilli, dried shrimp and $^1/_2$ teaspoon salt to a paste in a mortar and pestle. Whisk in the fish sauce, lime juice and sugar with a fork.

Spread the shredded coconut on a baking tray and bake for 1–2 minutes, shaking the tray occasionally to ensure even toasting. Watch the coconut closely, as it will burn easily.

Put the shredded mango in a large bowl and add the mint, coriander, lime leaves, ginger, coconut and crab meat. Pour the dressing over the top and toss together gently.

If using the banana leaves, place a square in each serving bowl (the leaves are for presentation only and are not edible). Mound some crab salad on top, sprinkle with the peanuts and serve immediately with lime wedges.

# prawn, mango and macadamia salad

serves 4–6

## ingredients

1 radicchio heart

25 g (1 oz/$^1$/$_2$ cup) basil leaves, torn

30 g (1 oz/1 cup) watercress sprigs

24 cooked king prawns (shrimp), peeled and deveined with tails intact

3 tablespoons macadamia oil

3 tablespoons extra virgin olive oil

150 g (5$^1$/$_2$ oz/1 cup) macadamia nuts, coarsely chopped

2 garlic cloves, crushed

3 tablespoons lemon juice

1 ripe mango, cut into small dice

## method

Remove the outer green leaves from the radicchio, leaving only the tender pink leaves. Tear any large leaves in half and arrange in a shallow serving bowl. Scatter with half of the basil leaves and the watercress, and toss lightly. Arrange the prawns over the salad leaves.

Heat the oils in a small frying pan over medium heat. Add the nuts and cook for 5 minutes, or until golden. Add the garlic and cook for a further 30 seconds, then remove from the heat and add the lemon juice and mango. Season to taste, pour over the salad and scatter with the remaining basil leaves.

# radicchio with figs and ginger vinaigrette

serves 4

## ingredients

1 radicchio lettuce
1 baby frisée (curly endive)
3 oranges
$1/2$ small red onion, thinly sliced into rings
8 small green figs, quartered
3 tablespoons extra virgin olive oil
1 teaspoon red wine vinegar
$1/8$ teaspoon ground cinnamon
2 tablespoons orange juice
2 tablespoons very finely chopped glacé ginger,
    with 2 teaspoons syrup
2 pomegranates, sliced in half (optional)

## method

Wash the radicchio and frisée leaves thoroughly and drain well. Tear any large leaves into bite-sized pieces and toss in a salad bowl.

Peel and segment the oranges, discarding all the bitter white pith. Add to the salad leaves with the onion and figs, reserving eight fig quarters. Whisk the oil, vinegar, cinnamon, orange juice, ginger and ginger syrup in a small jug. Season to taste, pour over the salad and toss lightly.

Arrange the reserved figs in pairs over the salad. If you are using the pomegranates, scoop out the seeds, scatter over the salad and serve.

# chargrilled polenta with shaved fennel salad

serves 4

## ingredients

500 ml (17 fl oz/2 cups) milk
175 g (6 oz) polenta (cornmeal)
35 g (1$^1$/$_4$ oz/$^1$/$_3$ cup) grated parmesan cheese,
   plus 100 g (3$^1$/$_2$ oz/1 cup) shaved parmesan
   cheese
20 g ($^3$/$_4$ oz) butter
2 baby fennel bulbs, trimmed (reserve the fronds)
40 g (1$^1$/$_2$ oz/1$^1$/$_3$ cups) picked watercress leaves
3 teaspoon lemon juice
1$^1$/$_2$ tablespoons olive oil

## method

Bring the milk and 500 ml (17 fl oz/2 cups) water to the boil in a heavy-based saucepan. Add the polenta in a thin, steady stream and whisk thoroughly. Reduce the heat as low as possible and simmer for 30–40 minutes, stirring occasionally. Remove from the heat, stir in the grated parmesan and butter and season well. Pour into an oiled square dish and leave for 30 minutes to set. When cold, cut into four squares, then cut each square diagonally to give eight triangles. Brush with a little oil and cook on a hot chargrill pan (griddle) or barbecue hotplate until crisp brown grill marks appear.

Slice the fennel very thinly and chop the fronds. Toss in a bowl with the watercress, lemon juice, oil and half the shaved parmesan. Season well. Stack two polenta triangles on four serving plates, pile the salad on top, scatter with the remaining shaved parmesan and serve.

# smoked trout and kipfler potato salad

serves 4

## ingredients

6 hickory woodchips
2 rainbow trout
1 tablespoon oil
750 g (1 lb 10 oz) even-sized kipfler (fingerling)
    potatoes, peeled
3 baby fennel bulbs, cut into quarters, then into
    eighths
2 tablespoons olive oil
40 g (1$^1/_2$ oz/2 cups) watercress sprigs

### dill and caper dressing
125 g (4$^1/_2$ oz/$^1/_2$ cup) whole-egg mayonnaise
2 garlic cloves, crushed
1 tablespoon chopped dill
1 tablespoon baby capers, drained, rinsed and
    chopped
1 tablespoon lemon juice

## method

Soak the woodchips in water overnight, or for a minimum of 30 minutes. Preheat a covered barbecue to low indirect heat. Allow the coals to burn down to ash, then add three hickory woodchips to each pile of coals. When the chips begin to smoke, brush the trout with the oil, place in the middle of the barbecue, then lower the lid and cook for 10–15 minutes, or until cooked through. Preheat the barbecue chargrill plate to medium–high.

Bring a saucepan of water to the boil on the stovetop. Add the potatoes to the pan and cook for 5 minutes, or until almost tender. Drain and allow to cool slightly. Combine the dill and caper dressing ingredients in a bowl and refrigerate.

Cut the potatoes into 1.5 cm ($^5/_8$ in) slices on the diagonal. Place in a bowl with the fennel and olive oil, season and toss to coat. Chargrill the potatoes for 5 minutes on each side, or until golden and cooked. Remove from the heat and place in a serving bowl. Chargrill the fennel for 2–3 minutes on each side, or until golden, then add to the potato slices. Remove the skin from the smoked trout and gently pull the flesh away from the bones. Flake the flesh into pieces and add to the potato with the watercress and fennel. Pour on the dressing and serve.

# nanna's favourites

We might be getting more sophisticated in our eating habits but
nothing can beat the taste of those old fashioned favourites.
scones, chocolate pudding, macaroons, shortbread, brownies,
apple pie, various jams and other
timeless goodies passed down through the generations
never go out of date ... mmmm, nobody cooks quite like nanna!

# easy sponge cake with strawberries and cream

serves 6

## ingredients

30 g (1 oz) butter, melted
60 g (2$^1/_4$ oz/$^1/_2$ cup) plain (all-purpose) flour
60 g (2$^1/_4$ oz/$^1/_2$ cup) cornflour (cornstarch)
2 teaspoons cream of tartar
1 teaspoon bicarbonate of soda (baking soda)
4 eggs
170 g (6 oz/$^3/_4$ cup) caster (superfine) sugar
2 tablespoons hot milk
300 ml (10$^1/_2$ fl oz) whipping (pouring) cream
1 tablespoon icing (confectioners') sugar, plus
   extra for dusting
2 tablespoons strawberry jam
500 g (1 lb 2 oz/3$^1/_3$ cups) strawberries, hulled
   and sliced in half

## method

Preheat the oven to 180°C (350°F/Gas 4). Grease two 20 cm (8 in) round cake tins with the melted butter and line the bases with baking paper. Dust the sides of the tins with a little flour, shaking out any excess.

Sift the flour, cornflour, cream of tartar and bicarbonate of soda into a bowl, then repeat the sifting twice more.

Whisk the eggs and sugar in a large bowl for 5 minutes, or until pale and thick. Using a large metal spoon, carefully fold in the sifted flour mixture and the hot milk until they are just incorporated; take care not to overmix. Divide the mixture evenly between the two tins, then bake for 18–20 minutes, or until the cakes are golden and have shrunk slightly from the side of the tins. Leave in the tins for 5 minutes, then turn out onto a wire rack to cool.

Combine the cream and icing sugar in a bowl, then whip until soft peaks form. Place one sponge cake on a serving plate and spread with jam. Top with half the cream and half of the sliced strawberries. Cover with the second sponge cake. Spread the remaining cream over the top and top with the remaining strawberries. Dust with icing sugar and serve immediately.

# anzac biscuits

makes about 25

## ingredients

125 g ($4^1/_2$ oz/1 cup) plain (all-purpose) flour
100 g ($3^1/_2$ oz/1 cup) rolled oats
65 g ($2^1/_4$ oz/$^3/_4$ cup) desiccated coconut
170 g (6 oz/$^3/_4$ cup) caster (superfine) sugar
125 g ($4^1/_2$ oz) butter
1 tablespoon golden syrup or honey
$1^1/_2$ teaspoons bicarbonate of soda (baking soda)
2 tablespoons boiling water

## method

Preheat the oven to 150°C (300°F/Gas 2). Lightly grease
two baking trays with melted butter or oil. Place the flour, oats,
coconut and sugar in a large mixing bowl. Stir until combined.

Combine the butter and golden syrup in a small saucepan and
stir over high heat until melted. Mix the soda with boiling
water, and add to the melted butter and syrup. Add to the
flour mixture and stir until combined.

Shape level tablespoonsful of mixture into balls and flatten
slightly. Place onto prepared trays about 6 cm ($2^1/_2$ in) apart.

Bake for 15–20 minutes, or until crisp and golden. Remove
from the oven and stand for 2 minutes. Loosen biscuits and
allow to cool on a wire rack.

# rock cakes

makes about 20

### ingredients

250 g (9 oz/2 cups) self-raising flour
90 g (3 1/4 oz) unsalted butter, chilled, cubed
125 g (4$^1$/$_2$ oz/$^1$/$_2$ cup) caster (superfine) sugar
95 g (3 oz/$^1$/$_2$ cup) mixed dried fruit
$^1$/$_2$ teaspoon ground ginger
1 egg
3 tablespoons milk

### method

Preheat the oven to 200°C (400°F/Gas 6). Grease two baking trays. Sift the flour into a large bowl and rub in the butter with your fingertips until the mixture resembles fine breadcrumbs. Stir in the sugar, fruit and ginger.

Whisk the egg into the milk in a bowl, add to the dry ingredients and mix to a stiff dough. Drop rough heaps of mixture, about 3 tablespoons at a time, onto the trays.

Bake for 10–15 minutes, or until golden. Allow to cool on a wire rack.

# coconut macaroons

makes about 64

## ingredients

4 egg whites, lightly beaten
450 g (1 lb/2 cups) caster (superfine) sugar
1¹/₂ tablespoons liquid glucose
1¹/₂ teaspoons natural vanilla extract
180 g (6 oz/2 cups) desiccated coconut
125 g (4¹/₂ oz/1 cup) plain (all-purpose) flour

## method

Combine the egg whites, sugar and liquid glucose in a large heatproof bowl and whisk to combine. Place the bowl over a saucepan of simmering water and whisk until the mixture is just warm. Remove from the heat and add the vanilla, coconut and flour and stir to combine well. Cover the bowl with plastic wrap and refrigerate the mixture until firm.

Meanwhile, preheat the oven to 150°C (300°F/Gas 2). Line two baking trays with baking paper.

Take a heaped teaspoonful of the mixture and, using wet hands, form the mixture into balls. Flatten the balls slightly and place them on the trays, spacing them apart. Bake for 15 minutes, or until the macaroons are light golden, swapping the position of the trays halfway through cooking. Allow to cool for 5 minutes on the tray, then transfer to a wire rack to cool completely.

# passionfruit melting moments

makes 14 filled biscuits

## ingredients

250 g (9 oz) unsalted butter
40 g (1$^1$/$_2$ oz/$^1$/$_3$ cup) icing (confectioners') sugar
1 teaspoon natural vanilla extract
185 g (6$^1$/$_2$ oz/1$^1$/$_2$ cups) self-raising flour
60 g (2$^1$/$_4$ oz/$^1$/$_2$ cup) custard powder

### passionfruit filling

60 g (2$^1$/$_4$ oz) unsalted butter
60 g (2$^1$/$_4$ oz/$^1$/$_2$ cup) icing (confectioners') sugar
1$^1$/$_2$ tablespoons passionfruit pulp

## method

Preheat the oven to 180°C (350°F/Gas 4). Line two baking trays with baking paper. Beat the butter and sugar until light and creamy. Beat in the natural vanilla extract. Sift in the flour and custard powder and mix to a soft dough.

Roll level tablespoons of the mixture into 28 balls and place on the trays. Flatten slightly with a floured fork.

Bake for 20 minutes, or until lightly golden. Allow to cool on a wire rack.

To make the filling, beat the butter and sugar until light and creamy, then beat in the passionfruit pulp. Use the filling to sandwich the biscuits together. Leave to firm before serving.

# brandy snaps

makes 15

## ingredients

60 g (2$^1/_4$ oz) unsalted butter
2 tablespoons golden syrup or honey
60 g (2$^1/_4$ oz/$^1/_3$ cup) soft brown sugar
30 g (1 oz/$^1/_4$ cup) plain (all-purpose) flour
1$^1/_2$ teaspoons ground ginger
60 g (2$^1/_4$ oz) dark chocolate, chopped

## method

Preheat the oven to 180°C (350°F/Gas 4). Line two baking trays with baking paper. Put the butter, golden syrup and sugar in a saucepan over low heat and stir until the butter has melted and the sugar has dissolved. Remove from the heat and add the sifted flour and ground ginger to the saucepan. Stir the mixture until the ingredients are well combined.

Using 3 level teaspoons of the mixture for each brandy snap, drop the mixture onto the trays about 12 cm (5 in) apart. Bake for 5–6 minutes, or until lightly browned. Leave the biscuits on the trays for 30 seconds then, while still hot, lift one biscuit off the tray, using a large flat knife or spatula, and wrap around the handle of a thin wooden spoon. Slide the biscuit off the spoon and set aside to cool while you curl the remaining brandy snaps. Repeat to use all the mixture.

Put the chopped chocolate in a heatproof bowl. Bring a saucepan of water to the boil, remove from the heat and place the bowl over the water, making sure the base of the bowl doesn't touch the water. Stir occasionally until melted.

Dip both ends of each brandy snap in the melted chocolate and leave to dry on a foil-lined tray.

# jam drops

makes about 45

## ingredients

250 g (9 oz) unsalted butter, softened
140 g (5 oz) icing (confectioners') sugar
1 egg yolk, lightly beaten
90 g (3$^1/_4$ oz) cream cheese, softened and cut into
   chunks
1$^1/_2$ teaspoons natural vanilla extract
1 teaspoon finely grated lemon zest
350 g (12 oz/2$^3/_4$ cups) plain (all-purpose) flour,
   sifted
$^1/_4$ teaspoon baking powder
$^1/_2$ teaspoon bicarbonate of soda (baking soda)
2 tablespoons each apricot, blueberry and
   raspberry jam

## method

Preheat the oven to 180°C (350°F/Gas 4) and grease three baking trays.

Cream the butter, icing sugar and egg yolk in a bowl using electric beaters until pale and fluffy, then beat in the cream cheese, vanilla and lemon zest until smooth. Combine the flour, baking powder, bicarbonate of soda and $^1/_4$ teaspoon salt in a large bowl and, using a wooden spoon, gradually stir into the creamed mixture until a soft dough forms. Set aside for 5–10 minutes, or until the dough firms up.

Break off small pieces of dough, shape into balls and flatten slightly to make 4 cm (1$^1/_2$ in) rounds. Transfer to the prepared trays and make a small indent in the centre of each with your thumb. Spoon about $^1/_4$ teaspoon of apricot jam into one-third of the biscuits, $^1/_4$ teaspoon blueberry jam into one-third, and $^1/_4$ teaspoon of raspberry jam into the remaining one-third of the biscuits. Bake for 10–12 minutes, or until light golden. Cool for a few minutes on the trays, then transfer to a wire rack.

# neenish tarts

makes 12

## ingredients

2 tablespoons plain (all-purpose) flour
60 g (2$^1$/$_4$ oz/$^2$/$_3$ cup) ground almonds
60 g (2$^1$/$_4$ oz/$^1$/$_2$ cup) icing (confectioners') sugar,
    sifted
1 egg white, lightly beaten

### creamy filling
1 tablespoon plain (all-purpose) flour
125 ml (4 fl oz/$^1$/$_2$ cup) milk
2 egg yolks
60 g (2$^1$/$_4$ oz) unsalted butter, softened
2 tablespoons caster (superfine) sugar
$^1$/$_4$ teaspoon natural vanilla extract

### icing
125 g (4$^1$/$_2$ oz/1 cup) icing (confectioners') sugar
2 tablespoons milk, extra
1 tablespoon unsweetened cocoa powder

## method

Lightly grease a 12-hole patty tin. Sift the flour into a bowl and add the almonds and icing sugar. Make a well in the centre, add the egg white and mix with a flat-bladed knife, until a stiff paste forms. Turn onto a floured surface and gather into a ball. Wrap in plastic wrap and refrigerate for 30 minutes. Preheat the oven to 190°C (375°F/Gas 5). Roll out the dough between two sheets of baking paper to 3 mm ($^1$/$_8$ in) thick. Cut the pastry into 12 circles with a 7 cm (2$^3$/$_4$ in) fluted cutter. Press the pastry circles into the greased patty tin and prick evenly with a fork. Bake for 10 minutes, or until lightly golden.

To make the filling, stir the flour and milk in a saucepan over medium heat for 2 minutes. Remove from the heat, then stir in the egg yolks. Cover with plastic wrap and set aside. Using electric beaters, beat the butter, sugar and vanilla until creamy. Add the egg mixture and beat until smooth. Spoon some of the mixture in the pastry shells. Smooth the tops with a spoon.

To make the icing, combine the icing sugar and milk in a heatproof bowl, place over a saucepan of simmering water and stir until smooth. Remove, transfer half the icing to a bowl, add the cocoa and stir until smooth. Using a flat-bladed knife, spread plain icing over half of each tart. Allow to set. Reheat the chocolate icing and ice the other half of each tart.

# custard tarts

makes 12

## ingredients

250 g (9 oz/2 cups) plain (all-purpose) flour
60 g (2$^1/_4$ oz/$^1/_3$ cup) rice flour
30 g (1 oz/$^1/_4$ cup) icing (confectioners') sugar
120 g (4$^1/_4$ oz) unsalted butter, chilled, cubed
1 egg yolk
3 tablespoons iced water
1 egg white, lightly beaten

### custard filling

3 eggs
375 ml (13 fl oz/1$^1/_2$ cups) milk
60 g (2$^1/_4$ oz/$^1/_4$ cup) caster (superfine) sugar
1 teaspoon natural vanilla extract
$^1/_2$ teaspoon ground nutmeg

## method

Sift the flours and icing sugar into a bowl and rub in the butter until the mixture resembles fine breadcrumbs. Make a well and add the egg yolk and almost all the water. Mix with a flat-bladed knife, until the mixture comes together in beads. Gather together and roll out between two sheets of baking paper. Divide the dough into 12 equal portions and roll each portion out to fit the base and side of a 10 cm (4 in) loose-based fluted tart tin. Line the tins with the pastry and roll the rolling pin over the tins to cut off any excess pastry. Refrigerate for 20 minutes.

Preheat the oven to 180°C (350°F/Gas 4). Line each pastry-lined tin with crumpled baking paper. Fill with baking beads or uncooked rice. Place the tins on two large baking trays and bake for 10 minutes. Remove the baking paper and beads and return the trays to the oven. Bake for 10 minutes, or until the pastry is lightly golden. Cool. Brush the base and side of each pastry case with beaten egg white. Reduce the oven temperature to 150°C (300°F/Gas 2).

To make the filling, whisk the eggs and milk in a bowl to combine. Add the sugar gradually, whisking to dissolve. Stir in the natural vanilla extract. Strain into a jug, then pour into the cooled pastry cases. Sprinkle with nutmeg and bake for 25 minutes, or until the filling is just set.

# chocolate chip cookies

makes 16

## ingredients

125 g (4$^1$/$_2$ oz) unsalted butter
185 g (6$^1$/$_2$ oz/1 cup) soft brown sugar
1 teaspoon natural vanilla extract
1 egg, lightly beaten
1 tablespoon milk
215 g (7$^1$/$_2$ oz/1$^3$/$_4$ cups) plain (all-purpose) flour
1 teaspoon baking powder
250 g (9 oz/1$^1$/$_2$ cups) dark chocolate chips

## method

Preheat the oven to 180°C (350°F/Gas 4). Line a large baking tray with baking paper.

Cream the butter and sugar with electric beaters in a large bowl. Mix in the natural vanilla extract and gradually add the egg, beating well. Stir in the milk. Sift the flour and baking powder into a large bowl, then fold into the butter and egg mixture. Stir in the dark chocolate bits.

Drop level tablespoons of the cookie mixture onto the baking tray, leaving about 4 cm (1$^1$/$_2$ in) between each cookie, then lightly press with a floured fork. Bake for 15 minutes, or until lightly golden. Cool on a wire rack.

# butterfly cupcakes

makes 12

## ingredients

120 g (4$^1$/$_2$ oz) unsalted butter, softened
180 g (6$^1$/$_2$ oz/$^3$/$_4$ cup) caster (superfine) sugar
185 g (6$^1$/$_2$ oz/1$^1$/$_2$ cups) self-raising flour
125 ml (4 fl oz/$^1$/$_2$ cup) milk
2 eggs
125 ml (4 fl oz/$^1$/$_2$ cup) thick (double/heavy)
    cream
1$^1$/$_2$ tablespoons strawberry jam
icing (confectioners') sugar, to dust

## method

Preheat the oven to 180°C (350°F/Gas 4). Line a flat-bottomed 12-hole cupcake tray with paper patty cases.

Beat the butter, sugar, flour, milk and eggs with electric beaters on low speed. Increase the speed and beat until smooth and pale. Divide evenly among the cases and bake for 30 minutes, or until cooked and golden. Transfer to a wire rack to cool.

Cut shallow rounds from the centre of each cake using the point of a sharp knife, then cut in half. Spoon 2 teaspoons of cream into each cavity, top with 1 teaspoon of jam and position two halves of the cake tops in the jam to resemble butterfly wings. Dust with icing sugar.

# coconut ice

makes 30 pieces

## ingredients

250 g (9 oz/2 cups) icing (confectioners') sugar
$^1/_4$ teaspoon cream of tartar
400 g (14 oz) tinned condensed milk
315 g (11 oz/3$^1/_2$ cups) desiccated coconut
2–3 drops pink food colouring

## method

Grease a 20 cm (8 in) square cake tin and line the base with baking paper.

Sift the icing sugar and cream of tartar into a bowl. Make a well and add the condensed milk. Using a wooden spoon, stir in half the coconut, then the remaining coconut. Mix well with your hands. Divide in half and tint one half pink. Using your hand, knead the colour through evenly.

Press the pink mixture over the base of the tin, cover with the white mixture and press down firmly. Refrigerate for 1–2 hours, or until firm. Remove from the tin, remove the paper and cut into pieces.

# classic shortbread

makes 16 wedges

## ingredients

225 g (8 oz) unsalted butter
115 g (4 oz/$^1/_2$ cup) caster (superfine) sugar, plus
   extra for dusting
225 g (8 oz/1$^3/_4$ cups) plain (all-purpose) flour
115 g (4 oz/$^2/_3$ cup) rice flour

## method

Preheat the oven to 190°C (375°F/Gas 5). Lightly grease two baking trays.

Cream the butter and sugar in a bowl using electric beaters until pale and fluffy. Sift in the flour, rice flour and a pinch of salt and, using a wooden spoon, stir into the creamed mixture until it resembles fine breadcrumbs. Transfer to a lightly floured work surface and knead gently to form a soft dough. Cover with plastic wrap and refrigerate for 30 minutes.

Divide the dough in half and roll out one half on a lightly floured work surface to form a 20 cm (8 in) round. Carefully transfer to a prepared tray. Using a sharp knife, score the surface of the dough into eight equal wedges, prick the surface lightly with a fork and, using your fingers, press the edges to form a fluted effect. Repeat this process using the remaining dough to make a second round. Lightly dust the shortbreads with the extra sugar.

Bake for 18–20 minutes, or until the shortbreads are light golden. Remove from the oven and while still hot, follow the score marks and cut into wedges. Cool on the baking tray for 5 minutes, then transfer to a wire rack.

# walnut brownies

makes 24 pieces

## ingredients

85 g (3 oz/$^2$/$_3$ cup) self-raising flour
85 g (3 oz/$^2$/$_3$ cup) cocoa powder
250 g (9 oz/1 cup) caster (superfine) sugar
330 g (11$^1$/$_2$ oz) unsalted butter, melted
4 eggs, lightly beaten
1 teaspoon natural vanilla extract
250 g (9 oz/1$^1$/$_2$ cups) dark chocolate chips
125 g (4$^1$/$_2$ oz/1 cup) walnut pieces
icing (confectioners') sugar, to dust

## method

Preheat the oven to 180°C (350°F/Gas 4). Grease a 20 x 30 cm (8 x 12 in) shallow baking tin and line with baking paper, leaving it hanging over the two long sides.

Sift together the flour and cocoa, then add the sugar. Make a well in the centre, then add the butter, eggs and vanilla and beat until smooth. Fold in the chocolate chips and walnuts.

Spoon into the tin and smooth the surface. Bake for 25 minutes, or until a skewer inserted into the centre comes out clean. Leave in the tin for 10 minutes, then turn onto a wire rack to cool. Dust with icing sugar.

# berry and apple slice

makes 12 pieces

## ingredients

150 g (5$^1$/$_2$ oz) unsalted butter
320 g (11$^1$/$_4$ oz/1$^1$/$_3$ cups) caster (superfine) sugar
2 eggs, lightly beaten
250 g (9 oz/2 cups) self-raising flour, sifted
160 ml (5$^1$/$_4$ fl oz/$^2$/$_3$ cup) buttermilk
1 teaspoon natural vanilla extract
2 large apples
150 g (5$^1$/$_2$ oz/1 cup) blueberries
150 g (5$^1$/$_2$ oz/1$^1$/$_4$ cups) blackberries
icing (confectioners') sugar, to dust

## method

Preheat the oven to 180°C (350°F/Gas 4). Lightly grease a 30 x 20 cm (12 x 8 in) shallow baking tin and line with baking paper, leaving it hanging over the two long sides.

Beat the butter and sugar with electric beaters until light and fluffy. Add the egg gradually, beating well after each addition. Stir in the flour and buttermilk alternately and mix until smooth. Stir through the vanilla. Spread a 5 mm ($^1$/$_4$ in) layer of mixture over the base of the tin.

Peel, quarter and core the apples. Cut into very thin slices and arrange on the mixture. Spoon the remaining mixture over the apple and smooth the surface, then scatter with the blueberries and blackberries. Bake on the middle rack for 40 minutes, or until cooked and golden.

Cool in the tin for 30 minutes before lifting onto a wire rack. Dust with icing sugar and cut into squares.

# gingerbread

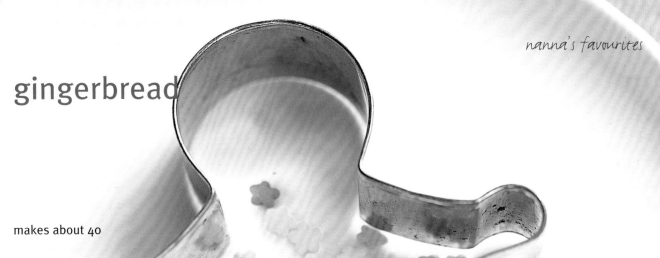

**makes about 40**

### ingredients

350 g (12 oz) plain (all-purpose) flour
2 teaspoons baking powder
2 teaspoons ground ginger
100 g ($3^1/_2$ oz) chilled unsalted butter, diced
175 g (6 oz/$^3/_4$ cup) soft brown sugar
1 egg, beaten
115 g (4 oz/$^1/_3$ cup) dark treacle
silver balls (optional)

### icing glaze

1 egg white
3 teaspoons lemon juice
155 g ($5^1/_2$ oz/$1^1/_4$ cups) icing (confectioners')
   sugar

### royal icing

1 egg white
200 g (7 oz) icing (confectioners') sugar

### method

Preheat the oven to 190°C (375°F/Gas 5). Lightly grease two baking trays. Sift the flour, baking powder, ground ginger and a pinch of salt into a bowl. Rub in the butter until the mixture resembles fine breadcrumbs, then stir in the sugar. Make a well in the centre, add the egg and treacle and stir until a soft dough forms. Transfer to a clean surface and knead until smooth.

Divide the dough in half and roll out on a lightly floured work surface until 5 mm ($^1/_4$ in) thick. Using various-shaped cutters, cut into desired shapes, then transfer to the trays. Bake in batches for 8 minutes, or until the biscuits are light brown. Cool on the trays for 2–3 minutes, then transfer to a wire rack.

To make the glaze, whisk the egg white and lemon juice together until foamy, then whisk in the icing sugar to form a smooth, thin icing. Cover the surface with plastic wrap.

To make the royal icing, lightly whisk the egg white until just foamy, then gradually whisk in enough icing sugar to form a soft icing. Cover the surface with plastic wrap until needed.

Brush a layer of glaze over some of the biscuits and leave to set. Use an icing bag filled with royal icing to decorate.

# finger buns

makes 12

## ingredients

500 g (1 lb 2 oz/4 cups) plain (all-purpose) flour
35 g (1$^1$/$_4$ oz/$^1$/$_3$ cup) full-cream milk powder
15 g ($^1$/$_2$ oz) dried yeast
125 g (4$^1$/$_2$ oz/$^1$/$_2$ cup) caster (superfine) sugar
80 g (2$^3$/$_4$ oz/$^1$/$_2$ cup) sultanas
60 g (2$^1$/$_4$ oz) unsalted butter, melted
1 egg, lightly beaten
1 egg yolk, extra, to glaze

### glacé icing

155 g (5$^1$/$_2$ oz/1$^1$/$_4$ cups) icing (confectioners')
  sugar
20 g ($^3$/$_4$ oz) unsalted butter, melted
pink food colouring

## method

Mix 375 g (12 oz/3 cups) of the flour with the milk powder, yeast, sugar, sultanas and $^1$/$_2$ teaspoon salt in a bowl. Make a well in the centre. Combine the butter, egg and 250 ml (9 fl oz/ 1 cup) of warm water and add to the flour. Stir for 2 minutes. Add enough of the remaining flour to make a soft dough. Turn out onto a lightly floured surface. Knead for 10 minutes, or until the dough is smooth and elastic, adding more flour if necessary. Place in a lightly oiled bowl and brush with oil. Cover with plastic wrap and leave in a warm place for 1 hour.

Lightly grease two large baking trays. Preheat the oven to 180°C (350°F/Gas 4). Punch down the dough and knead for 1 minute. Divide into 12 pieces. Shape each into a 15 cm (6 in) long oval. Put on the trays 5 cm (2 in) apart. Cover with plastic wrap and set aside in a warm place for 20–25 minutes.

Mix the extra egg yolk with 1$^1$/$_2$ teaspoons water and brush over the dough. Bake for 12–15 minutes, until firm and golden.

To make the glacé icing, stir the icing sugar, melted butter and 2–3 teaspoons water together in a bowl until smooth. Mix in the food colouring and spread over the tops of the buns.

# cream buns

makes 12

## ingredients

7 g ($^1/_4$ oz) dried yeast
2 tablespoons sugar
350 ml (12 fl oz) milk, warmed
435 g (15$^1/_4$ oz/3$^1/_2$ cups) plain (all-purpose) flour
60 g (2$^1/_4$ oz) unsalted butter, melted
160 g (5$^3/_4$ oz/$^1/_2$ cup) strawberry jam
315 ml (10$^3/_4$ fl oz/1$^1/_4$ cups) cream
1 tablespoon icing (confectioners') sugar, plus
    extra, to dust

## method

Put the yeast, 1 teaspoon of sugar and the milk in a bowl and leave in a warm place for 10 minutes, or until bubbles appear. Sift the flour into a large bowl, stir in the remaining sugar and $^1/_2$ teaspoon salt. Make a well and add the milk mixture and butter and mix to a dough. Turn onto a floured surface and knead for 10 minutes, or until smooth. Place in an oiled bowl, cover with plastic wrap, and leave in a warm place for 1 hour.

Punch down the dough and turn onto a floured surface. Knead for 2 minutes, or until smooth. Divide into 12 pieces. Knead one portion at a time for 30 seconds, then shape into a ball.

Preheat the oven to 210°C (415°F/Gas 6–7). Lightly grease two baking trays and dust with flour. Place balls of dough on the trays. Set aside, covered with plastic wrap, in a warm place for 15 minutes. Bake for 20 minutes, or until well browned. Set aside for 5 minutes, then transfer to a wire rack to cool completely. Using a serrated knife, cut diagonally into each bun, to a depth of 5 cm (2 in), from the top towards the base. Spread jam over the cut base of each bun. Using electric beaters, beat the cream and sugar in a bowl until firm peaks form. Spoon into a piping bag and pipe the cream into the buns. Dust the tops with icing sugar.

# blueberry muffins

makes 12

## ingredients

375 g (13 oz/3 cups) plain (all-purpose) flour
1 tablespoon baking powder
165 g (5$^3$/$_4$ oz/$^3$/$_4$ cup) firmly packed soft brown
   sugar
125 g (4$^1$/$_2$ oz) unsalted butter, melted
2 eggs, lightly beaten
250 ml (9 fl oz/1 cup) milk
185 g (6$^1$/$_2$ oz/1$^1$/$_4$ cups) fresh or thawed frozen
   blueberries

## method

Preheat the oven to 210°C (415°F/Gas 6–7). Grease or brush
12-hole standard muffin tin with melted butter or oil. Sift the
flour and baking powder into a large bowl. Stir in the sugar
and make a well in the centre.

Add the combined melted butter, eggs and milk all at once, and
fold until just combined. Do not overmix — the batter should
look quite lumpy.

Fold in the blueberries. Spoon the batter into the prepared tin.
Bake for 20 minutes, or until golden brown. Allow to cool on a
wire rack.

# double chocolate brownies

makes 12

## ingredients

80 g (2³/₄ oz) butter
40 g (1¹/₂ oz/¹/₃ cup) unsweetened cocoa powder
145 g (5 oz/²/₃ cup) caster (superfine) sugar
2 eggs
60 g (2¹/₄ oz/1/2 cup) plain (all-purpose) flour
¹/₂ teaspoon baking powder
100 g (3¹/₂ oz/¹/₂ cup) chocolate chips

## method

Preheat the oven to 180°C (350°F/Gas 4). Grease a 20 x 30 cm (8 x 12 in) shallow baking tin and line with baking paper, leaving it hanging over the two long sides.

Melt the butter in a saucepan. Remove from the heat and stir in the cocoa and sugar, followed by the eggs.

Put a sieve over the saucepan and add the flour, baking powder and a pinch of salt. Sift into the saucepan, then mix well to combine. Add the chocolate chips and stir well.

Pour the mixture into the tin and bake for 30 minutes, or until a skewer inserted into the centre comes out clean.

Leave in the tin for 10 minutes, then turn onto a wire rack to cool.

# jam roly poly

serves 4

## ingredients

250 g (9 oz/2 cups) self-raising flour, sifted
125 g ($4^1/_2$ oz) butter, roughly chopped
2 tablespoons caster (superfine) sugar
50 ml ($1^3/_4$ fl oz/$^1/_4$ cup) milk
210 g ($7^1/_2$ oz/$^2/_3$ cup) raspberry jam
1 tablespoon milk, extra

## method

Preheat the oven to 180°C (350°F/Gas 4) and line a baking tray with baking paper. Sift the flour into a bowl and add the butter. Using your fingertips, rub the butter into the flour until the mixture resembles fine breadcrumbs. Stir in the sugar.

Add the milk and 3 tablespoons of water, and stir with a flat-bladed knife to form a dough. Turn the dough out onto a lightly floured surface and gather together.

On a large sheet of baking paper, roll out the dough into a thin rectangle, 23 x 33 cm (9 x 13 in). Spread with the raspberry jam, leaving a narrow border around the edge.

Roll up lengthways like a Swiss roll and place on the tray seam-side down. Brush with the extra milk and bake for 35 minutes, or until golden. Leave to stand for a few minutes, then slice using a serrated knife. Serve warm.

# lamingtons

makes 16

## ingredients

185 g (6 oz/1$^1$/$_2$ cups) self-raising flour
40 g (1$^1$/$_2$ oz/$^1$/$_3$ cup) cornflour (cornstarch)
185 g (6$^1$/$_2$ oz) unsalted butter, softened
250 g (9 oz/1 cup) caster (superfine) sugar
2 teaspoons natural vanilla extract
3 eggs, lightly beaten
125 ml (4 fl oz/$^1$/$_2$ cup) milk
185 ml (6 fl oz/$^3$/$_4$ cup) thick (double/heavy)
  cream

### icing

500 g (1 lb 2 oz/4 cups) icing (confectioners')
  sugar
40 g (1$^1$/$_2$ oz/$^1$/$_3$ cup) unsweetened cocoa powder
30 g (1 oz) unsalted butter, melted
170 ml (5$^1$/$_2$ fl oz/$^2$/$_3$ cup) milk
270 g (9$^1$/$_2$ oz/3 cups) desiccated coconut

## method

Preheat the oven to 180°C (350°F/Gas 4). Lightly grease a shallow 23 cm (9 in) square cake tin and line the base and sides with baking paper.

Sift the flour and cornflour into a bowl. Add the butter, sugar, vanilla extract, eggs and milk. Using electric beaters, beat for 1 minute on low speed. Increase the speed to high and beat for 3 minutes. Pour into the tin. Bake for 50 minutes, or until a skewer comes out clean when inserted in the centre. Leave in the tin for 3 minutes, then turn out onto a wire rack to cool.

Trim the top of the cake until flat. Trim the crusts from the sides, then cut the cake in half horizontally. Using electric beaters, beat the cream in a bowl until stiff peaks form. Place the first layer of cake on a board and spread with cream. Place the remaining cake layer on top. Cut the cake into 16 squares.

To make the icing, sift the icing sugar and cocoa into a heatproof bowl and add the butter and milk. Stand the bowl over a saucepan of simmering water, stirring, until the icing is smooth, then remove from the heat. Place 90 g (3$^1$/$_4$ oz/1 cup) of the coconut on a sheet of baking paper. Using two forks, roll a piece of cake in chocolate icing. Roll the cake in coconut, then place on a wire rack. Repeat with remaining cake pieces.

# apple strudel

## ingredients

4 green cooking apples
30 g (1 oz) butter
2 tablespoons orange juice
1 tablespoon honey
60 g ($2^1/_4$ oz/$^1/_4$ cup) sugar
60 g ($2^1/_4$ oz/$^1/_2$ cup) sultanas
2 sheets frozen puff pastry, thawed
45 g ($1^1/_2$ oz/$^1/_4$ cup) ground almonds
1 egg, lightly beaten
2 tablespoons soft brown sugar
1 teaspoon ground cinnamon

## method

Preheat the oven to 220°C (425°F/Gas 7). Lightly grease two baking trays. Peel, core and thinly slice the apples. Heat the butter in a saucepan. Add the apples and cook for 2 minutes, or until lightly golden. Add the orange juice, honey, sugar and sultanas. Stir over medium heat until the sugar dissolves and the apples are just tender. Transfer the mixture to a bowl and leave until completely cooled.

Place a sheet of the pastry on a flat work surface. Fold it in half and make small cuts in the folded edge of the pastry at 2 cm ($^3/_4$ in) intervals. Open out the pastry and sprinkle with half of the ground almonds. Drain away the liquid from the apples and place half of the mixture in the centre of the pastry. Brush the edges with the lightly beaten egg, and fold together, pressing firmly to seal.

Place the strudel on a prepared tray, seam-side down. Brush the top with egg and sprinkle with half of the combined brown sugar and cinnamon. Repeat the process with the other sheet and the remaining filling. Bake for 20–25 minutes or until the pastry is golden and crisp. Serve hot with cream or ice cream, or at room temperature as a teatime treat.

# madeira cake

serves 6

## ingredients

180 g (6 oz) unsalted butter, softened
185 g (6$^1$/$_2$ oz/$^3$/$_4$ cup) caster (superfine) sugar
3 eggs, beaten
165 g (5$^3$/$_4$ oz/1$^1$/$_3$ cups) self-raising flour, sifted
2 teaspoons finely grated lemon zest
1 teaspoon lemon juice
2 teaspoons caster (superfine) sugar, extra,
   to sprinkle
icing (confectioners') sugar, to dust
lemon zest, extra, to garnish

## method

Preheat the oven to 160°C (315°F/Gas 2–3). Grease and flour a deep 18 cm (7 in) round cake tin, shaking out any excess.

Beat the butter and sugar with electric beaters until pale and creamy. Add the eggs gradually, beating well after each addition. Fold in the flour, lemon zest and juice until combined. When smooth, spoon into the prepared tin and level the surface. Sprinkle the extra caster sugar over the top.

Bake for 1 hour, or until a skewer comes out clean when inserted into the centre of the cake. Allow to cool for 15 minutes in the tin before turning out onto a wire rack. To serve, dust with icing sugar and garnish with lemon zest.

# bakewell slice

makes 15 pieces

## ingredients

125 g (4$^1$/$_2$ oz/1 cup) plain (all-purpose) flour
30 g (1 oz/$^1$/$_4$ cup) icing (confectioners') sugar
170 g (6 oz) unsalted butter, chilled and chopped
1 egg yolk
125 g (4$^1$/$_2$ oz/$^1$/$_2$ cup) caster (superfine) sugar
4 eggs
125 g (4$^1$/$_2$ oz/1$^1$/$_4$ cups) ground almonds
2 drops almond extract
160 g (5$^3$/$_4$ oz/$^1$/$_2$ cup) raspberry jam
25 g (1 oz/$^1$/$_4$ cup) flaked almonds

## method

Preheat the oven to 180°C (350°F/Gas 4). Lightly grease a 20 x 30 cm (8 x 12 in) baking tin and line with baking paper, hanging over the two long sides.

Sift the flour and 1 tablespoon of the icing sugar into a bowl, add 50 g (1$^3$/$_4$ oz) of the butter and rub it in until the mixture resembles breadcrumbs. Add the egg yolk and 2 tablespoons cold water and mix with a flat-bladed knife until the mixture comes together in beads. Gather into a ball, cover with plastic wrap and refrigerate for 30 minutes. Roll out between two sheets of baking paper, remove the paper and put in the tin, pressing into the edges. Bake for 10 minutes. Cool.

Beat the remaining butter and the caster sugar with electric beaters until creamy. Add the eggs and fold in the ground almonds and almond extract.

Spread the jam over the pastry base and pour over the filling. Sprinkle with almonds and bake for 30 minutes, or until firm.

Sift the remaining icing sugar into a bowl. Mix in 2 teaspoons warm water to form a free-flowing paste. Drizzle over the slice in a zigzag pattern and leave to set. Trim the edges and cut into squares.

# apple teacake

serves 8

## ingredients

150 g ($5^1/_2$ oz) unsalted butter, chopped
200 g (7 oz/1 cup) caster (superfine) sugar
2 eggs, lightly beaten
1 teaspoon natural vanilla extract
185 g ($6^1/_2$ oz/$1^1/_2$ cups) self-raising flour, sifted
185 g ($6^1/_2$ oz/$3/_4$ cup) vanilla-flavoured yoghurt
1 granny smith apple, peeled, cored and thinly
    sliced
1 teaspoon ground cinnamon

## method

Preheat the oven to 180°C (350°F/Gas 4). Grease a deep 20 cm (8 in) round cake tin and line the base with baking paper. Beat 130 g ($4^3/_4$ oz) of the butter and 185 g ($6^1/_2$ oz/$3/_4$ cup) of the sugar with electric beaters until light and creamy.

Gradually add the egg, beating well after each addition until combined. Add the natural vanilla extract. Fold in the flour, then the yoghurt and stir until smooth. Spoon the mixture into the prepared tin and smooth the surface.

Arrange the apple slices over the mixture in a circular pattern starting in the centre. Sprinkle with the cinnamon and remaining sugar. Melt the remaining butter, then drizzle over the top.

Bake for 1 hour, or until a skewer comes out clean when inserted into the centre of the cake. Leave in the tin for 30 minutes before turning out onto a wire rack to cool. If desired, combine a little extra cinnamon and sugar and sprinkle over the apple.

# banana cake

serves 8

## ingredients

125 g (4$^1/_2$ oz) butter
125 g (4$^1/_2$ oz/$^1/_2$ cup) caster (superfine) sugar
2 eggs, lightly beaten
1 teaspoon natural vanilla extract
4 ripe bananas, mashed
1 teaspoon bicarbonate of soda (baking soda)
125 ml (4 fl oz/$^1/_2$ cup) milk
250 g (9 oz/2 cups) self-raising flour

### butter frosting
125 g (4$^1/_2$ oz) butter
90 g (3 oz/$^3/_4$ cup) icing (confectioners') sugar
1 tablespoon lemon juice
15 g ($^1/_2$ oz/$^1/_4$ cup) flaked coconut, toasted

## method

Preheat the oven to 180°C (350°F/Gas 4). Brush a 20 cm (8 in) round cake tin with oil or melted butter and line the base with baking paper.

Using electric beaters, beat butter and sugar in a small bowl until light and creamy. Add the eggs gradually, beating thoroughly after each addition. Add the extract and mashed banana and beat until combined.

Transfer the mixture to a large bowl. Dissolve the soda in the milk. Using a metal spoon, fold in the sifted flour alternately with the milk. Stir until all the ingredients are just combined and the mixture is smooth. Spoon into the prepared tin and smooth the surface. Bake for 1 hour, or until a skewer comes out clean when inserted into the centre of the cake. Leave in the tin for 10 minutes before turning onto a wire rack to cool.

To make the frosting, using electric beaters, beat the butter, icing sugar and lemon juice until smooth and creamy. Spread onto the cooled cake, sprinkle with toasted coconut flakes.

# chocolate caramel slice

makes 24 triangles

## ingredients

200 g (7 oz) plain chocolate biscuits, crushed
100 g (3$^1$/$_2$ oz) unsalted butter, melted
2 tablespoons desiccated coconut
125 g (4$^1$/$_2$ oz) unsalted butter, extra
400 ml (14 fl oz) tin sweetened condensed milk
90 g (3$^1$/$_4$ oz/$^1$/$_3$ cup) caster (superfine) sugar
3 tablespoons maple syrup
250 g (9 oz) dark chocolate
2 teaspoons oil

## method

Grease a 30 x 20 cm (12 x 8 in) shallow baking tin and line with baking paper, leaving it hanging over the two long sides.

Combine the biscuits, melted butter and coconut in a bowl, then press into the tin and smooth the surface.

Combine the butter, condensed milk, sugar and maple syrup in a small saucepan. Stir over low heat for 15 minutes, or until the sugar has dissolved and the mixture is smooth, thick and lightly coloured. Remove from the heat and cool slightly. Pour over the biscuit base and smooth the surface. Refrigerate for 30 minutes, or until firm.

Chop the chocolate into small even-sized pieces and place in a heatproof bowl. Bring a saucepan of water to the boil and remove from the heat.

Sit the bowl over the saucepan, making sure the bowl doesn't touch the water. Allow to stand, stirring occasionally, until the chocolate has melted. Add the oil and stir until smooth. Spread over the caramel and leave until partially set before marking into 24 triangles. Refrigerate until firm. Cut into triangles before serving.

# carrot cake

serves 10–12

## ingredients

125 g (4$^1$/$_2$ oz/1 cup) self-raising flour
125 g (4$^1$/$_2$ oz/1 cup) plain (all-purpose) flour
2 teaspoons ground cinnamon
1 teaspoon ground ginger
$^1$/$_2$ teaspoon ground nutmeg
1 teaspoon bicarbonate of soda (baking soda)
250 ml (9 fl oz/1 cup) oil
185 g (6$^1$/$_2$ oz/1 cup) soft brown sugar
4 eggs
175 g (6 oz/$^1$/$_2$ cup) golden syrup
400 g (14 oz/2$^1$/$_2$ cups) grated carrot
60 g (2$^1$/$_4$ oz/$^1$/$_2$ cup) chopped pecans or walnuts

### lemon icing

175 g (6 oz) cream cheese, softened
60 g (2$^1$/$_4$ oz) butter, softened
185 g (6$^1$/$_2$ oz/1$^1$/$_2$ cups) icing (confectioners')
    sugar
1 teaspoon natural vanilla extract
1–2 teaspoons lemon juice

## method

Preheat the oven to 160°C (315°F/Gas 2–3). Lightly grease a 23 cm (9 in) round cake tin and line the base and side with baking paper.

Sift the flours, spices and soda into a large bowl and make a well in the centre.

Whisk together the oil, sugar, eggs and golden syrup in a jug until combined. Add this mixture to the well in the flour and gradually stir into the dry ingredients with a metal spoon until smooth. Stir in the carrot and nuts, then spoon into the tin and smooth the surface. Bake for 1 hour 30 minutes, or until a skewer comes out clean when inserted into the centre of the cake.

Leave the cake in the tin for at least 15 minutes before turning out onto a wire rack to cool completely.

For the lemon icing, beat the cream cheese and butter with electric beaters until smooth. Gradually add the icing sugar alternately with the vanilla and lemon juice, beating until light and creamy. Spread the icing over the cooled cake using a flat-bladed knife. Can be sprinkled with freshly grated nutmeg.

# hummingbird cake

serves 8

## ingredients

2 ripe bananas, mashed
125 g (4$^1/_2$ oz/$^1/_2$ cup) drained crushed pineapple
310 g (11 oz/1$^1/_4$ cups) caster (superfine) sugar
210 g (7$^1/_2$ oz/1$^2/_3$ cups) self-raising flour
2 teaspoons ground cinnamon or mixed spice
170 ml (5$^1/_2$ fl oz/$^2/_3$ cup) oil
3 tablespoons pineapple juice
2 eggs

### icing

60 g (2$^1/_4$ oz) unsalted butter, softened
125 g (4$^1/_2$ oz) cream cheese, softened
185 g (6 oz/1$^1/_2$ cups) icing (confectioners') sugar
1–2 teaspoons lemon juice

## method

Preheat the oven to 180°C (350°F/Gas 4). Lightly grease a 20 cm (8 in) square cake tin and line with baking paper.

Place the banana, pineapple and sugar in a large bowl. Add the sifted flour and cinnamon or mixed spice. Stir together with a wooden spoon until well combined.

Whisk together the oil, juice and eggs in a jug. Pour onto the banana mixture and stir until combined and the mixture is smooth.

Spoon into the tin and smooth the surface. Bake for 1 hour, or until a skewer comes out clean when inserted into the centre of the cake. Leave in the tin for 15 minutes before turning out onto a wire rack to cool.

For the icing, beat the butter and cream cheese with electric beaters until smooth. Gradually add the icing sugar alternately with the juice. Beat until thick and creamy.

Spread the icing thickly over the top of the cooled cake, or thinly over the top and side.

# vanilla slice

makes 9 pieces

## ingredients

500 g (1 lb 2 oz) block ready-made puff pastry,
  thawed
250 g (9 oz/1 cup) caster (superfine) sugar
90 g (3$^1$/$_4$ oz/$^3$/$_4$ cup) cornflour (cornstarch)
60 g (2$^1$/$_4$ oz/$^1$/$_2$ cup) custard powder
1 litre (35 fl oz/4 cups) pouring (whipping) cream
60 g (2$^1$/$_4$ oz) unsalted butter, cubed
2 teaspoons natural vanilla extract
3 egg yolks

## icing

185 g (6$^1$/$_2$ oz/1$^1$/$_2$ cups) icing (confectioners')
  sugar
60 g (2$^1$/$_4$ oz/$^1$/$_4$ cup) passionfruit pulp
15 g ($^1$/$_2$ oz) unsalted butter, melted

## method

Preheat the oven to 210°C (415°F/Gas 6–7). Lightly grease two baking trays with oil. Line the base and sides of a shallow 23 cm (9 in) square cake tin with foil, leaving the foil hanging over two opposite sides.

Divide the pastry in half, roll each piece to a 25 cm (10 in) square 3 mm ($^1$/$_4$ in) thick and put on a baking tray. Prick all over with a fork and bake for 8 minutes, or until golden. Trim each pastry sheet to a 23 cm (9 in) square. Put one sheet top-side-down in the cake tin.

Combine the sugar, cornflour and custard powder in a saucepan. Add the cream, stirring constantly over medium heat for 2 minutes, or until it boils and thickens. Add the butter and vanilla and stir until smooth. Remove from the heat and whisk in the egg yolks until combined. Spread the custard over the pastry in the tin, then cover with the other pastry sheet, top-side-down. Allow to cool completely.

To make the icing, combine the icing sugar, passionfruit pulp and butter in a bowl, and stir until smooth.

Lift the slice out of the tin using the foil as handles. Ice the top and leave to set before cutting with a serrated knife.

# chocolate mud cake

serves 10–12

## ingredients

125 g (4$^1/_2$ oz/1 cup) plain (all-purpose) flour
125 g (4$^1/_2$ oz/1 cup) self-raising flour
60 g (2$^1/_4$ oz/$^1/_2$ cup) dark cocoa powder
$^1/_2$ teaspoon bicarbonate of soda (baking soda)
625 g (1 lb 6 oz/2$^3/_4$ cups) sugar
450 g (1 lb) dark chocolate, chopped
450 g (1 lb) unsalted butter
125 ml (4 fl oz/$^1/_2$ cup) buttermilk
2 tablespoons oil
2 tablespoons instant espresso coffee granules
    or powder
4 eggs

## method

Preheat the oven to 160°C (315°F/Gas 2–3). Lightly grease a deep 23 cm (9 in) square cake tin. Line the base and sides with baking paper, extending at least 2 cm ($^3/_4$ in) above the rim.

Sift the flours, cocoa and bicarbonate of soda into a large bowl. Stir in the sugar and make a well in the centre. Put 250 g (9 oz) of the chocolate and 250 g (9 oz) of the butter in a saucepan. Add 185 ml (6 fl oz/$^3/_4$ cup) of water and stir over low heat until melted. Stir the chocolate mixture into the dry ingredients using a large metal spoon.

Whisk together the buttermilk, oil, coffee and eggs in a large jug and add to the mixture, stirring until smooth. Pour into the tin and bake for 1 hour 40 minutes, or until a skewer comes out clean when inserted in the centre. Cool in the tin, then turn out.

Combine the remaining chocolate and butter in a small saucepan and stir over low heat until smooth. Cool to room temperature, stirring often, until thick enough to spread. Turn the cake upside down so that the uneven top becomes the base, and spread the icing over the entire cake. Allow the icing to set slightly before serving.

# caramel peach cake

serves 10–12

## ingredients

250 g (9 oz) unsalted butter, softened
60 g (2$^1$/$_4$ oz/$^1$/$_3$ cup) soft brown sugar
825 g (1 lb 13 oz) tinned peach halves in
    natural juice
250 g (9 oz/1 cup) caster (superfine) sugar
3 teaspoons finely grated lemon zest
3 eggs, lightly beaten
310 g (11 oz/2$^1$/$_2$ cups) self-raising flour, sifted
250 g (9 oz/1 cup) plain yoghurt

## method

Preheat the oven to 180°C (350°F/Gas 4). Grease a deep 23 cm (9 in) round cake tin and line the base with baking paper. Melt 50 g (1$^3$/$_4$ oz) of the butter and pour on the base of the tin. Evenly sprinkle the brown sugar on top. Drain the peaches, reserving 1 tablespoon of the liquid. Arrange the peach halves, cut-side-up, over the sugar mixture.

Beat the caster sugar, lemon zest and remaining butter with electric beaters for 5–6 minutes, or until pale and creamy. Add the egg gradually, beating well after each addition—the mixture may look curdled but once you add the flour, it will bring it back together. Using a metal spoon, fold in the flour alternately with the yoghurt (in two batches) then the reserved peach liquid. Spoon the mixture over the peaches in the tin and smooth the surface. Bake for 1 hour 25 minutes, or until a skewer comes out clean when inserted into the centre of the cake. Leave to cool in the tin for 30 minutes before carefully turning out onto a large serving plate.

# baked cheesecake

serves 10–12

## ingredients

375 g (13 oz) plain sweet biscuits (cookies)
175 g (6 oz) unsalted butter, melted

### filling

500 g (1 lb 2 oz) cream cheese
200 g (7 oz) caster (superfine) sugar
4 eggs
300 ml (10$^1$/$_2$ fl oz) pouring (whipping) cream
2 tablespoons plain (all-purpose) flour
1 teaspoon ground cinnamon
$^1$/$_4$ teaspoon freshly grated nutmeg
1 tablespoons lemon juice
2 teaspoon vanilla extract

freshly grated nutmeg, ground cinnamon,
pouring (whipping) cream and strawberries,
to decorate

## method

Preheat the oven to 180°C (350°F/Gas 4) oven. Lightly grease a 23 cm (9 in) shallow spring-form cake tin. Process the biscuits in a food processor until crushed into fine crumbs. Add the melted butter and process for a further 10 seconds. Press the mixture into the base and side of the tin, then refrigerate for 1 hour.

Beat the cream cheese and sugar together, then add the eggs and cream and beat for 4 minutes. Fold in the flour, cinnamon, nutmeg, lemon juice and vanilla. Pour the mixture into the chilled crust. Bake for 1 hour, without opening the oven door, or until the cheesecake is golden brown on top.

Turn off the heat and let the cake stand in the oven for 2 hours.

Then open the oven door and let it stand for a further 1 hour. Refrigerate overnight.

To decorate, sprinkle with nutmeg and cinnamon and then serve with cream and strawberries.

# blueberry shortcake

serves 8–10

## ingredients

100 g (3$\frac{1}{2}$ oz/$\frac{3}{4}$ cup) hazelnuts
280 g (10 oz/2$\frac{1}{4}$ cups) self-raising flour
1$\frac{1}{2}$ teaspoons ground cinnamon
165 g (5$\frac{3}{4}$ oz/$\frac{3}{4}$ cup) demerara sugar
150 g (5$\frac{1}{2}$ oz) unsalted butter, chopped
2 eggs
160 g (5$\frac{3}{4}$ oz/$\frac{1}{2}$ cup) blueberry jam
1 tablespoon demerara sugar, extra

## method

Preheat the oven to 180°C (350°F/Gas 4). Grease a deep 20 cm (8 in) round cake tin and line the base with baking paper.

Spread the hazelnuts on a baking tray. Bake for 5–10 minutes, or until lightly golden. Place in a tea towel (dish towel) and rub together to remove the skins, then roughly chop.

Mix the flour, cinnamon, sugar, butter and half the hazelnuts in a food processor in short bursts until finely chopped. Add the eggs and process until well combined. Press half the mixture onto the base of the tin, then spread the jam evenly over the mixture. Lightly knead the remaining hazelnuts into the remaining dough, then press evenly over the jam layer.

Sprinkle the extra sugar over the top and bake for 50 minutes, or until a skewer comes out clean when inserted into the centre. Leave in the tin for 15 minutes before turning out onto a wire rack to cool. If desired, garnish with fresh blueberries and serve with thick cream.

# cinnamon tea cake

serves 8

## ingredients

60 g (2$^1/_4$ oz) butter
115 g (4 oz/$^1/_2$ cup) caster (superfine) sugar
1 egg, lightly beaten
1 teaspoon natural vanilla extract
90 g (3$^1/_4$ oz/$^3/_4$ cup) self-raising flour
30 g (1 oz/$^1/_4$ cup) plain (all-purpose) flour
125 ml (4 fl oz/$^1/_2$ cup) milk
20 g ($^3/_4$ oz) butter, melted
1 tablespoon caster (superfine) sugar, extra
1 teaspoon ground cinnamon

## method

Preheat oven to 180°C (350°F/Gas 4). Lightly grease a 20 cm (8 in) round cake tin. Line the base with baking paper.

Using electric beaters, beat the butter and sugar in a small bowl until light and creamy. Add the beaten egg gradually, beating well after each addition. Add the vanilla extract and beat until combined.

Transfer the mixture to a large bowl. Using a metal spoon, fold in the sifted flours, alternately with the milk. Stir until smooth. Spoon into the prepared tin and smooth the surface. Bake for 30 minutes, or until a skewer comes out clean when inserted into the centre. Stand the cake in the tin for 5 minutes before turning out onto a wire rack to cool.

Brush the cake with melted butter while still warm. Sprinkle the cake with the combined extra sugar and cinnamon.

# hot cross buns

makes 16

## ingredients

12 g ($^1/_4$ oz) instant dried yeast
80 g (2$^3/_4$ oz/$^1/_3$ cup) caster (superfine) sugar
625 g (1 lb 6 oz/5 cups) white bread (strong) flour
1$^1/_2$ teaspoons mixed (pumpkin pie) spice
1 teaspoon ground cinnamon
1 teaspoon ground nutmeg
250 ml (9 fl oz/1 cup) warm milk
100 g (3$^1/_2$ oz) unsalted butter, melted
2 eggs, lightly beaten
200 g (7 oz/1$^1/_3$ cups) currants
70 g (2$^1/_2$ oz/$^1/_3$ cup) mixed peel

### glaze

2 tablespoons caster (superfine) sugar

### cross dough

60 g (2$^1/_4$ oz/$^1/_2$ cup) plain (all-purpose) flour

## method

Sprinkle the yeast and a pinch of the sugar over 125 ml (4 fl oz/ $^1/_2$ cup) of warm water in a bowl. Stir. Leave for 10 minutes, or until foamy. Combine the flour, spices and $^1/_2$ teaspoon of salt in a bowl and set aside. Combine the milk, butter, remaining sugar, eggs and 125 g (4$^1/_2$ oz/1 cup) of the flour mixture in the bowl of an electric mixer. Mix for 1 minute, or until smooth. Add the yeast mixture, currants and mixed peel and stir. Add the flour, 125 g (4$^1/_2$ oz/1 cup) at a time, stirring. Grease a bowl with oil, then transfer the dough to the bowl, turning the dough to coat in the oil. Cover with plastic wrap and leave to rise for 1$^1/_2$–2 hours, or until the dough has doubled in size. Knock back the dough by punching it, then turn out onto a floured surface. Divide the dough into 16 equal portions. Roll each portion into a ball, then place on greased baking trays. Cover with a damp cloth and leave for 30 minutes. Preheat the oven to 180°C (350°F/Gas 4). To make the glaze, combine the sugar with 2 tablespoons water in a saucepan. Bring to the boil over high heat, then remove. To prepare the cross dough, put the flour in a bowl and add 3 tablespoons of water, stirring to form a dough. Roll out the dough on a floured surface to a 2 mm ($^1/_{16}$ in) thickness. Cut into 5 mm ($^1/_4$ in) wide strips, about 12 cm (4$^1/_2$ in) long. Brush the strips with water and place two strips over each bun to form a cross. Bake for 15–20 minutes, or until golden brown. Brush the hot buns with the glaze.

# pineapple upside-down cake

serves 6–8

## ingredients

20 g ($^3/_4$ oz/$^1/_2$ oz) unsalted butter, melted
2 tablespoons firmly packed soft brown sugar
440 g (1 lb) tinned pineapple rings in natural juice
90 g ($3^1/_4$ oz) unsalted butter, extra, softened
125 g ($4^1/_2$ oz/$^1/_2$ cup) caster (superfine) sugar
2 eggs, lightly beaten
1 teaspoon natural vanilla extract
125 g ($4^1/_2$ oz/1 cup) self-raising flour

## method

Preheat the oven to 180°C (350°F/Gas 4). Grease a 20 cm (8 in) ring tin. Pour the melted butter into the base of the tin and tip to evenly coat. Sprinkle with the brown sugar. Drain the pineapple and reserve 4 tablespoons of the juice. Cut the pineapple rings in half and arrange on the base.

Beat the extra butter and the caster sugar with electric beaters until light and creamy. Gradually add the egg, beating well after each addition.

Add the natural vanilla extract and beat until combined. Fold in the flour alternately with the reserved juice, using a metal spoon.

Spoon the mixture evenly over the pineapple and smooth the surface. Bake for 35–40 minutes, or until a skewer comes out clean when inserted into the centre of the cake. Leave in the tin for 10 minutes before turning out onto a wire rack to cool.

# orange poppy seed cake with citrus icing

serves 8–10

## ingredients

50 g ($1^3/_4$ oz/$^1/_3$ cup) poppy seeds
185 ml (6 fl oz/$^3/_4$ cup) warm milk
250 g (9 oz/1 cup) caster (superfine) sugar
3 eggs
250 g (9 oz/2 cups) self-raising flour, sifted
210 g ($7^1/_2$ oz) unsalted butter, softened
$1^1/_2$ tablespoons finely grated orange zest
250 g (9 oz/2 cups) icing (confectioners') sugar

## method

Preheat the oven to 180°C (350°F/Gas 4). Lightly grease a 23 cm (9 in) fluted baba tin. Combine the poppy seeds and milk in a bowl and set aside for at least 15 minutes.

Place the caster sugar, eggs, flour, 185 g ($6^1/_2$ oz) of the butter and 3 teaspoons of the orange rind in a large bowl. Add the poppy seed mixture and beat with electric beaters on low speed until combined. Increase to medium speed and beat for 3 minutes, or until the mixture is thick and pale. Pour the mixture evenly into the prepared tin. Bake for 50 minutes, or until a skewer comes out clean when inserted into the centre of the cake. Leave in the tin for 5 minutes then turn out onto a wire rack.

To make the icing, melt the remaining butter, then place in a bowl with the icing sugar, remaining zest and 3 tablespoons boiling water. Mix to make a soft icing, then spread over the warm cake.

# marble cake

serves 6

## ingredients

1 vanilla bean or 1 teaspoon natural vanilla extract
185 g (6$^1/_2$ oz) unsalted butter, chopped
230 g (8 oz/1 cup) caster (superfine) sugar
3 eggs
280 g (10 oz/2$^1/_4$ cups) self-raising flour
185 ml (6 fl oz/$^3/_4$ cup) milk
2 tablespoons unsweetened cocoa powder
1$^1/_2$ tablespoons warm milk, extra

## method

Preheat the oven to 200°C (400°F/Gas 6). Lightly grease a 25 x 11 x 7.5 cm (10 x 4$^1/_4$ x 3 in) loaf (bar) tin and line the base with baking paper.

If using the vanilla bean, split it down the middle and scrape out the seeds. Put the seeds (or vanilla extract) in a bowl with the butter and sugar and, using electric beaters, cream the mixture until pale and fluffy. Add the eggs one at a time, beating well after each addition. Sift the flour, then fold it into the creamed mixture alternately with the milk until combined. Divide the mixture in half and put the second half into another bowl.

Combine the cocoa powder and warm milk in a small bowl and stir until smooth, then add to one half of the cake mixture, stirring to combine well. Spoon the two mixtures into the prepared tin in alternate spoonfuls. Using a metal skewer, cut through the mixture four times to create a marble effect. Bake for 50–60 minutes, or until a skewer inserted into the centre of the cake comes out clean. Leave in the tin for 5 minutes before turning out onto a wire rack to cool.

# boiled fruit cake

serves 8

## ingredients

320 g (11 oz/2 cups) raisins, chopped
320 g (11 oz/2 cups) sultanas
150 g (5$^{1}/_{2}$ oz/1 cup) currants
100 g (3$^{1}/_{2}$ oz/$^{2}/_{3}$ cup) blanched almonds, chopped
100 g (3$^{1}/_{2}$ oz/$^{1}/_{2}$ cup) red glacé cherries
230 g (7$^{1}/_{2}$ oz/1 cup) soft brown sugar
125 g (4$^{1}/_{2}$ oz) unsalted butter, chopped
3 tablespoons brandy
2 eggs, lightly beaten
90 g (3$^{1}/_{4}$ oz/$^{3}/_{4}$ cup) plain (all-purpose) flour
90 g (3$^{1}/_{4}$ oz/$^{3}/_{4}$ cup) self-raising flour
2 teaspoons mixed spice

## method

Put the dried fruits, almonds, glacé cherries, sugar, butter, brandy and 250 ml (9 fl oz/1 cup) water in a large saucepan. Bring to the boil, stirring occasionally until the sugar has dissolved and the butter has melted. Remove from the heat and set aside to cool to room temperature.

Preheat the oven to 160°C (315°F/Gas 2–3). Grease and line a 20 cm (8 in) round or 18 cm (7 in) square cake tin.

Add the eggs to the fruit, then sift in the flours and spice. Mix together, working quickly and lightly, but don't overmix. Spoon into the tin, tap the tin on the bench to remove any air bubbles, then smooth the surface with wet fingers. Wrap newspaper around the outside of the tin. Sit the tin on several more layers of newspaper in the oven and bake for 1$^{1}/_{2}$–2 hours, until a skewer inserted into the centre comes out clean. Allow to cool completely in the tin, covered with a tea towel (dish towel), then turn out. Store in an airtight container or wrapped in plastic wrap for 2–3 months.

# rich butter cake

serves 6–8

## ingredients

250 g (9 oz) unsalted butter, softened
250 g (9 oz/1 cup) caster (superfine) sugar
4 eggs
1 teaspoon natural vanilla extract
185 g (6$^1$/$_2$ oz/1$^1$/$_2$ cups) self-raising flour
60 g (2$^1$/$_4$ oz/$^1$/$_2$ cup) plain (all-purpose) flour
185 ml (6 fl oz/$^3$/$_4$ cup) milk
icing (confectioners') sugar, to dust

## method

Preheat the oven to 180°C (350°F/Gas 4). Lightly grease a deep 20 cm (8 in) round cake tin and line the base with baking paper. Beat the butter and sugar with electric beaters until light and creamy. Add the eggs one at a time, beating well after each addition.

Add the natural vanilla extract and beat until combined. Sift the flours together and fold in alternately with the milk. Stir until the ingredients are just combined and the mixture is almost smooth. Spoon the mixture into the tin and smooth the surface.

Bake for 1 hour 10 minutes, or until a skewer comes out clean when inserted into the centre. Leave in the tin for 10 minutes before turning onto a wire rack to cool. Dust with the icing sugar and, if desired, serve with fresh raspberries and cream.

# chocolate pudding

serves 4

## ingredients

160 g (5$^3/_4$ oz) dark chocolate, chopped
butter, for greasing
80 g (2$^3/_4$ oz) caster (superfine) sugar
60 g (2$^1/_4$ oz) milk chocolate, chopped
4 eggs
whipped cream, to serve

## method

Preheat the oven to 200°C (400°F/Gas 6). Put the dark chocolate in a glass bowl and set it above a saucepan of simmering water. Stir until smooth.

Grease four 200 ml (7 fl oz) ramekins with butter. Add $^1/_2$ teaspoon of the sugar to each and shake it around until the insides are coated. Divide the chopped milk chocolate among the ramekins.

Beat the rest of the sugar with the egg yolks, using electric beaters, for about 3 minutes, or until you have a pale, creamy mass. Clean the beaters and dry them thoroughly. Whisk the egg whites until they are thick enough to stand up in peaks.

Fold the melted chocolate into the yolk mixture and then fold in the whites. Use a large spoon or rubber spatula to do this and try not to squash out too much air. Divide the mixture among the four ramekins. Bake for 15–20 minutes. The puddings should be puffed and spongelike. Serve with cream.

# sago plum pudding

serves 6–8

## ingredients

65 g (2¼ oz/⅓ cup) sago
250 ml (9 fl oz/1 cup) milk
1 teaspoon bicarbonate of soda (baking soda)
140 g (5 oz/¾ cup) dark brown sugar
160 g (5¾ oz/2 cups) fresh white breadcrumbs
80 g (2¾ oz/½ cup) sultanas
75 g (2½ oz/½ cup) currants
80 g (2¾ oz/½ cup) dried dates, chopped
2 eggs, lightly beaten
60 g (2¼ oz) unsalted butter, melted and cooled
raspberries and blueberries, to decorate
icing (confectioners') sugar, to dust

## method

Combine the sago and milk in a bowl, cover and refrigerate overnight. Lightly grease a 1.5 litre (52 fl oz/6 cup) pudding basin (steamed pudding mould) with butter and line the base with baking paper. Place the empty basin in a large saucepan on a trivet or upturned saucer and pour in enough cold water to come halfway up the side of the basin. Remove the basin and put the water on to boil. Transfer the soaked sago and milk to a large bowl and stir in the bicarbonate of soda until dissolved. Stir in the sugar, breadcrumbs, dried fruit, beaten eggs and melted butter and mix well. Spoon into the basin and smooth the surface with wet hands. Cover the pudding.

Cover the basin with the lid and make a string handle. Gently lower the basin into the boiling water, reduce to a fast simmer and cover the saucepan with a tight-fitting lid. Cook for 3½–4 hours, or until a skewer inserted into the centre of the pudding comes out clean. Check the water level every hour and top up with boiling water as necessary. Carefully remove the pudding basin from the saucepan, remove the coverings and leave for 5 minutes before turning out the pudding onto a large serving plate. Loosen the edges with a palette knife, if necessary. Serve decorated with raspberries and blueberries and lightly dusted with icing sugar.

# spiced quince charlotte

serves 4–6

## ingredients

460 g (1 lb/2 cups) caster (superfine) sugar
1 vanilla bean
1 cinnamon stick
1 teaspoon ground allspice
1.5 kg (3 lb 5 oz) quinces, peeled, quartered and
    cored
unsalted butter
2 loaves thinly sliced brioche
crème anglaise, to serve

## method

Preheat the oven to 180°C (350°F/Gas 4). Combine 1 litre (35 fl oz/4 cups) of water and the sugar in a saucepan and stir over medium heat until the sugar dissolves. Split the vanilla bean down the middle and scrape out the seeds. Put the bean and its seeds in the saucepan with the cinnamon and allspice. Remove from the heat.

Place the quinces in a roasting tin or baking dish and pour over the syrup. Cover with foil and bake for 2 hours, or until the fruit is very tender. Drain the quinces.

Butter the slices of brioche. Cut out a circle from two slices of brioche (cut a half-circle from each slice), large enough to fit the base of a 2 litre (70 fl oz/8 cup) capacity charlotte mould or ovenproof bowl. Reserving 4 slices of brioche for the top, cut the remaining brioche into 2 cm ($^3/_4$ in) wide fingers, and long enough to fit the height of the mould. Press the brioche vertically around the side of the dish, overlapping the strips slightly.

Put the quinces in the brioche-lined mould and cover with the reserved slices of brioche. Sit the mould on a baking tray and bake for 25–30 minutes. Allow to cool for 10 minutes, then unmould onto a serving plate. Serve with crème anglaise.

# lemon delicious

serves 4–6

## ingredients

70 g (2$^1$/$_2$ oz) unsalted butter, at room
  temperature
185 g (6$^1$/$_2$ oz/$^3$/$_4$ cup) sugar
2 teaspoons finely grated lemon zest
3 eggs, separated
30 g (1 oz/$^1$/$_4$ cup) self-raising flour
185 ml (6 fl oz/$^3$/$_4$ cup) milk
4 tablespoons lemon juice
icing (confectioners') sugar, to dust
thick (double/heavy) cream, to serve

## method

Preheat the oven to 180°C (350°F/Gas 4). Melt 10 g ($^1$/$_4$ oz)
of the butter and use to lightly grease a 1.25 litre (44 fl oz/
5 cups) ovenproof ceramic dish.

Using an electric beater, beat the remaining butter, the sugar
and grated zest together in a bowl until the mixture is light
and creamy. Gradually add the egg yolks, beating well after
each addition. Fold in the flour and milk alternately to make a
smooth but runny batter. Stir in the lemon juice. Don't worry
if the batter looks like it has separated.

Whisk the egg whites in a clean, dry bowl until firm peaks form
and, with a large metal spoon, fold a third of the whites into
the batter. Gently fold in the remaining egg whites, being
careful not to overmix.

Pour the batter into the prepared dish and place in a large
roasting tin. Pour enough hot water into the tin to come
one-third of the way up the side of the dish and bake for
55 minutes, or until the top of the pudding is golden, risen
and firm to the touch. Leave for 5 minutes before serving.
Dust with icing sugar and serve with cream.

# steamed ginger pudding

serves 8

## ingredients

60 g (2$\frac{1}{4}$ oz/$\frac{1}{2}$ cup) plain (all-purpose) flour
185 g (6$\frac{1}{2}$ oz/1$\frac{1}{2}$ cups) self-raising flour
2 teaspoons ground ginger
1 teaspoon mixed spice
$\frac{1}{2}$ teaspoon ground cinnamon
125 g (4$\frac{1}{2}$ oz) unsalted butter, cut into cubes
125 ml (4 fl oz/$\frac{1}{2}$ cup) golden or maple syrup
3 tablespoons treacle or molasses
2 eggs, lightly whisked
75 g (2$\frac{1}{2}$ oz/$\frac{1}{3}$ cup) glacé ginger, chopped
custard, to serve

## method

Lightly grease a 1.5 litre (52 fl oz/6 cup) capacity heatproof pudding basin with melted butter, and line the base with a round of baking paper. Brush a sheet of foil with butter. Lay a sheet of baking paper on top, creating a pleat in the centre.

Sift the flours, ground ginger, mixed spice, and cinnamon into a large bowl and make a well in the centre. Put the butter, golden syrup, and treacle into a saucepan, and stir over medium–low heat until the butter has melted and is well combined, then allow to cool slightly. Pour into the flour well, along with the eggs and chopped ginger. Stir until well combined, but do not over-beat.

Pour the mixture into the prepared basin, cover with the foil and paper, paper side down. Tie securely with string under the lip of the basin. Place the basin on a trivet in a large deep saucepan. Carefully pour boiling water into the pan down the side of the basin to come halfway up the side of the basin, and bring to the boil over high heat. Reduce the heat to medium–low, cover with a lid and simmer for 2 hours, or until a skewer inserted into the centre comes out clean. Add more boiling water to the pan when necessary. Remove the pudding from the pan. Allow to stand for 5 minutes before turning out onto a serving plate. Cut into slices and serve with custard.

# sticky date pudding

serves 6–8

## ingredients

200 g (7 oz) dates, pitted and chopped
250 ml (9 fl oz/1 cup) water
1 teaspoon bicarbonate of soda (baking soda)
100 g (3$^1$/$_2$ oz) butter
160 g (5$^1$/$_4$ oz/$^2$/$_3$ cup) caster (superfine) sugar
2 eggs, lightly beaten
1 teaspoon natural vanilla extract
185 g (6$^1$/$_2$ oz/1$^1$/$_2$ cups) self-raising flour

### sauce

185 g (6$^1$/$_2$ oz/1 cup) soft brown sugar
125 ml (4 fl oz/$^1$/$_2$ cup) pouring (whipping) cream
100 g (3$^1$/$_2$ oz) butter

## method

Preheat the oven to 180°C (350°F/Gas 4). Lightly grease a 20 cm (8 in) square cake tin. Line the base with baking paper. Combine the dates and water in a small saucepan. Bring to the boil, then remove from the heat. Stir in the soda and set aside to cool to room temperature.

Using electric beaters, beat the butter and sugar in a small bowl until light and creamy. Add the eggs gradually, beating thoroughly after each addition. Add the extract and beat until combined. Transfer to a large bowl.

Using a metal spoon, fold in the flour and dates with the liquid and stir until just combined—do not over-beat. Pour into the prepared tin and bake for 50 minutes, until a skewer comes out clean when inserted into the centre. Leave in tin for 10 minutes before turning out.

To make the sauce, combine the sugar, cream and butter in a small saucepan. Stir until the butter melts and the sugar dissolves. Bring to the boil, reduce the heat and simmer for 2 minutes. Cut the pudding into wedges and place on serving plates. Pour the hot sauce over. Serve immediately, with extra cream and raspberries, if desired.

# queen of puddings

serves 6

## ingredients

500 ml (17 fl oz/2 cups) milk
50 g (1³/₄ oz) unsalted butter
140 g (5 oz/1³/₄ cups) fresh breadcrumbs
115 g (4 oz/¹/₂ cup) caster (superfine) sugar,
    plus 1 tablespoon extra
finely grated zest from 1 orange
5 eggs, separated
210 g (7¹/₂ oz/²/₃ cup) orange marmalade
1 teaspoon honey
whipped cream, to serve

## method

Preheat the oven to 180°C (350°F/Gas 4). Lightly grease a 1.25 litre (44 fl oz/5 cup) rectangular ovenproof dish.

Combine the milk and butter in a small saucepan and heat over low heat until the butter has melted. Put the breadcrumbs, the extra sugar and orange zest in a large bowl. Stir in the milk mixture and set aside for 10 minutes.

Lightly whisk the egg yolks, then stir into the breadcrumb mixture. Spoon into the prepared dish, then bake for 25–30 minutes, or until firm to touch.

Combine the marmalade and honey in a saucepan and heat over low heat until melted. Pour evenly over the pudding.

Whisk the egg whites in a clean, dry bowl until stiff peaks form. Gradually add the sugar, whisking well, until the mixture is stiff and glossy and the sugar has dissolved. Spoon the meringue evenly over the top of the pudding and bake for 12–15 minutes, or until the meringue is golden. Serve the pudding warm with whipped cream.

# bread and butter pudding

serves 6

## ingredients

2 tablespoons sultanas (golden raisins)
1 tablespoon Grand Marnier
10 slices day-old white bread, crusts removed
$2^1/_2$ tablespoons marmalade
2 eggs
2 tablespoons caster (superfine) sugar
500 ml (/17 fl oz/2 cups) milk
1 teaspoon natural vanilla extract

## method

Place the sultanas in a bowl, add the Grand Marnier, toss to coat and leave for 30 minutes. Preheat the oven to 160°C (315°F/Gas 2–3).

Spread the slices of bread with $1^1/_2$ tablespoons of the marmalade. Cut each slice into four triangles. Lightly grease a 1.5 litre (52 fl oz/6 cup) ovenproof dish with oil. Layer the bread in the dish, sprinkling the sultanas between the layers.

Whisk the eggs, sugar, milk and natural vanilla extract together in a bowl. Pour over the bread and leave to soak for at least 30 minutes.

Place the pudding dish in a large roasting tin and pour in boiling water to come halfway up the side of the pudding dish. Bake for 35–40 minutes. Remove the pudding dish from the roasting tin and brush with the remaining marmalade. Leave for 10 minutes, then serve.

# summer pudding

serves 6

## ingredients

150 g ($5^1/_2$ oz) blackcurrants
150 g ($5^1/_2$ oz) redcurrants
150 g ($5^1/_2$ oz) raspberries
150 g ($5^1/_2$ oz) blackberries
200 g (7 oz) strawberries, hulled and quartered or halved
125 g ($4^1/_2$ oz/$^1/_2$ cup) caster (superfine) sugar
6–8 slices sliced white bread, crusts removed

## method

Put all the berries, except the strawberries, in a large saucepan with 125 ml (4 fl oz/$^1/_2$ cup) of water and heat for 5 minutes, or until the berries begin to collapse. Add the strawberries and remove from the heat. Add the sugar, to taste. Allow to cool.

Line a 1 litre (35 fl oz/4 cup) pudding basin or six 170 ml ($5^1/_2$ oz/$^2/_3$ cup) moulds with the bread. For the large mould, cut a large circle out of one slice for the base and cut the rest of the bread into wide fingers. For the small moulds, use one slice of bread for each, cutting a small circle to fit the base and strips to fit snugly around the sides. Drain a little of the juice off the fruit mixture. Dip one side of each piece of bread in the juice before fitting it, juice-side-down, into the basin.

Fill the centre of the basin with the fruit and add a little juice. Cover the top with the remaining dipped bread, juice-side-up, trimmed to fit. Cover with plastic wrap. Place a small plate which fits inside the dish onto the plastic wrap, then weigh it down with heavy cans or a glass bowl. Place on a baking tray to catch any juices. For the small moulds, cover with plastic and sit a small can, or a similar weight, on top of each. Refrigerate overnight. Turn out the pudding and serve with any leftover fruit mixture. Served with cream.

# trifle

serves 6

## ingredients

4 slices of Madeira (pound) cake or trifle sponges
3 tablespoons sweet sherry or Madeira
250 g (9 oz) raspberries
4 eggs
2 tablespoons caster (superfine) sugar
2 tablespoons plain (all-purpose) flour
500 ml (17 fl oz/2 cups) milk
$^1/_4$ teaspoon natural vanilla extract
125 ml (4 fl oz/$^1/_2$ cup) whipping cream
3 tablespoons flaked almonds, to decorate
raspberries, to decorate

## method

Put the cake in the base of a bowl, then sprinkle it with the sherry. Scatter the raspberries over the top and crush them gently into the sponge with the back of a spoon to release their tart flavour, leaving some of them whole.

Mix the eggs, sugar and flour together in a bowl. Heat the milk in a pan, pour it over the egg mixture, stir well and pour back into a clean pan. Cook over medium heat until the custard boils and thickens and coats the back of a spoon. Stir in the vanilla, cover the surface with plastic wrap and leave to cool.

Pour the cooled custard over the raspberries and leave to set in the fridge — it will firm up but not become solid. Spoon the whipped cream over the custard. Decorate with almonds and raspberries and refrigerate until needed.

# baked rice pudding

serves 4–6

## ingredients

20 g ($^1/_2$ oz) unsalted butter, melted
3 tablespoons short-grain rice
3 eggs
60 g ($2^1/_4$ oz/$^1/_4$ cup) caster (superfine) sugar
440 ml ($15^1/_4$ fl oz/$1^3/_4$ cups) milk
125 ml (4fl oz/$^1/_2$ cup) pouring (whipping) cream
1 teaspoon natural vanilla extract
$^1/_4$ teaspoon ground nutmeg

## method

Preheat the oven to 160°C (315°F/Gas 2–3). Lightly grease a 1.5 litre (52 fl oz/6 cup) ovenproof dish with the melted butter. Cook the rice in a saucepan of boiling water for 12 minutes, or until tender, then drain well.

Place the eggs in a bowl and beat lightly. Add the sugar, milk, cream and natural vanilla extract, and whisk until well combined. Stir in the cooked rice, pour into the prepared dish and sprinkle with nutmeg.

Place the dish in a deep roasting tin and pour enough hot water into the tin to come halfway up the side of the pudding dish. Bake for 45 minutes, or until the custard is lightly set and a knife inserted into the centre comes out clean. Remove the pudding dish from the roasting tin and leave for 5 minutes before serving. Serve the pudding with poached or stewed fruit.

# baked custard

serves 4

## ingredients

10 g ($^1/_4$ oz) unsalted butter, melted
3 eggs
90 g ($3^1/_4$ oz/$^1/_3$ cup) caster (superfine) sugar
500 ml (17 fl oz/2 cups) milk
125 ml (4 fl oz/$^1/_2$ cup) pouring (whipping) cream
$1^1/_2$ teaspoons natural vanilla extract
ground nutmeg, to sprinkle

## method

Preheat the oven to 160°C (315°F/Gas 2–3). Lightly grease four 250 ml (9 fl oz/1 cup) ramekins or a 1.5 litre (52 fl oz/6 cups) ovenproof dish with the melted butter.

Whisk together the eggs and sugar in a large bowl until they are combined. Place the milk and cream in a small saucepan and stir over medium heat for 3–4 minutes, or until the mixture is warmed through, then stir into the egg mixture with the natural vanilla extract. Strain into the prepared dishes and sprinkle with the ground nutmeg.

Place the dishes in a deep roasting tin and add enough hot water to come halfway up the side of the dishes. Bake for 25 minutes for the individual custards, or 30 minutes for the large custard, or until it is set and a knife inserted into the centre comes out clean.

Remove the custards from the roasting tin and leave for 10 minutes before serving.

# pavlova

serves 6

## ingredients

4 egg whites
230 g ($8^1/_2$ oz/1 cup) caster (superfine) sugar
2 teaspoons cornflour (cornstarch)
1 teaspoon white vinegar
500 ml (17 fl oz/2 cups) pouring (whipping) cream
3 passionfruit, to decorate
strawberries, to decorate

## method

Preheat the oven to 160°C (315°F/Gas 2–3). Line a 32 x 28 cm (13 x 11 in) baking tray with baking paper.

Place the egg whites and a pinch of salt in a small bowl. Using electric beaters, beat until stiff peaks form. Add the sugar gradually, beating constantly after each addition, until the mixture is thick and glossy and all the sugar has dissolved.

Using a metal spoon, fold in the cornflour and vinegar. Spoon the mixture into a mound on the prepared tray. Lightly flatten the top of the pavlova and smooth the sides. (This pavlova should have a cake shape and be about 2.5 cm (1 in) high.) Bake for 1 hour, or until pale cream and crisp. Remove from the oven while warm and carefully turn upside down onto a plate. Allow to cool.

Lightly whip the cream until soft peaks form and spread over the soft centre. Decorate with pulp from the passionfruit and halved strawberries. Cut into wedges to serve.

# apple pie

serves 8

## ingredients

### pastry
250 g (9 oz/2 cups) self-raising flour
85 g (3 oz/$^2$/$_3$ cup) cornflour (cornstarch)
180 g (6 oz) unsalted butter, chilled and cubed
90 g (3$^1$/$_4$ oz/$^1$/$_3$ cup) caster (superfine) sugar
1 egg, lightly beaten

40 g (1$^1$/$_2$ oz) unsalted butter
6 green apples, peeled, cored and thinly sliced
1 tablespoon lemon juice
140 g (5 oz/$^3$/$_4$ cup) soft brown sugar
1 teaspoon ground nutmeg
2 tablespoons plain (all-purpose) flour mixed
    with 3 tablespoons water
25 g (1 oz/$^1$/$_4$ cup) ground almonds
milk, to brush
sugar, to sprinkle

## method

Lightly grease a 1 litre (35 fl oz/4 cups), 20 cm (8 in) metal pie dish. Sift the flours into a large bowl and rub in the butter with your fingers until mixture resembles fine breadcrumbs. Stir in the sugar and a pinch of salt. Make a well, add the egg and mix with a knife, using a cutting action, until the mixture comes together in beads. Put the dough on a floured surface and press into a smooth disc, cover with plastic wrap and refrigerate for 20 minutes.

Use two-thirds of the dough to line the base and side of the dish. Roll out the remaining dough to make a lid. Cover and refrigerate for 20 minutes. Preheat the oven to 200°C (400°F/ Gas 6) and heat a baking tray.

Melt the butter in a large frying pan, add the apple and toss. Stir in the lemon juice, sugar and nutmeg and cook for 10 minutes, or until tender. Add the flour and water mixture, then the almonds. Bring to the boil and cook, stirring, for 2–3 minutes. Pour into a bowl and cool. Put the apple in the pastry case. Cover with the pastry lid and press lightly onto the rim. Trim the edges and pinch together to seal. Prick over the top, brush with milk and sprinkle with sugar. Bake on the hot tray for 40 minutes, or until golden.

# rhubarb pie

serves 6

## ingredients

**pastry**

250 g (9 oz/2 cups) plain (all-purpose) flour
30 g (1 oz) unsalted butter, chilled and cubed
70 g (2$^1/_2$ oz) copha (white vegetable shortening)
2 tablespoons icing (confectioners') sugar
160 ml (5$^1/_4$ fl oz/$^2/_3$ cup) iced water

1.5 kg (3 lb 5 oz) rhubarb, trimmed and cut into
    2 cm ($^3/_4$ in) pieces
250 g (9 oz/1 cup) caster (superfine) sugar
$^1/_2$ teaspoon ground cinnamon
2$^1/_2$ tablespoons cornflour (cornstarch), mixed
    with 3 tablespoons water
30 g (1 oz) unsalted butter, cubed
1 egg, lightly beaten
icing (confectioners') sugar, to dust

## method

Grease a 25 x 20 x 4 cm (10 x 8 x 1$^1/_2$ in) ceramic pie dish. Sift the flour and $^1/_2$ teaspoon of salt into a bowl and rub in the butter and copha until mixture looks like breadcrumbs. Stir in the icing sugar. Make a well, add most of the water and mix with a flat-bladed knife, using a cutting action, until it comes together in beads. Gather dough together and put on a floured surface. Press into a ball, flatten a little and cover in plastic wrap. Refrigerate for 30 minutes.

Put the rhubarb, sugar, cinnamon and 2 tablespoons water in a pan and stir over low heat until the sugar dissolves. Simmer, covered, for 5–8 minutes, or until the rhubarb is tender. Add the cornflour and water mixture. Bring to the boil, stirring until thickened. Allow to cool. Preheat the oven to 180°C (350°F/Gas 4) and heat a baking tray.

Roll out two-thirds of the dough to a 30 cm (12 in) circle and put into pie dish. Spoon in the rhubarb and dot with butter. Roll out remaining pastry for a lid. Brush the pie rim with egg and press the top in place. Trim the edges and make a slit in the top. Decorate with pastry scraps and brush with egg. Bake on the tray for 35 minutes, or until golden. Dust with icing sugar.

# lemon meringue pie

serves 4–6

### ingredients

375 g (13 oz) sweet shortcrust (pie) pastry
30 g (1 oz/$^1$/$_4$ cup) plain (all-purpose) flour
30 g (1 oz/$^1$/$_4$ cup) cornflour (cornstarch)
250 g (9 oz/1 cup) caster (superfine) sugar
185 ml (6 fl oz/$^3$/$_4$ cup) lemon juice
1 tablespoon grated lemon zest
50 g (1$^3$/$_4$ oz) unsalted butter, chopped
6 egg yolks

### meringue
6 egg whites
pinch of cream of tartar
345 g (11$^3$/$_4$ oz/1$^1$/$_2$ cups) caster (superfine) sugar

### method

Grease a 25 x 18 x 3 cm (10 x 7 x 1$^1$/$_4$ in) pie plate. Roll pastry out between two sheets of baking paper into a 30 cm (12 in) circle. Invert the pastry into the plate. Trim the edges. Re-roll pastry trimmings and cut into three 10 x 2 cm (4 x $^3$/$_4$ in) strips. Brush the pie rim with water and place the pastry strips around the top. Prick over the base with a fork. Cover and refrigerate for 20 minutes. Preheat the oven to 180°C (350°F/Gas 4). Blind bake the pastry for 15 minutes. Remove the beads and bake for 15–20 minutes. Cool.

Increase the oven to 200°C (400°F/Gas 6). Put the flours, sugar, lemon juice and zest in a saucepan. Gradually add 315 ml (10$^3$/$_4$ fl oz/1$^1$/$_4$ cups) of water and whisk over medium heat until smooth. Cook, stirring, for 2 minutes, or until thick. Remove from the heat and whisk in the butter and egg yolks. Return to low heat and stir, for 2 minutes, or until thick.

To make the meringue, beat the eggwhites and cream of tartar in a dry bowl using an electric mixer until soft peaks form. Gradually pour in the sugar, beating until the meringue is thick. Spread the lemon filling into the pastry base, then cover with the meringue, piling high in the centre and making peaks with a knife. Bake for 8–10 minutes, or until lightly browned.

# baked apples

serves 4

## ingredients

4 granny smith apples
50 g (1³/₄ oz) dried apricots, finely chopped
50 g (1³/₄ oz) dates, finely chopped
1 tablespoon dry breadcrumbs
¹/₂ teaspoon ground cinnamon
1 tablespoon honey, warmed
2 teaspoons apricot jam, warmed
20 g (¹/₂ oz) firm butter
ground nutmeg, for sprinkling

## method

Preheat the oven to 180°C (350°F/Gas 4) and lightly grease an ovenproof dish.

Core the apples and, using a sharp knife, run a small slit around the circumference of each apple to stop it splitting during baking.

Combine the apricots, dates, breadcrumbs, cinnamon, honey and jam in a bowl. Divide the mixture into four, and push it into the apples using your fingers. Dot the top of each apple with the butter, and put the apples in the prepared dish.

Bake for about 45–50 minutes, or until the apples are tender all the way through—test with a skewer to be absolutely sure. Serve hot with cream or ice cream. Sprinkle some nutmeg over the top before serving.

# plum cobbler

serves 4

## ingredients

825 g (1 lb 13 oz) tin dark plums, pitted
1 tablespoon honey
2 ripe pears, peeled, cored and cut into eighths

### topping

250 g (9 oz/1 cup) self-raising flour
1 tablespoon caster (superfine) sugar
$^1/_4$ teaspoon ground cardamom or ground
    cinnamon
40 g ($1^1/_2$ oz) unsalted butter, chilled and
    chopped
3 tablespoons milk
extra milk, for brushing
1 tablespoon caster (superfine) sugar, extra
$^1/_4$ teaspoon ground cardamom or ground
    cinnamon, extra

## method

Preheat the oven to 200°C (400°F/Gas 6). Grease an 18 cm (7 in) round 1.5 litre (52 fl oz/6 cup) ovenproof dish. Drain the plums, reserving 185 ml (6 fl oz/$^3/_4$ cup) of the syrup. Place the syrup, honey and pear in a large wide saucepan and bring to the boil. Reduce the heat and simmer for 8 minutes, or until the pear is tender. Add the plums.

To make the topping, sift the flour, sugar, cardamom and a pinch of salt into a large bowl. Rub in the butter with your fingers until it resembles fine breadcrumbs. Stir in the milk using a flat-bladed knife, mixing lightly to form a soft dough—add a little more milk if necessary. Turn onto a floured surface and form into a smooth ball. Roll out to a 1 cm ($^1/_2$ in) thickness and cut into rounds with a 4 cm ($1^1/_2$ in) cutter.

Spoon the hot fruit into the dish, then arrange the circles of dough in an overlapping pattern over the fruit, on the inside edge of the dish only—leave the fruit in the centre exposed. Brush the dough with the extra milk. Mix the extra sugar and cardamom and sprinkle over the dough.

Place the dish on a baking tray and bake for 30 minutes, or until the topping is golden and cooked.

# apple crumble

serves 4

## ingredients

8 apples
90 g (3$^1$/$_4$ oz/$^1$/$_3$ cup) caster (superfine) sugar
zest of 1 lemon
120 g (4 oz) butter
125 g (4$^1$/$_2$ oz/1 cup) plain (all-purpose) flour
1 teaspoon ground cinnamon
pouring (whipping) cream, to serve

## method

Turn the oven to 180°C (350°/Gas 4). Peel and core the apples, then cut into chunks. Put the apple, 2 tablespoons of the sugar and the lemon zest in a small baking dish and mix them together. Dot 2 tablespoons of butter over the top.

Rub the remaining butter into the flour until you have a texture that resembles coarse breadcrumbs.

Stir in the rest of the sugar and cinnamon. Add 1–2 tablespoons of water and stir the crumbs together so they form bigger clumps.

Sprinkle the crumble mixture over the apple and bake the crumble for 1 hour 15 minutes, by which time the top should be browned and the juice bubbling up through the crumble. Serve with cream.

# iced tea bun

makes 1

## ingredients

250 g (9 oz/2 cups) plain (all-purpose) flour
7 g ($^1/_4$ oz) dried yeast
2 tablespoons caster (superfine) sugar
2 teaspoons grated orange zest
60 g ($2^1/_4$ oz/$^1/_2$ cup) sultanas
4 tablespoons orange juice
1 egg, lightly beaten
30 g (1 oz) butter, melted
4 tablespoons warm water

### glacé icing
125 g ($4^1/_2$ oz/1 cup) icing (confectioners') sugar
15 g ($^1/_2$ oz) butter
1 tablespoon boiling water
pink food colouring
desiccated coconut, to sprinkle

## method

Lightly grease a baking tray. Sift the flour into a large bowl. Add the yeast, sugar, zest and sultanas. Stir to combine and make a well in the centre. Add the combined orange juice, beaten egg and melted butter and almost all the water. Mix to a soft dough, adding more water if necessary. Turn out onto a lightly floured surface. Knead for 10 minutes, or until smooth and elastic.

Place the dough in a lightly oiled bowl. Cover with plastic wrap and leave in a warm place for 45 minutes, or until risen. Punch down the dough and knead for 1 minute. Shape the dough into a ball and roll or pat out to a 25 cm (10 in) circle. Place on the tray, cover and leave in a warm place to rise for 30 minutes.

Preheat the oven to 180°C (350°F/Gas 4). Mark the dough into 8 wedges with the edge of a ruler. Cook for 20 minutes, or until golden brown. Turn out onto a wire rack. When cold, spread the glacé icing over the bun and sprinkle with coconut.

To make the glacé icing, sift the icing sugar into a heatproof bowl. Combine the butter and water in a saucepan. Stir over low heat until the butter has melted. Add to the sugar. Mix to a paste. Stand the bowl over saucepan of simmering water. Stir until glossy. Remove from heat. Tint the icing with food colouring.

# cherry pie

serves 6

## ingredients

500 g (1 lb 2 oz) shortcrust (pie) pastry
850 g (1 lb 14 oz) tinned seedless black cherries,
    drained well
60 g (2$^1/_4$ oz/$^1/_3$ cup) soft brown sugar
1$^1/_2$ teaspoons ground cinnamon
1 teaspoon finely grated lemon zest
1 teaspoon finely grated orange zest
1–2 drops almond extract
25 g (1 oz/$^1/_4$ cup) ground almonds
1 egg, lightly beaten

## method

Preheat the oven to 190°C (375°F/Gas 5). Roll out two-thirds of the dough between two sheets of baking paper to form a circle large enough to fit a 22 x 20 x 2 cm (8$^1/_2$ x 8 x $^3/_4$ in) pie dish. Remove the top sheet of baking paper and invert the pastry into the pie plate. Cut away the excess pastry with a small knife. Roll out the remaining pastry large enough to cover the pie. Refrigerate, covered in plastic wrap, for 20 minutes.

Place the cherries, sugar, cinnamon, lemon and orange zests, and almond extract in a bowl and mix to coat the cherries.

Line the pastry base with the ground almonds. Spoon in the filling and brush the pastry edges with beaten egg. Cover with the pastry lid. Use a fork to seal the edges pastry. Cut four slits in the top of the pie to allow steam to escape. Brush the pastry with beaten egg. Bake for 1 hour, or until the pastry is golden and the juices are bubbling through the slits in the pastry. Serve warm.

# peach pie

serves 6

## ingredients

500 g (1 lb 2 oz) shortcrust (pie) pastry
1.6 kg (3 lb 8 oz) tinned peach slices, well-drained
125 g ($4^1/_2$ oz/$^1/_2$ cup) caster (superfine) sugar
30 g (1 oz/$^1/_4$ cup) cornflour (cornstarch)
$^1/_4$ teaspoon almond extract
20 g ($^1/_2$ oz) unsalted butter, chopped
1 tablespoon milk
1 egg, lightly beaten
caster (superfine) sugar, to sprinkle

## method

Roll out two-thirds of the dough between two sheets of baking paper until large enough to line a 23 x 18 x 3 cm (9 x 7 x $1^1/_4$ in) pie tin. Remove the top sheet of paper and invert the pastry into the tin. Use a small ball of pastry to press the pastry into the tin. Trim any excess pastry with a knife. Refrigerate for 20 minutes.

Preheat the oven to 200°C (400°F/Gas 6). Line the pastry with crumpled baking paper and pour in baking beads or rice. Bake for 10 minutes, remove the paper and beads and return to the oven for 5 minutes, or until the pastry base is dry and lightly coloured. Allow to cool.

Mix the peaches, sugar, cornflour and almond essence in a bowl, then spoon into the pastry shell. Dot with butter and moisten the edges with milk.

Roll out remaining dough to a 25 cm (10 in) square. Using a fluted pastry cutter, cut into 10 strips 2.5 cm (1 in) wide. Lay the strips in a lattice pattern over the filling, pressing firmly on the edges and trim. Brush with egg and sprinkle with sugar. Bake for 10 minutes, reduce the heat to 180°C (350°F/Gas 4) and bake for 30 minutes, or until golden. Cool before serving.

# damper

serves 4

## ingredients

375 g (13 oz/3 cups) self-raising flour, plus extra,
    for dusting
1–2 teaspoons salt
90 g ($3^1/_4$ oz) butter, melted, plus extra, to serve
125 ml ($4^1/_2$ oz/$^1/_2$ cup) milk, plus extra,
    for glazing
golden syrup or honey, to serve

## method

Preheat the oven to 210°C (375°F/Gas 5). Lightly grease a baking tray. Sift the flour and salt into a large mixing bowl. Make a well in the centre. Combine the butter, milk and 125 ml (4 fl oz/$^1/_2$ cup) of water and add to the flour. Stir with a knife until just combined.

Turn onto a lightly floured surface. Knead for 20 seconds, or until smooth. Transfer the dough to the tray. Press out to a 20 cm (8 in) round.

Using a sharp pointed knife, score into 8 sections 1 cm ($^1/_2$ in) deep. Brush with milk and dust with flour. Bake for 10 minutes.

Reduce the heat to 180°C (350°F/Gas 4). Bake for 15 minutes, or until the damper is golden and sounds hollow when tapped. Serve with extra butter and golden syrup or honey.

# scones

makes 12

## ingredients

**plain scones**
250 g (9 oz/2 cups) self-raising flour
pinch of salt (optional)
30 g ( 1 oz) butter, cut into small pieces
125 ml ($4^1/_2$ oz/$^1/_2$ cup) milk
milk, extra, for glazing
jam and whipped cream, to serve

## method

Preheat the oven to 210°C (415°F/Gas 6–7). Lightly grease a baking tray. Sift the flour and salt into a bowl. Add the chopped butter and rub in lightly using your fingertips.

Make a well in the centre of the flour. Add almost all of the combined milk and 3 tablespoons of water. Mix with a flat-bladed knife to a soft dough, adding more liquid if necessary.

Turn the dough onto a lightly floured surface (use self-raising flour). Knead the dough briefly and lightly until smooth. Press or roll out the dough to form a round 1–2 cm thick.

Cut the dough into rounds using a floured round 5 cm (2 in) cutter. Place the rounds on the prepared tray. Glaze the rounds with milk. Bake for 10–12 minutes, or until golden brown. Serve the scones with jam and whipped cream.

# currant cream scones

makes 12 scones

## ingredients

375 g (13 oz/3 cups) plain (all-purpose) flour
1$^1$/$_2$ teaspoons bicarbonate of soda (baking soda)
3 teaspoons cream of tartar
1 teaspoon mixed (pumpkin pie) spice
2 teaspoons caster (superfine) sugar, plus extra
  for sprinkling
50 g (1$^3$/$_4$ oz) unsalted butter, chilled and diced
150 ml (5 fl oz) pouring (whipping) cream
150 ml (5 fl oz) milk, plus extra for brushing
125 g (4$^1$/$_2$ oz/$^3$/$_4$ cup) currants
jam and thick (double/heavy) cream, to serve

## method

Preheat the oven to 220°C (425°F/Gas 7). Lightly grease a baking tray.

Sift the flour, bicarbonate of soda, cream of tartar, mixed spice and sugar into a large bowl. Using your fingertips, rub in the butter until the mixture resembles breadcrumbs. Add the cream, milk and currants and mix with a flat-bladed knife to form a soft dough, adding a little extra flour if the mixture is too sticky.

Using floured hands, gently gather the dough together and lift out onto a lightly floured work surface. Pat into a smooth ball, then press out to a 2 cm ($^3$/$_4$ in) thickness. Using a 6 cm (2$^1$/$_2$ in) pastry cutter, cut the dough into rounds, or use a knife dipped in flour to cut 4 cm (1$^1$/$_2$ in) squares.

Place the scones on the baking tray, brush the tops lightly with milk and sprinkle with the extra sugar. Bake for 10–12 minutes, or until golden. Transfer to a wire rack lined with a tea towel (dish towel). Serve the scones warm with marmalade or jam and thick cream.

# strawberry jam

Fills six 250 ml (9 fl oz) jars

## ingredients

1.25 kg (2 lb 12 oz/5 cups) sugar
1.5 kg (3 lb 5 oz) strawberries
125 ml (4 fl oz/$^1/_2$ cup) lemon juice

## method

Warm the sugar by spreading in a large baking dish and heating in a 120°C (250°F/Gas $^1/_2$) oven for 10 minutes, stirring occasionally. Put two plates in the freezer.

Hull the strawberries and put in a large saucepan with the lemon juice, sugar and 125 ml (4 fl oz/$^1/_2$ cup) water. Warm gently, without boiling, stirring carefully with a wooden spoon. Try not to break up the fruit too much.

Increase the heat and, without boiling, continue stirring for 10 minutes, until the sugar has thoroughly dissolved. Increase the heat and boil, without stirring, for 20 minutes. Start testing for setting point. Place $^1/_4$ teaspoon jam on one of the plates. A skin will form and the jam will wrinkle when pushed with your finger when setting point is reached.

Remove from the heat and leave for 5 minutes before removing any scum that forms on the surface. Pour into hot sterilized jars and seal. Allow to cool, then label and date each jar.

# raspberry jam

Fills seven 250 ml (9 fl oz) jars

## ingredients

1.5 kg (3 lb 5 oz) raspberries
4 tablespoons lemon juice
1.5 kg (3 lb 5 oz/6 cups) sugar

## method

Put two small plates in the freezer. Place the raspberries and lemon juice in a large saucepan. Gently stir over low heat for 10 minutes, or until the raspberries have softened. Warm the sugar by spreading in a baking dish and heating in a 120°C (250°F/Gas $^1/_2$) oven for 10 minutes, stirring occasionally.

Add the sugar to the pan and stir, without boiling, for 5 minutes or until the sugar has completely dissolved.

Bring the jam to the boil and boil for 20 minutes, then start testing for setting point. Place $^1/_4$ teaspoon jam on one of the plates. A skin will form and the jam will wrinkle when pushed with your finger when setting point is reached. Cool for 5 minutes, then remove any scum from the surface.

Pour into hot sterilized jars and seal. Allow to cool, then label and date each jar.

# plum and star anise jam

makes 4 cups

## ingredients

1 kg (2 lb 4 oz) firm plums, quartered
1 kg (2 lb 4 oz) caster (superfine) sugar
125 ml (4 fl oz/$^1/_2$ cup) lemon juice
3 star anise
1 teaspoon ground ginger

## method

In a heavy-based saucepan, put the plums, sugar, lemon juice, 125 ml (4 fl oz/$^1/_2$ cup) of water, star anise, and ground ginger.

Bring the ingredients in the saucepan to a boil, stirring until the sugar has dissolved. Reduce the heat to medium and simmer for 35–40 minutes, stirring occasionally.

Place a saucer in the freezer to chill. Test the setting consistency of the jam by placing a spoonful onto the chilled saucer. Cool slightly and run your finger through the jam, if it crinkles it is ready.

Remove any froth from the surface of the jam and remove the whole star anise with a metal spoon. Pour the jam into prepared hot sterilized jars and seal.

# kumquat marmalade

makes 1.75 litres (61 fl oz/7 cups)

## ingredients

1 kg (2 lb 4 oz) kumquats
3 tablespoons lemon juice
1.25 kg (2 lb 12 oz/5$^2$/$_3$ cups) sugar
10 cm (4 in) square of muslin (cheesecloth)

## method

Cut the kumquat in half lengthways, reserving any pips, slice thinly and put in a large non-metallic bowl with the water. Tie any pips securely in the muslin (cheesecloth) and add to the bowl. Cover and leave overnight. Put two plates in the freezer. Put the kumquats, lemon juice, 1.25 litres (44 fl oz/5 cups) water and muslin bag in a saucepan. Bring to the boil, then reduce the heat and simmer, covered, for 30–45 minutes.

Meanwhile, to warm the sugar, preheat the oven to 150°C (300°F/Gas 2). Spread the sugar evenly in a baking dish and heat in the oven for 10–15 minutes. Add the warmed sugar to the jam and stir over low heat, without boiling, for 5 minutes, or until dissolved. Return to the boil and boil rapidly, stirring often, for 20 minutes. When the syrup falls from a wooden spoon in thick sheets, test for setting point. Place $^1$/$_4$ teaspoon marmalade on one of the plates. A skin will form and the marmalade will wrinkle when pushed with your finger when setting point is reached. If not, return to the heat and retest a few minutes later with the other plate. Discard the muslin bag. Pour into hot sterilized jars and seal. Allow to cool, then label and date each jar. Store in a cool, dark place for 6–12 months. Refrigerate after opening for up to 6 weeks.

# lime marmalade

Fills ten 250 ml (9 fl oz) jars

## ingredients

1 kg (2 lb 4 oz) limes
2.25 kg (5 lb) sugar

## method

Scrub the limes under hot, running water to remove the wax coating. Cut them in half lengthways, then slice thinly. Place in a large non-metal bowl with 2 litres (70 fl oz/8 cups) water. Cover with plastic wrap and leave overnight.

Place two small plates in the freezer. Place the fruit and water in a large saucepan. Bring slowly to the boil, then reduce the heat and simmer, covered, for 45 minutes, or until the fruit is tender. Warm the sugar by spreading in a large baking dish and heating in a 120°C (250°F/Gas $^1/_2$) oven for 10 minutes, stirring occasionally.

Add the sugar to the fruit and stir over low heat, without boiling, for 5 minutes, or until all the sugar has dissolved. Then boil rapidly, without stirring, for 20 minutes. When the syrup falls from a wooden spoon in thick sheets, start testing for setting point. Place $^1/_4$ teaspoon of marmalade on one of the plates. A skin will form and the marmalade will wrinkle when pushed with your finger when setting point is reached. Cool for 5 minutes, then remove any scum.

Spoon the marmalade into hot, sterilized jars and seal. Turn upside down for 2 minutes, then invert. Allow to cool, then label and date each jar.

# swish sweets

Our **sweet horizons have widened** over the past few decades. Now we are just as likely to make a **soufflé** as a steamed pudding, or a **pannacotta** as a sponge cake. Having trawled the global larder, we now **enjoy the best** the food world has to offer, without completely forgetting our traditional culinary roots.

# grilled figs with ricotta

serves 4

## ingredients

2 tablespoons honey
1 cinnamon stick
3 tablespoons flaked almonds
4 large or 8 small fresh figs
125 g ($4^1/_2$ oz/$^1/_2$ cup) ricotta cheese
$^1/_2$ teaspoon natural vanilla extract
2 tablespoons icing (confectioners') sugar, sifted
pinch of ground cinnamon
$^1/_2$ teaspoon finely grated orange zest

## method

Put the honey and cinnamon stick in a small saucepan with 4 tablespoons of water. Bring to the boil, then reduce the heat and simmer gently for 6 minutes, or until thickened and reduced by half. Discard the cinnamon stick and stir in the almonds.

Preheat the grill (broiler) to hot and grease a shallow ovenproof dish large enough to fit all the figs side by side. Slice the figs into quarters from the top to within 1 cm ($^1/_2$ in) of the bottom, keeping them attached at the base. Arrange in the prepared dish.

Combine the ricotta, vanilla, icing sugar, ground cinnamon and orange zest in a small bowl. Divide the filling among the figs, spooning it into their cavities. Spoon the syrup over the top. Place under the grill and cook until the juices start to come out from the figs and the almonds are lightly toasted. Cool for 2–3 minutes. Spoon the juices and any fallen almonds from the bottom of the dish over the figs and serve.

# almond semifreddo

serves 8–10

## ingredients

300 ml (10$^1/_2$ fl oz) pouring (whipping) cream
4 eggs, at room temperature, separated
85 g (3 oz/$^2/_3$ cup) icing (confectioners') sugar
3 tablespoons Amaretto
80 g (2$^3/_4$ oz/$^1/_2$ cup) blanched almonds, toasted
   and chopped
8 Amaretti biscuits, crushed

fresh fruit or extra Amaretto

## method

Whip the cream until firm peaks form, cover and chill. Line a 10 x 21 cm (4 x 8$^1/_2$ in) loaf tin with plastic wrap so that it overhangs the two long sides.

Put the egg yolks and icing sugar in a large bowl and beat until pale and creamy.

Whisk the egg whites in a separate bowl until firm peaks form. Stir the Amaretto, almonds and amaretti biscuits into the egg yolk mixture, then carefully fold in the chilled cream and the egg whites until well combined.

Carefully pour or spoon into the lined loaf tin and cover with the overhanging plastic. Freeze for 4 hours, or until frozen but not rock hard. Serve in slices with fresh fruit or a sprinkling of Amaretto.

# hazelnut biscotti with Frangelico shots

makes 40

## ingredients

215 g  (7$^1/_2$ oz/1$^3/_4$ cups) plain (all-purpose) flour
160 g (5$^3/_4$ oz/$^2/_3$ cup) caster (superfine) sugar
$^1/_2$ teaspoon baking powder
60 g (2$^1/_4$ oz) chilled unsalted butter, cubed
2 eggs
150 g (51/2 oz/1$^1/_4$ cups) roughly chopped
    roasted hazelnuts
2 teaspoons grated orange zest
$^1/_2$ teaspoon caster (superfine) sugar, extra

### Frangelico shot

3 tablespoons double-strength coffee per person
1–2 teaspoons Frangelico per person

## method

Preheat the oven to 180°C (350°F/Gas 4). Line two baking trays with baking paper. Place the sifted flour, sugar, baking powder and a pinch of salt in a food processor and mix for 2 seconds. Add the butter and pulse until the mixture resembles fine breadcrumbs. Add the eggs and process until it comes together.

Transfer the dough to a floured surface and knead in the hazelnuts and zest. Divide into two portions and, using floured hands, shape each into a log about 20 cm (8 in) long. Place on the baking trays and sprinkle with the extra sugar. Press the top of each log down gently to flatten slightly. Bake for 20 minutes, or until golden. Remove and cool for 20 minutes. Reduce the oven temperature to 160°C (315°F/Gas 2–3).

Cut the logs into 5 mm–1 cm ($^1/_4$–$^1/_2$ in) slices on the diagonal (at least 6 cm/2$^1/_2$ in long). Turn the baking paper over, then spread on the tray in a single layer. Return to the oven and bake for a further 20–25 minutes, or until just begining to colour. Cool completely.

To make the Frangelico shot, pour hot coffee into shot glasses and top with Frangelico to taste.

# crème caramel

serves 6

## ingredients

250 ml (9 fl oz/1 cup) milk
250 ml (9 fl oz/1 cup) pouring (whipping) cream
375 g (13 oz/1$^1$/$_2$ cups) caster (superfine) sugar
1 teaspoon natural vanilla extract
4 eggs, lightly beaten
90 g (3$^1$/$_4$ oz/$^1$/$_3$ cup) caster (superfine) sugar, extra

## method

Preheat the oven to 200°C (400°F/Gas 6). Place the milk and cream in a saucepan and gradually bring to boiling point.

Put the sugar in a frying pan and cook over medium heat for 8–10 minutes. Stir occasionally as the sugar melts to form a golden toffee. The sugar may clump together—break up any lumps with a wooden spoon. Pour the toffee into the base of six 125 ml (4 fl oz/$^1$/$_2$ cup) ramekins or ovenproof dishes.

Combine the vanilla, eggs and extra sugar in a bowl. Remove the milk and cream from the heat and gradually add to the egg mixture, whisking well. Pour the custard mixture evenly over the toffee. Place the ramekins in a baking dish and pour in boiling water until it comes halfway up the sides of the dishes. Bake for 20 minutes, or until set. Use a flat-bladed knife to run around the edges of the dishes and carefully turn out the crème caramel onto a serving plate, toffee-side-up.

# madeleines

makes 14 (or 30 small ones)

## ingredients

3 eggs
100 g (3$^1$/$_2$ oz/$^1$/$_2$ cup) caster (superfine) sugar
150 g (5$^1$/$_2$ oz/1$^1$/$_4$ cups) plain (all-purpose) flour
100 g (3$^1$/$_2$ oz) unsalted butter, melted
grated zest of 1 lemon and 1 orange

## method

Preheat the oven to 200°C (400°F/Gas 6). Lightly grease a tray of madeleine moulds and coat with flour, then tap the tray to remove the excess flour.

Whisk the eggs and sugar until the mixture is thick and pale and the whisk leaves a trail when lifted. Gently fold in the flour, then the melted butter and grated lemon and orange zest. Spoon into the moulds, leaving a little room for rising. Bake for 12 minutes (small madeleines will only need 7 minutes), or until very lightly golden and springy to the touch. Remove from the tray and cool on a wire rack.

# nougat

makes 1 kg (2 lb 4 oz)

## ingredients

500 g (1 lb 2 oz/2 cups) sugar
250 ml (9 fl oz/1 cup) liquid glucose
175 g (6 oz/$^1/_2$ cup) honey (preferably blossom
   honey)
2 egg whites
1 teaspoon natural vanilla extract
125 g (4$^1/_2$ oz) unsalted butter, softened
60 g (2$^1/_4$ oz) almonds, unblanched and toasted
100 g (3$^1/_2$ oz) glacé cherries

## method

Grease a 18 x 28 cm (7 x 11$^1/_4$ in) baking dish and line with
baking paper. Stir the sugar, glucose, honey, 3 tablespoons
water and $^1/_4$ teaspoon salt over low heat in a heavy-based
saucepan until dissolved. Bring to the boil and cook at a rolling
boil for 8 minutes, or until the mixture forms a hard ball
when tested in water or reaches 122°C (225°F) on a sugar
thermometer. The correct temperature is very important,
otherwise it will not set properly.

Beat the egg whites with electric beaters until stiff peaks form.
Slowly add a quarter of the sugar mixture to the egg whites
and beat for 5 minutes, or until it holds its shape. Cook the
remaining syrup for 2 minutes, or until a small amount forms
brittle threads when dropped in cold water, or reaches 157°C
(315°F) on a sugar thermometer. Add slowly to the meringue
mixture with the beaters running, and beat until very thick.

Add the vanilla and butter, and beat for another 5 minutes. Stir
in the almonds and cherries with a metal spoon. Turn the mixture
into the tin and smooth the top. Chill for at least four hours,
or until firm. Turn onto a large board and cut into 2 x 4 cm
($^3/_4$ x 1$^1/_2$ in) pieces. Wrap each piece in cellophane and store
in the refrigerator.

# caramelized pears

serves 4

## ingredients

4 ripe corella pears, or other small sweet pears
4 tablespoons demerara or soft brown sugar
40 g (1$^1$/$_2$ oz) butter, softened
1 tablespoon brandy
200 g (7 oz) crème fraîche, to serve
4 lemon wedges, to serve

## method

Heat the grill (broiler) to high. Peel the pears and halve them from top to bottom, keeping the stems intact if possible. Core the pears using a melon baller or a spoon.

Mix the sugar and butter together in a small bowl, then stir in the brandy. Sit the pears, cut side down, on the grill tray, and brush the tops with some of the sugar mixture. Grill for about 5 minutes, or until lightly browned.

Turn the pears, brush with a little more of the sugar mixture, then fill the cavities with the remaining mixture. Grill for another 3 minutes, or until the sugar is bubbling and brown. Baste again, then grill for a further 3 minutes.

Remove from the heat and leave the pears for 5 minutes, then serve with a scoop of crème fraîche, a squeeze of lemon juice and any juices from the grill tray.

# panforte

serves 10

## ingredients

110 g (3³/₄ oz/³/₄ cup) hazelnuts
110 g (3³/₄ oz/³/₄ cup) almonds
125 g (4¹/₂ oz/²/₃ cup) candied mixed peel,
   chopped
100 g (3¹/₂ oz/²/₃ cup) candied pineapple,
   chopped
grated zest of 1 lemon
75 g (2¹/₂ oz/²/₃ cup) plain (all-purpose) flour
1 teaspoon ground cinnamon
¹/₄ teaspoon ground coriander
¹/₄ teaspoon ground cloves
¹/₄ teaspoon grated nutmeg
pinch of white pepper
150 g (5¹/₂ oz/²/₃ cup) sugar
4 tablespoons honey
50 g (1³/₄ oz) unsalted butter
icing (confectioners') sugar, to dust

## method

Line a 20 cm (8 in) spring-form cake tin with baking paper and grease well with butter.

Toast the nuts under a hot grill (broiler), turning so they brown on all sides, then allow to cool. Put the nuts in a bowl with the mixed peel, pineapple, lemon zest, flour and spices and toss together. Preheat the oven to 150°C (300°F/Gas 2).

Put the sugar, honey and butter in a saucepan and melt. Cook the syrup until it reaches 118°C (245°F) on a sugar thermometer, or a little of it dropped into cold water forms a firm ball when moulded between your fingers.

Pour the syrup into the nut mixture and mix well, working fast before it stiffens too much. Pour straight into the prepared tin, smooth the surface and bake for 35 minutes. (Unlike other cakes, this cake will neither firm up as it cooks nor colour at all, so you need to time it carefully.)

Cool in the tin until the cake firms up enough to remove the side of the tin. Peel off the paper and leave to cool completely. Dust with icing sugar.

# sticky fig and hazelnut puddings

makes 6

## ingredients

70 g (2$^1/_2$ oz/$^1/_2$ cup) toasted hazelnuts
150 ml (5 fl oz) fresh orange juice
100 g (3$^1/_2$ oz/$^1/_2$ cup) chopped dried figs, plus
    6 dried figs, extra, cut horizontally
$^1/_4$ teaspoon ground ginger
$^1/_4$ teaspoon ground cinnamon
3 teaspoons finely grated orange zest
$^1/_2$ teaspoon bicarbonate of soda (baking soda)
80 g (2$^3/_4$ oz) butter, softened
115 g (4 oz/$^1/_2$ cup) soft brown sugar
1 egg
90 g (3$^1/_4$ oz/$^3/_4$ cup) self-raising flour
2 tablespoons maple syrup
boiling water, for steaming
thick (double/heavy) cream, to serve

## method

Preheat the oven to 200°C (400°F/Gas 6). Spread the hazelnuts out on a tray and place in the oven for 10–15 minutes. Tip the nuts onto a tea towel (dish towel) and rub to remove the skins. Put the nuts in a food processor and pulse until finely ground. Grease six 250 ml (9 fl oz/1 cup) ramekins and place a square of baking paper in the base of each. Pour the orange juice into a saucepan and bring to the boil over medium heat. Add the chopped figs, ginger, cinnamon and 1 teaspoon of the orange zest and cook for 1 minute. Remove from the heat and add the bicarbonate of soda, then set aside to cool for 10 minutes. Combine the butter and sugar in a bowl and beat with electric beaters until light and fluffy. Add the egg and beat until well combined. Fold in the hazelnuts, and add the flour in three batches Pour the orange sauce into the pudding mixture and stir well to combine. Pour the maple syrup into the base of the ramekins and top with the remaining orange zest. Arrange two of the extra fig halves in the base of each ramekin. Spoon in the pudding mixture until it is three-quarters full, then cover each ramekin with foil. Arrange the puddings in the base of a deep roasting tin. Fill the baking tin with enough boiling water to come halfway up the sides of the ramekins, and bake the puddings for 35 minutes, or until cooked. Set the ramekins aside for 5 minutes before inverting onto a plate and serving with cream.

# tiramisu

serves 4

## ingredients

5 eggs, separated
180 g (6 oz) caster (superfine) sugar
250 g (9 oz) mascarpone cheese
250 ml (9 fl oz/1 cup) cold strong coffee
3 tablespoons brandy or sweet Marsala
44 small sponge fingers
80 g (2$^3/_4$ oz) dark chocolate, finely grated

## method

Beat the egg yolks with the sugar until the sugar has dissolved and the mixture is light and fluffy and leaves a ribbon trail when dropped from the whisk. Add the mascarpone and beat until the mixture is smooth. Whisk the egg whites in a dry glass bowl until soft peaks form. Fold into the mascarpone mixture.

Pour the coffee into a shallow dish and add the brandy. Dip some of the sponge finger biscuits into the coffee mixture, using enough biscuits to cover the base of a 25 cm (10 in) square dish. The biscuits should be fairly well soaked on both sides but not so much so that they break up. Arrange the biscuits in one tightly packed layer in the base of the dish.

Spread half the mascarpone mixture over the layer of biscuits. Add another layer of soaked biscuits and then another layer of mascarpone, smoothing the top layer neatly. Refrigerate for at least 2 hours or overnight. Dust with grated chocolate to serve.

# chocolate raspberry ice cream sandwich

serves 4

## ingredients

300 g (10$^1/_2$ oz) frozen chocolate pound cake
2 tablespoons raspberry liqueur (optional)
250 g (9 oz/2 cups) fresh or thawed raspberries
250 g (9 oz/1 cup) sugar
1 teaspoon lemon juice
1 litre (35 fl oz/4 cups) vanilla ice cream, softened
icing (confectioners') sugar, to dust

## method

Using a sharp knife, cut the pound cake lengthwise into four thin slices. Using a 6.5 cm (2$^1/_2$ in) plain cutter, cut eight rounds from the slices of cake. You will need two rounds of cake per person. Brush each round with half of the raspberry liqueur if using, then cover and set aside.

Line a 20 x 20 cm (8 x 8 in) tin or dish with baking paper, leaving a generous overhang of paper on two opposite sides. Place the raspberries, sugar, lemon juice and remaining liqueur in a blender and blend to a smooth purée. Reserving 125 ml (4 fl oz/$^1/_2$ cup) of the purée, fold the remainder through the ice cream and pour into the tin. Freeze for 2 hours, or until firm.

Remove the ice cream from the freezer and use the overhanging baking paper to lift from the tin. Using a 6.5 cm (2$^1/_2$ in) cutter, cut four rounds from the ice cream.

To assemble, place four slices of cake on a tray, top each with a round of ice cream and then the remaining slices of cake. Smooth the sides of the ice cream to neaten, if necessary. Return the sandwiches to the freezer for 5 minutes to firm. Dust with icing sugar and serve with the remaining raspberry sauce.

# praline semi freddo

serves 6

## ingredients

200 g (7 oz/1$^1$/$_4$ cups) blanched almonds
200 g (7 oz/1 cup) caster (superfine) sugar
600 ml (21 fl oz/2$^1$/$_2$ cups) thick (double) cream
2 eggs, separated
100 g (3$^1$/$_2$ oz/$^3$/$_4$ cup) icing (confectioners')
   sugar, sifted
2 tablespoons Mandorla (almond-flavoured
   Marsala) or brandy

## method

To make the praline, put the blanched almonds in a hot frying pan and dry-fry until well browned all over, then set aside. Melt the sugar in a saucepan over medium heat until golden, tipping the pan from side to side so the sugar melts evenly. Remove from the heat and stir in the almonds. Carefully pour into a greased baking tray and smooth out with the back of a spoon. Allow to cool completely, then finely crush the praline in a food processor. Pour the cream into a large bowl and whisk until soft peaks form.

Beat the egg yolks with a quarter of the icing sugar until pale. Whisk the egg whites in a glass bowl until firm peaks form, then gradually add the rest of the icing sugar and whisk until glossy firm peaks form. Fold the egg yolks into the cream, then fold in the egg whites. Fold in the praline and Mandorla.

Line six 250 ml (9 fl oz/1 cup) metal dariole moulds with two long strips of foil each, leaving the ends to overhang the edge. Spoon in the mixture, level the surface and tap each mould on the bench. Cover with foil and freeze for 24 hours. To unmould, leave at room temperature for 5 minutes, then lift out with the foil 'handles'.

# grilled mango cheeks with coconut ice cream

serves 6

## ingredients

1 litre (35 fl oz/4 cups) vanilla ice cream, softened
30 g (1 oz/$^1/_2$ cup) shredded coconut, toasted
3 large ripe mangoes
2 tablespoons soft brown sugar
1 lime, halved

## method

Mix the ice cream and coconut together in a large bowl, stirring only until just combined. Do not allow the ice cream to melt too much or it will become too icy. Return the mixture to the ice cream container and freeze for several hours, or overnight, until firm.

Preheat a barbecue flatplate, grill plate or chargrill pan to medium. Cut 2 cheeks off each mango, so you have 6 cheeks. If you prefer to serve the mangoes without their skins, scoop the cheeks away from the skin using a large spoon, then sprinkle the cheeks with the sugar. Alternatively, leave the skin on and score the flesh in a criss-cross pattern, then sprinkle the flesh with sugar.

Put the mango cheeks flesh-side-down on the barbecue and grill for 1–2 minutes, or until the sugar has caramelized. Divide the cheeks among six serving bowls and drizzle with a squeeze of lime. Add a scoop or two of coconut ice cream and serve.

# lemon gelato

serves 6

## ingredients

5 egg yolks
125 g (4$^1$/$_2$ oz/$^1$/$_2$ cup) sugar
500 ml (17 fl oz/2 cups) milk
2 tablespoons grated lemon zest
185 ml (6 fl oz/$^3$/$_4$ cup) lemon juice
3 tablespoons thick (double/heavy) cream

## method

Whisk the egg yolks and half the sugar together until pale and creamy. Place the milk, lemon zest and remaining sugar in a saucepan and bring to the boil. Pour over the egg mixture and whisk to combine. Pour the custard back into the saucepan and cook over low heat, stirring continuously until the mixture is thick enough to coat the back of a wooden spoon—do not allow the custard to boil.

Strain the custard into a bowl, add the lemon juice and cream and then cool over ice. Churn in an ice-cream maker following the manufacturer's instructions. Alternatively, pour into a plastic freezer box, cover and freeze. Stir every 30 minutes with a whisk during freezing to break up the ice crystals and give a better texture. Keep in the freezer until ready to serve.

# berries in Champagne jelly

serves 8

## ingredients

1 litre (35 fl oz/4 cups) Champagne or sparkling
   white wine
$1^1/_2$ tablespoons gelatine
250 g (9 oz/1 cup) sugar
4 strips lemon zest
4 strips orange zest
250 g (9 oz/$1^2/_3$ cups) small hulled and halved
   strawberries
255 g (9 oz/$1^2/_3$ cups) blueberries

## method

Pour 500 ml (17 fl oz/2 cups) Champagne into a bowl and let the
bubbles subside. Sprinkle the gelatine over the Champagne in
an even layer. Leave until the gelatine is spongy — do not stir.
Place the remaining Champagne in a large saucepan with
the sugar, lemon and orange zest, and heat gently, stirring
constantly for 3–4 minutes, or until the sugar has dissolved.

Remove the pan from the heat, add the gelatine mixture and
stir until thoroughly dissolved. Leave the jelly to cool
completely, then remove the lemon and orange zest.

Divide the berries among eight 125 ml (4 fl oz/$^1/_2$ cup)
stemmed wine glasses and gently pour the jelly over the top.
Refrigerate for 6 hours or overnight, or until the jelly has fully
set. Remove from the refrigerator 15 minutes before serving.

# spiced caramelized bananas

serves 4

## ingredients

50 g ($1^3/_4$ oz) unsalted butter
2 tablespoons soft brown sugar
$^1/_2$ teaspoon ground nutmeg
$^1/_4$ teaspoon ground allspice
4 bananas, peeled and sliced lengthways
grated zest and juice of 1 orange
1 tablespoon rum
2 tablespoons lightly roasted pecans or walnuts,
    chopped
freshly grated nutmeg, to sprinkle
ice cream, to serve

## method

Put the butter, sugar, nutmeg and allspice in a frying pan over medium heat. Mix until combined and cook for 1 minute, or until the sugar has dissolved. Add the bananas, cut side down, and cook for 2 minutes, or until a little softened.

Remove the bananas to a serving plate. Add the orange zest and juice to the frying pan and stir for 2 minutes, or until mixture thickens and is syrupy. Stir in the rum. Spoon the sauce over the bananas. Sprinkle with the chopped nuts and sprinkle with some freshly grated nutmeg. Serve warm with ice cream.

# pannacotta with blueberry compote

serves 4

## ingredients

300 ml (10$^1$/$_2$ fl oz) low-fat milk
1 vanilla bean, halved
1 cinnamon stick
$^1$/$_2$ teaspoon natural vanilla extract
1 tablespoon caster (superfine) sugar
2 sheets gelatine
200 g (7 oz) plain yoghurt

### blueberry compote

150 g (5$^1$/$_2$ oz) blueberries
15 g ($^1$/$_2$ oz) caster (superfine) sugar
100 ml (3$^1$/$_2$ fl oz) sweet Marsala
1 cinnamon stick
2 cm ($^3$/$_4$ in) strip lemon zest, white pith removed
$^1$/$_2$ vanilla bean, halved
$^1$/$_2$ teaspoon arrowroot

## method

Pour the milk into a heavy-based saucepan. Scrape in the seeds from the vanilla bean and add the pod, cinnamon stick, vanilla extract and the sugar. Bring to the boil, stirring, then remove from the heat and leave to infuse for 10 minutes.

Soak the gelatine in cold water for 5 minutes, or until soft. Squeeze out and add the leaves to the milk. Stir over low heat until the leaves dissolve (do not boil). Remove the vanilla pod and the cinnamon stick. Cool to room temperature. Whisk in the yoghurt. Pour into four 125 ml (4 fl oz/$^1$/$_2$ cup) ramekins and chill for 6 hours, or until set.

To make the compote, place the berries in a saucepan and add the sugar, Marsala, cinnamon stick and zest. Scrape in the seeds from the vanilla bean and add the pod. Cook over low heat for 15 minutes, stirring occasionally. Make sure the fruit does not break up. Mix the arrowroot with 2 teaspoons water and add to the fruit. Cook, stirring, until the mixture thickens. Leave to cool for 2 hours.

Run a knife around the edge of each ramekin and invert the pannacotta onto plates. Remove the cinnamon, zest and pod from the compote, and serve with the pannacotta.

# peaches cardinal

serves 4

## ingredients

4 large ripe peaches
300 g (10$^1$/$_2$ oz/2$^1$/$_2$ cups) raspberries
2 dessertspoons icing (confectioners') sugar,
    plus extra, to dust

## method

If the peaches are very ripe, put them in a bowl and pour boiling water over them. Leave for 1 minute, then drain and carefully peel away the skin. If the fruit you have is not so ripe, dissolve 2 tablespoons sugar in a saucepan of water, add the peaches and cover the pan. Gently poach the peaches for 5–10 minutes, or until they are tender. Drain and peel.

Let the peaches cool and then halve each one and remove the stone. Put two halves in each serving glass. Put the raspberries in a food processor or blender and mix until puréed (or mix by hand). Pass through a fine nylon sieve to get rid of the seeds.

Sift the icing sugar over the raspberry purée and stir in. Drizzle the purée over the peaches, cover and chill thoroughly. Dust a little icing sugar over the top to serve.

# pistachio crème brûlée

serves 6

## ingredients

500 ml (17 fl oz/2 cups) pouring (whipping) cream
35 g (1$^1/_4$ oz/$^1/_4$ cup) finely chopped pistachios
$^1/_2$ vanilla bean, halved lengthways
$^1/_2$ teaspoon grated orange zest
100 g (3$^1/_2$ oz/$^1/_2$ cup) caster (superfine) sugar
5 egg yolks
1–3 tablespoons caster (superfine) sugar, extra
pistachio biscotti, to serve

## method

Preheat the oven to 140°C (275°F/Gas 1). Put the cream, pistachios, vanilla bean, zest and half the sugar in a saucepan over medium heat and stir to dissolve the sugar, then bring to the boil. Remove from the heat and infuse for 10 minutes.

Whisk the egg yolks and remaining sugar in a bowl. Strain the cream mixture into a bowl, then add to the egg mixture, stirring continuously. Ladle the custard into six 125 ml (4 fl oz/$^1/_2$ cup) ramekins and place in a roasting tin. Pour in cold water to come halfway up the sides of the ramekins, then put in the oven and cook for 1 hour, or until the custard has set and is only just wobbly. Cool the ramekins on a wire rack, then refrigerate for 4 hours.

Preheat the grill (broiler) to very hot. Sprinkle 1–2 teaspoons of the extra sugar over the top of each brûlée. Put the brûlées in a roasting tin full of ice, then put the tin under the grill for 4 minutes, or until the tops of the brûlées have melted and caramelized. Remove the ramekins from the roasting tin and dry around the outside edges. Refrigerate for 1–2 hours but not more than 3 hours (or the toffee will start to go sticky and lose its crunch). Serve with pistachio biscotti.

# chocolate soufflés

serves 8

## ingredients

40 g ($1^1/_2$ oz) unsalted butter, softened
185 g ($6^1/_2$ oz) caster (superfine) sugar
90 g ($3^1/_4$ oz) unsweetened cocoa powder
3 tablespoons chocolate or coffee liqueur
80 g ($2^3/_4$ oz) dark chocolate, chopped
12 egg whites
3 tablespoons caster (superfine) sugar
icing (confectioners') sugar, to dust

### crème pâtissière
6 egg yolks
125 g ($4^1/_2$ oz) caster (superfine) sugar
30 g (1 oz) cornflour (cornstarch)
10 g ($^1/_4$ oz) plain (all-purpose) flour
550 ml (19 fl oz) milk
1 vanilla pod
15 g ($^1/_2$ oz) butter

## method

Brush the insides of eight 300 ml ($10^1/_2$ fl oz) soufflé dishes with the butter. Pour a little caster sugar into each one, turn the dishes round to coat. Preheat the oven to 190°C (375°F/Gas 5). Put a baking tray in the oven.

To make the crème pâtissière, whisk together the egg yolks and half the sugar until creamy. Sift in the cornflour and flour and mix. Put the milk, remaining sugar and vanilla pod in a saucepan. Bring just to the boil and then strain over the egg yolk mixture, stirring. Pour back into a saucepan and bring to the boil, stirring. Boil for 2 minutes, then stir in the butter. Allow to cool. Put the crème pâtissière in a bowl over a saucepan of simmering water, then remove from the heat. Whisk the cocoa powder, chocolate liqueur and chocolate into the crème pâtissière.

Beat the egg whites in a bowl until firm peaks form. Whisk in the sugar. Whisk half the egg white into the crème pâtissière, and then fold in the remainder with a spatula. Pour into the soufflé dishes. Put the dishes on the hot baking tray and bake for 15–18 minutes, or until well risen. Test with a skewer through a crack in the side of a soufflé—the skewer should come out clean. Serve immediately, dusted with icing sugar.

# hazelnut friands

makes 10

## ingredients

165 g (5$^3$/$_4$ oz/1$^1$/$_3$ cups) icing (confectioners')
    sugar, plus extra, to dust
40 g (1$^1$/$_2$ oz/$^1$/$_3$ cup) plain (all-purpose) flour
125 g (4$^1$/$_2$ oz/1 cup) ground hazelnuts
160 g (5$^3$/$_4$ oz) unsalted butter, melted
5 egg whites, lightly beaten
$^1$/$_2$ teaspoon natural vanilla extract
55 g (2 oz/$^1$/$_4$ cup) caster (superfine) sugar
35 g (1$^1$/$_4$ oz/$^1$/$_4$ cup) chopped hazelnuts

## method

Preheat the oven to 190°C (375°F/Gas 5). Lightly grease ten
125 ml (4 fl oz/$^1$/$_2$ cup) friand tins.

Sift the icing sugar and flour into a bowl. Add the ground
pistachios, butter, egg whites and vanilla and stir with a metal
spoon until just combined.

Spoon the mixture into the prepared tins. Place on a baking
tray and bake for 15–20 minutes, or until a skewer inserted into
the centre of a friand comes out clean. Leave in the tins for
5 minutes, then turn out onto a wire rack to cool.

Meanwhile, put the sugar and 3 tablespoons of water in a
small saucepan and stir over low heat until the sugar has
dissolved. Increase the heat, then boil for 4 minutes, or
until thick and syrupy. Remove from the heat and stir in the
chopped pistachios, then, working quickly, spoon the mixture
over the tops of the friands. Dust with icing sugar and serve.

# mixed berry tartlets

makes 10

## ingredients

### pastry

350 g (12 oz/2³/₄ cups) plain (all-purpose) flour
pinch of salt
150 g (5¹/₂ oz) unsalted butter
100 g (3¹/₂ oz/³/₄ cup) icing (confectioners') sugar
2 eggs, beaten

### frangipane

250 g (9 oz) unsalted butter, softened
250 g (9 oz/2 cups) icing (confectioners') sugar
250 g (9 oz/2¹/₂ cups) ground almonds
40 g (1¹/₂ oz/¹/₃ cup) plain (all-purpose) flour
5 eggs, lightly beaten

400 g (14 oz) mixed berries
3 tablespoons apricot jam

## method

To make the pastry, sift the flour and salt onto a work surface and make a well in the centre. Put the butter into the well and work, using a pecking action with your fingertips and thumb, until it is very soft. Add the sugar to the butter and mix. Add the eggs to the butter and mix together. Gradually incorporate the flour, flicking it onto the mixture, then chop through it until you have a rough dough. Bring together and knead a few times until smooth. Roll into a ball, cover in plastic wrap and refrigerate for 1 hour.

To make the frangipane, beat the butter until soft. Add the icing sugar, almonds and flour and beat well. Add the egg gradually, beating well. Put in a clean bowl, cover with plastic wrap and refrigerate for up to 24 hours.

Preheat the oven to 180°C (350°F/Gas 4). Roll out pastry to 2 mm (¹/₈ in) thick and use to line ten 8 cm (3 in) wide tartlet tins. Put the frangipane in a piping bag and pipe into the tartlet tins. Put the tins on a baking tray and bake for 10 minutes, or until golden. Cool slightly on a wire rack, then arrange berries on top. Melt the jam with 1 teaspoon water, sieve out any lumps and brush over the berries.

# mango cakes with lime syrup

makes 4

## ingredients

425 g (15 oz) tinned mango slices in syrup,
    drained
90 g (3$^1/_4$ oz) unsalted butter, softened
185 g (6$^1/_2$ oz/$^3/_4$ cup) caster (superfine) sugar
2 eggs, lightly beaten
60 g (2$^1/_4$ oz/$^1/_2$ cup) self-raising flour
2 tablespoons ground almonds
2 tablespoons coconut milk
2 tablespoons lime juice

## method

Preheat the oven to 200°C (400°F/Gas 6). Grease four 250 ml (9 oz/1 cup) muffin holes and line with mango slices. Beat the butter and 125 g (4$^1/_2$ oz/$^1/_2$ cup) of the sugar in a bowl with electric beaters until light and creamy. Gradually add the egg, beating well after each addition. Fold in the sifted flour, then add the almonds and coconut milk, then spoon into the muffin holes. Bake for 25 minutes, or until a skewer comes out clean when inserted into the centre of the cakes.

To make the syrup, put the lime juice, the remaining sugar and 125 ml (4 fl oz/$^1/_2$ cup) of water in a small saucepan and stir over low heat until the sugar dissolves. Increase the heat and simmer for 10 minutes. Pierce holes in each cake with a skewer. Drizzle the syrup over the top and allow to stand for 5 minutes to soak up the liquid. Turn out and serve.

# apricot honey soufflé

serves 4

## ingredients

180 g (6$^1/_2$ oz/1 cup) dried whole apricots, chopped
2 tablespoons caster (superfine) sugar
2 egg yolks
1$^1/_2$ tablespoons honey, warmed
1 teaspoon finely grated lemon zest
4 egg whites
icing (confectioners') sugar, to dust

## method

Place the apricots in a saucepan with 125 ml (4 fl oz/$^1/_2$ cup) of cold water, or enough to cover. Bring to the boil, then reduce the heat and simmer for 20 minutes, or until the apricots are soft and pulpy. Drain, then process in a food processor to a purée.

Preheat the oven to 200°C (400°F/Gas 6). Lightly grease a 1.25 litre (52 fl oz/5 cup) soufflé dish and sprinkle the base and side with 1 tablespoon of caster sugar. Put the egg yolks, honey, zest and apricot purée in a bowl and beat until smooth.

Whisk the egg whites in a dry bowl until soft peaks form, then whisk in the remaining sugar. Fold 1 tablespoon into the apricot mixture and mix well. Lightly fold in the remaining egg white, being careful to keep the mixture light and aerated. Spoon into the soufflé dish and level the surface. Run your thumb around the inside rim to create a gap between the mixture and the wall of the dish (this will encourage even rising).

Bake on the upper shelf in the oven for 25–30 minutes, or until risen and just set. Cover loosely with foil if the surface starts to overbrown. Dust with icing sugar and serve immediately.

# strawberries with balsamic vinegar

serves 4

## ingredients

750 g (1 lb 10 oz) ripe small strawberries
60 g (21/4 oz/$^1$/$_4$ cup) caster (superfine) sugar
2 tablespoons balsamic vinegar
125 g (4$^1$/$_2$ oz/$^1$/$_2$ cup) mascarpone

## method

Wipe the strawberries with a clean damp cloth and carefully remove the green stalks. If the strawberries are large, cut each one in half.

Place all the strawberries in a large glass bowl, sprinkle the caster sugar evenly over the top and toss gently to coat. Set aside for 2 hours to macerate, then sprinkle the balsamic vinegar over the strawberries. Toss them again, then refrigerate for about 30 minutes.

Spoon the strawberries into four glasses, drizzle with the syrup and top with a dollop of mascarpone.

# tarte tatin

serves 8

## ingredients

70 g (2¹/₂ oz) unsalted butter
185 g (6¹/₂ oz) caster (superfine) sugar
1.5 kg (3 lb 5 oz) dessert apples, peeled, cored
    and cut into quarters

### tart pastry
220 g (7³/₄ oz) plain (all-purpose) flour
pinch of salt
150 g (5¹/₂ oz) unsalted butter, chilled and diced
1 egg yolk

### crème chantilly
200 ml (7 fl oz) thick (double/heavy) cream
1 teaspoon icing (confectioners') sugar
¹/₂ teaspoon natural vanilla extract

## method

Heat the butter and sugar in a deep 25 cm (10 in) frying pan until melted. Arrange the apples tightly in the frying pan. Cook over low heat for 35–40 minutes, or until the apple is soft and the caramel is lightly browned. Baste the apple with a pastry brush often. Preheat the oven to 190°C (375°F/Gas 5).

To make the tart pastry, sift the flour and salt into a bowl, add the butter and rub in until the mixture resembles breadcrumbs. Add the egg yolk and a little cold water and mix with the blade of a palette knife until the dough just starts to come together. Shape the dough into a ball. Wrap in plastic wrap and refrigerate for at least 30 minutes. Roll out the pastry on a floured surface into a circle slightly larger than the frying pan and about 3 mm (¹/₈ in) thick. Lay the pastry over the apple and press down around the edge to enclose it completely. Roughly trim the edge of the pastry and then fold the edge back on itself. Bake for 25–30 minutes, or until the pastry is golden. Remove from the oven and leave to rest for 5 minutes before turning out.

To make the crème chantilly, put the cream, icing sugar and vanilla extract in a chilled bowl. Whisk until soft peaks form and then serve with the hot tarte tatin.

# fruit poached in red wine

serves 6

## ingredients

3 pears, peeled, quartered and cored
3 apples, peeled, quartered and cored
50 g (1³/₄ oz/¹/₄ cup) sugar
1 vanilla bean, cut in half lengthways
2 small cinnamon sticks
400 ml (14 fl oz) red wine
200 ml (7 fl oz) dessert wine or port
700 g (1 lb 9 oz) red-skinned plums, halved

## method

Put the pears and apples in a large saucepan. Add the sugar, vanilla bean, cinnamon sticks, red wine and dessert wine and bring to the boil. Reduce the heat and gently simmer for 5–10 minutes, or until just soft.

Add the plums, stirring them through the pears and apples, and bring the liquid back to a simmer. Cook for a further 5 minutes, or until the plums are soft.

Remove the saucepan from the heat, cover with a lid and leave the fruit to marinate in the syrup for at least 6 hours. Reheat gently to serve warm, or serve at room temperature with cream or ice cream.

# easy flourless chocolate cake

serves 10

## ingredients

500 g (1 lb 2 oz) dark chocolate, chopped
6 eggs
2 tablespoons Frangelico or brandy
165 g (5³/₄ oz/1¹/₂ cups) ground hazelnuts
250 ml (9 fl oz/1 cup) pouring (whipping) cream
icing (confectioners') sugar, to dust
thick (double/heavy) cream, to serve

## method

Preheat the oven to 150ºC (300ºF/Gas 2). Grease a deep 20 cm (8 in) round cake tin and line the base with baking paper. Place the chocolate in a heatproof bowl. Half-fill a saucepan with water, boil, then remove from the heat and sit the bowl over the pan—don't let the bowl touch the water. Stir occasionally until the chocolate melts.

Put the eggs in a large heatproof bowl and add the Frangelico. Put the bowl over a saucepan of barely simmering water— don't let it touch the water. Beat the mixture using an electric beater on high speed for 7 minutes, or until light and foamy. Remove from the heat.

Using a metal spoon, quickly and lightly fold the chocolate and ground nuts into the egg mixture until just combined. Fold in the whipped cream and pour into the cake tin. Put the cake tin in a shallow roasting tin. Pour hot water into the roasting tin to come halfway up the side of the cake tin. Bake for 1 hour, or until just set. Remove the cake tin from the oven and allow to cool. Cover with plastic wrap and refrigerate overnight.

Invert the cake onto a plate, remove the paper and cut into slices. Dust with icing sugar and serve with cream.

# praline ice cream with caramel bark

makes 1 litre (35 fl oz/4 cups)

## ingredients

100 g ($3^{1}/_{2}$ oz/$^{2}/_{3}$ cup) blanched almonds, toasted
115 g (4 oz/$^{1}/_{2}$ cup) caster (superfine) sugar
185 ml (6 fl oz/$^{3}/_{4}$ cup) pouring (whipping) cream
250 g (9 oz) mascarpone cheese
125 g ($4^{1}/_{2}$ oz) white chocolate, melted and
   cooled
2 tablespoons sugar
fresh figs, to serve (optional)

## method

Line a baking tray with foil, brush the foil lightly with oil and scatter the almonds on top. Put the caster sugar in a small saucepan over low heat. Tilt the pan slightly (do not stir) and watch until the sugar melts and turns golden caramel—this should take 3–5 minutes.

Pour the caramel over the almonds and leave until set and cold. Break into chunks, put in a plastic bag and crush with a rolling pin, or process briefly in a food processor until crumbly. Whip the cream until stiff peaks form. In a large bowl, mix together the mascarpone and melted chocolate. Using a metal spoon, fold in the whipped cream and crushed praline. Transfer to a 1 litre (35 fl oz/4 cup) loaf (bar) tin, cover with baking paper and freeze for 5 hours, or overnight.

To make the caramel bark, line a baking tray with foil and brush lightly with oil. Sprinkle the sugar evenly onto the tray and place under a hot grill (broiler) for 2 minutes, or until the sugar is melted and golden—check frequently towards the end of the cooking time, as the sugar may burn quickly. Remove from the heat, leave until set and completely cold, then break the caramel into shards. Soften in the fridge for 30 minutes before serving. Serve with the caramel shards and fresh figs, if desired.

# watermelon granita

serves 4

## ingredients

450 g (1 lb) watermelon, skin and seeds removed
1 tablespoon liquid glucose or caster (superfine)
   sugar
$1/_2$ teaspoon lemon juice

## method

Purée the watermelon in a blender or food processor, or chop finely and push through a metal sieve.

Heat the glucose, lemon juice and 75 ml ($2^1/_4$ fl oz) water in a small saucepan for 4 minutes, or until dissolved. Add the watermelon and stir well.

Pour into a plastic freezer box, cover and freeze. Stir every 30 minutes with a fork during freezing to break up the ice crystals and give a better texture. Keep in the freezer until ready to serve, then roughly fork to break up the ice crystals.

index

# index